Population Education

Population Education

Editor

V. C. Pandey

ISHA BOOKS

DELHI-110 033

Population Education

ISBN: 81-8205-176-2

Published in 2006 in India by
Isha Books, D-43, Prithviraj Road,
Adarsh Nagar, Delhi-110 033

Laser Typesetting at: Shree Vaishnavi Creations, Delhi
Printed at: Mehra Offset Press, Delhi

PREFACE

'Population education' is generally defined as the transmission of knowledge about population processes and characteristics, the causes of population change and the consequences of that change for the individual and society. The concept of population education which emerged as an educational innovation in response to population problems only about four decades ago, is now being experimented in over a hundred countries of the world in non-too-uniform a manner. It has been introduced in the education systems of different countries as an important component of the multi-pronged strategy employed to help nations attain the goals of population stabilisation and sustainable development.

Very few educational programmes have matched its pace of expansion and adopted such varied conceptual frameworks and strategies of curriculum transaction. Perhaps no other educational concept has experienced such frequent changes in its framework and been subjected to so many misunderstandings as the concept of population education. This has been so because of not only the nature of the context in which it emerged but also its newness and its complex characteristics.

This book includes all relevant information regarding different area of population education. It deals with the topics on population education concepts, its need and importance, its historical development and present situation, population growth, population explosion, population policies and programmes. It is hoped that the book will prove useful for teacher-educators, school teachers, student teachers, research scholars, policy makers, administrators and other interested in the field.

Editor

CONTENTS

1

Nature and Scope of Population Education

In the most common sense of the word, a population is the collection of people—or organisms of a particular species—living in a given geographic area. Populations are studied in a wide variety of ways and disciplines. In population dynamics, size, age and sex structure, mortality, reproductive behaviour, and growth of a population are studied. Demography is the study of human population dynamics. Other aspects are studied in sociology, economics, and geography. Plant and animal populations are studied in biology, in particular in that branch of ecology known as population biology, and in population genetics. In biology, a population denotes a breeding group whose members breed mostly or solely among themselves, usually as a result of physical isolation, although biologically they could breed with any members of the species.

Population density is a measure of the number of people or organisms per unit of area. Variants may express the population per unit of habitable, inhabited, productive (or potentially productive), or cultivated area. A particular geographic area of land is said to have a carrying capacity, representing the maximum population which it can support. Some observers of human societies believe that the concept of carrying capacity also applies to human population, and that unchecked population growth can result in a "Malthusian catastrophe". Others dispute this view.

OVERPOPULATION

Overpopulation may indicate any case in which the population of any species of animal may exceed the carrying capacity of its ecological niche. In common parlance, the term specifically refers to the relationship of human population to the planet Earth.

Malthus's theory

Early in the 19th century, Thomas Malthus argued in An Essay on the Principle of Population that, if left unrestricted, human populations would continue to grow until they would become too large to be supported by the available agricultural land. He proposed that, while resources tend to grow arithmetically, population grows exponentially. At that point, the population would be restrained through mass famine and starvation. Malthus argued for population control, through "moral restraint", to avoid this happening.

Over the two hundred years which followed, famine has overtaken numerous individual regions; proponents of this theory state that these famines were examples of Malthusian catastrophes. On a global scale, however, food production has grown faster than population. It has often been argued that future pressures on food production, combined with threats to other aspects of the earth's habitat such as global warming, make overpopulation a still more serious threat in the future. Perhaps the best-known example of such an argument is The Limits to Growth, a report produced for the Club of Rome in the early 1970s.

The optimist's viewpoint on population growth

Other studies have countered with the claim that the current population level of over six billion may be supported by current resources, or that the global population may grow to ten billion and still be within the Earth's carrying capacity. Buckminster

Fuller and Barry Commoner were both proponents of the idea that human technology could keep up with population growth indefinitely. The assumptions that underlie these claims, however, have been strongly criticised.

In any case, many proponents of population control have averred that famine is far from being the only problem attendant to overpopulation. These critics point out ultimate shortages of energy sources and other natural resources, as well as the importance of serious communicable diseases in dense populations and war over scarce resources such as land area.

Fossil-fuel subsidies in agriculture

One of the strongest criticisms of an optimistic outlook is that of the fossil fuel subsidy of modern agriculture. The extremely high agricultural outputs of modern farms depend entirely on immense fossil fuel (mostly petroleum) subsidies in the forms of fertilizers, equipment fuel, and other chemicals such as pesticides. With proven reserves of petroleum steadily falling from year to year, fossil-fuel subsidies would seem to be ultimately doomed.

Effects of unregulated population growth

The world's current agricultural production, if it were distributed evenly, would be sufficient to feed everyone living on the Earth today. However, many critics hold that, in the absence of other measures, simply feeding the world's population well would only make matters worse, natural growth will cause the population to grow to unsustainable levels, and will directly result in famines and deforestation and indirectly in pandemic disease and war.

Some other characteristics of overpopulation:

— Birth rate is high

— Life expectancy is low

— Low level of literacy

— High rate of unemployment in urban areas (leading to social problems)

— Rural people are not gainfully employed (caught in cycle of poverty)

— Insufficient arable land

— Little surplus food

— Poor diet with ill health and diet-deficiency diseases (e.g. rickets)

— GDP per capita is low (under US$765 per annum)

— Many live in unhygienic conditions

— Government is stretched economically

The demographic transition

However, others contend that within a generation after the standard of living and life expectancy starts increasing, family sizes start dropping in what is termed the demographic transition. In support they point to the contention that every estimate of maximum global population since the 1960s, when the "population explosion" became a worry, has been significantly lower than the previous estimates. Among those holding this view are the ecologist Paul Colinvaux, who writes on the topic in Why Big Fierce Animals are Rare, and The Fates of Nations.

The status of women

Another point of view on population vs. the standard of living is that of Virginia Abernethy in Population Politics, in which she shows evidence that this effect only holds true in nations where women enjoy a relatively high status. In strongly patriarchal nations, where women enjoy few rights, a higher standard of living tends to result in population growth. She argues that foreign aid to poor countries must include significant components designed to improve the education, human rights, political rights, political power, and economic status and power of women.

Survival of the fittest

Some approach overpopulation with a "survival of the fittest," "laissez-faire" attitude, arguing that if the Earth's ecosystem becomes overtaxed, it will naturally regulate itself. In this mode of thought, disease or starvation are "natural" means of lessening population. Two particular objections to this argument are that a) in the meantime, a huge number of plant and animal species become extinct, and b) this would result in terrible pollution in some areas that would be difficult to abate. As well, it obviously creates certain moral problems, as this would cause great suffering in the people that die.

Others argue that economic development is the best way to reduce population growth. Many developed countries in the world today, such as Italy, now have declining populations (ignoring the effects of immigration).

In either case, it is often held that the most productive approach is to provide a combination of help targeted towards population control and self-sufficiency. One of the most important measures proposed for this effort is the empowerment of women educationally, economically, politically, and in the family. The value of this philosophy has been substantially borne out in cases where great strides have been taken to this goal: where women's status has dramatically improved, there has generally been a drastic reduction in the birthrate to more sustainable levels. Other measures include effective family planning programs, local renewable energy systems, sustainable agriculture methods and supplies, reforestation, and measures to protect the local environment.

Overpopulation as a social issue

The density of population has an impact on a broad range of social and economic issues, such as land prices and housing costs. For example, relatively densely populated countries such as Japan have higher land prices than less densely populated countries such as Australia, and even in that country, land prices have doubled and redoubled as the population has increased. It is sometimes argued that reducing the populations of some areas, such as large cities, would have positive benefits for these reasons.

CURRENT STATUS OF WORLD POPULATION

The current estimated world human population is 6,350,538,084. This figure is deceptively precise, however, since there is no complete database on the world's population, and humans are constantly being born (at the rate of about 3 per second) and dying. However, it is clear that the world's population continues to grow, and at rates that are unprecedented prior to the 20th century.

By some estimates, there are now one billion young people in the world between the ages of 15 and 24.

The United Nations Population Fund designated October 12, 1999 as the approximate day on which world population reached six billion. This was about 12 years after world population reached five billion, in 1987.

Rate of population increase

The last 70 years of the 20th century saw the biggest increase in the world's population in human history. The following table shows when each billion milestone was met:

1 billion reached in — 1802.

2 billion reached in — 1927.

3 billion reached in — 1961.

4 billion reached in — 1971.

5 billion reached in — 1987.

6 billion reached in — 1999.

From the figures above, the world's population tripled in 72 years, and doubled in 38.

The UN estimated in 2000 that the world's population was then growing at the rate of 1.2 percent (or 77 million people) per year. This represents a decrease in the growth rate in 1990, mostly due to decreased birth rates.

Every year the world's population gains nearly 90 million people, as of 2004.

Forecast of world population

The future growth of population is difficult to predict. Birth rates are declining slightly on average, but vary greatly between developed countries (where birth rates are often at or below replacement levels) and developing countries. Death rates can change unexpectedly due to disease, wars and catastrophes, or advances in medicine. The UN itself has issued multiple projections of future world population, based on different assumptions.

The current projections from the UN's Population Division, from their 2002 World Population Prospects database, are:

Year	Population (billions)
2010	6.8
2020	7.5
2030	8.1
2040	8.6
2050	8.9

Table 1. Population evolution in different continents

Year	World	Africa	Asia	Europe	Latin-America	North America	Oceania
1950	2518629	221214	1398488	547403	167097	171616	12812
1955	2755823	246746	1541947	575184	190797	186884	14265
1960	3021475	277398	1701336	604401	218300	204152	15888
1965	3334874	313744	1899424	634026	250452	219570	17657
1970	3692492	357283	2143118	655855	284856	231937	19443
1975	4068109	408160	2397512	675542	321906	243425	21564
1980	4434682	469618	2632335	692431	361401	256068	22828
1985	4830979	541814	2887552	706009	401469	269456	24678
1990	5263593	622443	3167807	721582	441525	283549	26687
1995	5674380	707462	3430052	727405	481099	299438	28924
2000	6070581	795671	3579737	727986	520229	315915	31043
2005	6453628	887964	3917508	724722	558281	332156	32998
2010	6830283	984225	4148948	719714	594436	348139	34821
2015	7197247	1084540	4370522	713402	628260	363953	36569
2020	7540237	1187584	4570131	705410	659248	379589	38275
2025	7851455	1292085	4742232	696036	686857	394312	39933
2030	8130149	1398004	4886647	685440	711058	407532	41468
2035	8378184	1504179	5006700	673638	731591	419273	42803
2040	8593591	1608329	5103021	660645	747953	429706	43938
2045	8774394	1708407	5175311	646630	759955	439163	44929
2050	8918724	1803298	5222058	631938	767685	447931	45815

Other projections of population growth predict that the world's population will eventually crest, though it is uncertain exactly when or how. In some scenarios, the population will crest as early as the mid-21st century at under 10 billion, due to gradually decreasing birth rates.

In less optimistic scenarios, disasters triggered by a growing population's demand for scarce resources will cause a sudden population crash, or even a Malthusian catastrophe.

Doomsayers

In 1798, Thomas Malthus predicted that population growth would eventually outrun food supply, resulting in catastrophe. In 1968 Paul R. Ehrlich reignited this argument with his book The Population Bomb, which helped give the issue significant mindshare throughout the 1960s and 1970s. The dire predictions of Ehrlich and other neo-Malthusians were vigourously challenged by a number of economists, notably Julian Simon. More recently, some scholars have applied bayesian probability to world population to argue that the end of humanity will come sooner than we usually think.

EMERGENCE OF THE CONCEPT OF POPULATION EDUCATION

'Population education' is generally defined as the transmission of knowledge about population processes and characteristics, the causes of population change and the consequences of that change for the individual and society.

The concept of population education which emerged as an educational innovation in response to population problems only about four decades ago, is now being experimented in over a hundred countries of the world in non-too-uniform a manner. It has been introduced in the education systems of different countries as an important component of the multi-pronged strategy employed to help nations attain the goals of population stabilisation and sustainable development.

Very few educational programmes have matched its pace of expansion and adopted such varied conceptual frameworks and strategies of curriculum transaction. Perhaps no other educational concept has experienced such frequent changes in its framework and been subjected to so many misunderstandings as the concept of population education. This has been so because of not only the nature of the context in which it emerged but also its newness and its complex characteristics.

The concept of population education emerged in the context of population and development - the two most pressing issues before humankind today. Both are closely interrelated and both encompass a number of complex factors. Viewed as an epiphenomenon of the process of development, population issues have aroused widespread concern among almost all the members of the comity of nations.

There have been undaunted endeavours to accelerate the pace of socioeconomic development through the instrumentalities of science and technology and to secure distributive justice for the people through different institutional mechanisms. But those are confronted with some basic population related questions of how many people are going to inhabit the earth, how they are to be supported and enabled to make their contributions to development efforts, what they are going to bequeath to posterity and how long they are going to be sustained by the natural and human resource base.

The rapid population growth and the concomitant problems of poverty, lack of adequate health and educational facilities, malnutrition, non-fulfilment of even the basic needs of a vast majority of the populace, paucity of employment opportunities, dwindling natural resources and consequent environmental degradation constitute critical dimensions of the present population and development phenomena. It is also pertinent to note that the population phenomenon today embraces issues beyond development. While the size, growth, composition and distribution of population have a close bearing on socioeconomic development, the population related issues also bring forth concerns for the "carrying capacity" of biological and ecological system and the future of mankind.

HISTORY OF POPULATION EDUCATION

The ideà that population education can play a potential role in addressing population problems, was first mooted in Sweden in 1935. The Population Commission of Swėden, which expressed its concern on the declining rates of birth in that country, recommended a comprehensive and truly vigorous educational campaign to clarify population related issues aimed at influencing the fertility behaviour of individuals.

A similar view was expressed in the United States during 1937-38. Since the birth rate continued to decline and population seemed to be dwindling, it was suggested that population studies be included as a content area in the school curriculum. However, nothing noteworthy happened during the next two decades. It was in the 1960s that the matter was seriously reconsidered in the United States. Warren S. Thompson and Philip M. Hauser published papers in march 1962 issue of Teachers College Record, Columbia University reiterating the inclusion of population content in the school curriculum.

Interestingly, they made such recommendations in a completely different context, as the perception of population problem had changed during 1960s and the concern had shifted from decline in growth rate to rapid population growth in both the industrialized and developing worlds. In the fifties and sixties, therefore, efforts were initiated in a number of countries to arrest population growth; and motivational activities for adults provided information about the consequences of high birth rate. The information, education and communication (IEC) or information education and motivation (IEM) strategy was employed in family planning programmes to achieve the desired objectives. However, in the developing world the "IEC" activities of family planning programmes were not always as successful as had been expected. It was in this context that the potential of education was realised in order to overcome deeply entrenched traditional learning that influenced demographic behaviour of the people.

The school education, in particular, was considered effective for achieving this objective. However, the nomenclature of population education was given to this educational innovation at a later date. Sloan Wayland was the first to use the term "population education". The first national endeavour to evolve and concretise the concept of population education was made in India in 1969 and then in the Philippines and the Republic of Korea in 1970.

The Workshop on Population and Family Education sponsored by the UNESCO Regional Office for Education in Asia held in September 1970 at Bangkok, was a land-mark in the history of population education. It not only facilitated the identification of objectives of population education, the selection of suitable contents and the consideration of strategies for introduction of population education into formal and non-formal education systems but also resulted in the launching of national population education programmes by many countries in Asia.

Similar activities were initiated by UNESCO Regional Offices in Santiago and Dakar. The United Nations Population Fund (UNFPA), previously known as United Nations Fund for Population Activities, played a vital role in appreciating the potential of population education and providing funds for national programmes from the late sixties onwards. Population education emerged as an educational innovation during 1970s and various countries initiated activities to introduce it into their ongoing education systems.

The recommendations of the World Population Plan of Action adopted at the 1974 World Population Conference held in Bucharest, also encouraged nations to adopt the strategy of population education.

The Plan of Action recommended that "the Governments should consider making provision, in both the formal and non-formal educational programmes, for informing their people on the consequences of existing or alternative fertility behaviour for the well-being of the family, for the educational and psychological development of children and for the general welfare of society, so that an informed and responsible attitude to marriage and reproduction will be promoted".

In India, the Family Planning Association for the first time sent a Memorandum to the State Government of Maharashtra in 1968 recommending that education in population dynamics should be made a part of school curriculum. However, the idea of population education was crystallised in the National Seminar on Population Education organised in Bombay in August 1969. It recommended that population education should be introduced into curriculum of schools and colleges. The Seminar made an attempt to define population education in the context of Indian situation, but more importantly, expressed the national consensus for introducing this educational innovation in the education system of the country.

NEED OF POPULATION EDUCATION

It has been gradually realized that since the interrelationship between population and development is highly complex and population problems are multidimensional, it will not yield to any single solution. It is basically related to the developmental needs of a nation and its people.

Demographic trends influence, and are influenced by, the level of development and the quality of life of the people. The population situation of any nation largely depends on the demographic behaviour of its people. Changes in the demographic profile of a nation depend largely on attitudes and behaviours of individuals in respect of population and development issues.

The demographic behaviour is to a great extent informed by population socialization, a process by which people acquire norms, values, attitudes and belief systems in respect of population related issues and which is embedded within the larger complexes of social practices reflecting the society's internal logical system.

This process is greatly influenced by education which enables the individual to know the phenomenon of population change and its consequences. It is commonly observed in many countries that the knowledge of the simple facts of population change, let alone the complex interrelationships with other parameters, is very low even among educated people. It is precisely because of these complexities that population education has emerged as an integral part of the multi-pronged strategy employed to solve contemporary population problems that face the nations.

POPULATION EDUCATION AND RELAED CONCEPTS

In the initial phase of its evolution, there were several misconceptions regarding population education, and some of those still continue to affect its proper understanding. Population education was popularly equated with family planning or family planning education, primarily because of its emergence in close association with the "IEC" or "IEM' activities of the family planning programmes. It was also regarded as a euphemism for sex education and family life education, as in some countries the concerned programmes approached population issues in terms of sexuality.

Population education was also equated with population studies, and even now both the terms are sometimes used interchangeably, because the core of the knowledge base of population education, contained the elements of population studies. While population education is none of these "educations" in the true sense, it draws contents from all those educational areas the objectives of which are mutually supportive. It is necessary, therefore, to discuss the nature and objectives of certain related areas, as it may help in proper understanding of the distinction and complementarity between population education and them.

Family planning

In many countries population programmes were initiated as family planning programmes which had a special "IEC" or "IEM" component. This component came to be popularly known also as family planning education. In some countries this campaign was launched in a very narrow sense aimed at creating awareness about controlling birth by using contraceptives. It helped in the supply and use of contraceptives to eligible couples.

But over the years family planning also has adopted a broad orientation. It is now increasingly being regarded more than an intervention to promote the use of contraception. It is a means of caring for the health of mother and child, enhancing the quality of families by regulating and spacing child birth, raising the age at marriage and improving the position of girls and women, helping sub-fertile couples to beget children and providing counseling for parents and potential parents. Despite these changes, the family planning education continues to address itself primarily to adults and youth, and its approach also remains predominantly prescriptive, explaining the oversimplified dogmatism of assertions like "small family is a happy family".

Population education shares all the content of the family planning education and also focuses on its objectives. But the scheme of contents of population education is broader and its specific objectives are more varied than those of the family planning education. Both have basic differences in their approach. Population education does not follow prescriptive and didactic approaches.

Whereas family planning education aims at conveying specific messages of family size and quality of life issues, population education focuses on influencing attitude and behaviour of individuals and developing basic thinking and decision-making skills in them.

Sex education

Sex education is an educational programme designed to provide learners with adequate and accurate knowledge about human sexuality in its biological, psychological, socio-cultural and moral dimensions. It largely, though not exclusively, focuses on the individual self-awareness, personal relationships, human sexual development, reproduction and sexual behaviour. It also covers the anatomy and physiology of reproductive systems, physical, emotional and psychological changes during puberty and conception, pregnancy, and birth. It deals with sexual behaviour, sex roles and sexually transmitted diseases. Whereas population education deals with many of these contents, it focuses on their interrelationships with population issues and also on population processes other than fertility.

Family life education

Closely related to sex education, the family life education is an educational process designed to assist young people in their physical, social, emotional and moral development, as they prepare themselves for adulthood, marriage and parenthood. It deals with issues like ageing as well as social relationships in the sociocultural context of family and society. It provides an opportunity to the learners to study family relationships and peer relationships. It does not simply deal with physiology and anatomy of reproduction and human sexuality. While population education includes these concerns in its scheme ot content, it also covers many other issues that are beyond the scope of the family life education.

Population studies is the body of knowledge, concepts and theories, which describe and attempt at explaining the dynamics of human populations and their relationships with social, cultural, economic, political and biological environments. It focuses on population issues related to the demographic processes of fertility, mortality and migration. It also covers components such as population size, age and sex composition, its spatial distribution and socioeconomic characteristics.

Population studies as a general body of knowledge, therefore, has made substantial contribution to the knowledge base of population education. During the initial years of the evolution of population education it was thought to be the be-all and end-all of population education, and the curriculum framers were expected to perform the simple task of including and hierarchically arranging the facts, theories and concepts of population studies into the scheme of content of population education.

But over the years, the conceptual framework of population education has broadened to incorporate those components which do not belong to population studies but to other disciplines and professional fields, such as life sciences, medical sciences, social sciences, pedagogy, psychology and so on. Moreover, population related attitudes, behaviour and decisions, rather than the internal logic of population studies are characteristically the major concerns of population education.

Population education differs from all the areas delineated above in that its need arose under special historical circumstances and some typical contemporary issues. Family planning education was initiated with a view to conveying specific messages focussed on the need to control population growth.

Sex education originally developed in response to the concern for changing sexual mores and increasing incidence of deviant sexual behaviour, venereal diseases and out of wedlock pregnancies. Family life education grew out of a recognition of the growing evidence of family instability and disintegration.

Population studies evolved, not as a separate discipline but as an interdisciplinary body of knowledge by bringing together facts, theories and concepts based on the research studies conducted by the specialists of different disciplines and professional fields for explaining various facets of population phenomenon.

Population education emerged as an educational response to the concern for population problems emanating from the changing inter-relationship between population and development. It is primarily because of the context in which it emerged that population education, by its very nature, has been treated as a culture and region specific concept. Its definition in one country or region differs from that in the other.

The numerosity of definitions is also the result of the constant changes being effected in the concept by including new areas of concern based on the experiences of international regional and national experimentation. Moreover, the definitions have been construed in various ways.

Population education has been defined by describing the nature of activity or by stating objectives or contents or by spelling out behavioural outcomes. However, not all the definitions are actually different from one another; there is a substantial commonality among them with certain differences in the emphasis on some aspect or the other.

Population education is broadly defined as an educational intervention aimed at helping individuals in understanding the interrelationship between population and development, in appreciating the determinants and consequences of population processes and changes, in assessing the possible actions that they and their respective families and communities can take to modify these processes and in carrying out selected actions. It is a part of total social learning process and based on the premise that an educational intervention which helps the learners define problems and search for solutions will have greater impact than the prescriptive programme that employs only assertions.

2

POPULATION EDUCATION IN INDIA

Since its inception the conceptual framework of population education has been changing quite frequently because of the changes in the perception of population phenomenon and its relationships with development variables. Every time when there was a change in the perception pattern of population issues, a need was felt to reconceptualise population education.

Although the changes that have occurred in the conceptual framework of population education in different countries over the years have reflected the context-specific variations, there has been an overarching commonness in them. And hence, the understanding of the process of evolution of the concept of sometimes erroneously, population education in one country such as India will provide adequate insight into its evolution throughout the world.

The first attempt to conceptualise population education in India was made during late 1960s. The National Seminar on Population Education held in August 1969 made the following recommendations to define the concept:

— "The objective of population education should be to enable the students to understand that family size is controllable, that population limitation can facilitate the development of a higher quality of life.... It should also enable the students to appreciate the fact that for preserving the health and welfare of the members of the family, ensuring economic stability to the family ... the Indian family of today should be small ... with only two or three children."

— "Students at all levels have a right to accurate information about the effect of changes in family size and in national population on the individual, the family and the nation so that this body of knowledge is utilized to control family size and national population

— "Population should not be treated merely as a quantitative phenomenon.... It is the quality of the population that is most relevant both as a factor of growth and an end product of growth...."

In pursuance of the recommendations of the National Seminar, a Population Education Syllabus was developed by National Council of Educational Research and Training in 1971. It defined population education as an educational intervention to make the target groups aware of the multi-faceted population phenomenon so that it leads them eventually to take rational decisions concerning population matters.

The Syllabus contained a scheme of content which was developed by drawing contents from the six major content areas - population growth, population and economic development, population and social development, population health and nutrition, population, biological factors and family life and ecological considerations and population. Population education thus was treated as a demography-laden concept, predominantly as education in demography and population studies.

The need to reconceptualise population education was felt for the first time during the early part of 1980s because of certain specific reasons. Evaluation studies on various facets of the implementation of the National Population Education Project identified significant gaps in the integration of elements of population education in content and process of school education. It was realized that since population education had been treated as a demography-laden concept, its ambitious conceptual framework, with excessive elements of population dynamics, had hindered the process of effective integration of its elements into the school curriculum.

The need for modification in the conceptual framework was also felt in the background of the recommendations adopted by the International Conference on Population held in Mexico City in 1984, which unfolded new dimensions of population phenomenon.

The initial step in reconceptualising population education was taken at the UNESCO Regional Seminar held in 1984, in which five major themes were identified as the core elements of the conceptual framework of population education. Those were: Family Size and Family Welfare, Delayed Marriage, Responsible Parenthood, Population Change and Resource Development, and Population related Beliefs and Values.

The National Policy on Education 1986 which reflected the magnitude of the major causes and consequences of rapid population growth also specified "promotion of observance of small family norm" as one of the core curricular areas to be reflected in the national system of education. It provided an appropriate context to reconceptualise population education.

Moreover, nearly half of the ten core curricular areas identified by the policy document such as equality of sexes, protection of environment, removal of social barriers, and inculcation of scientific temper were considered critical for realising population education objectives.

During the process of revision of the conceptual framework of population education in India, six major themes: family size and family welfare, delayed marriage, responsible parenthood, population change and resource development, population related values and beliefs, and status of women were identified.

The scheme of content was prepared by drawing contents relating to these major themes from the following six content areas: economic development, social development, environment and resources, family life, health and nutrition, and demographic implications.

The reconceptualised framework also emphasised the strategy of integrating maximum contents at minimum points in order to provide comprehensive treatment to contents to make the integration of population education elements in the textbooks more effective.

The new conceptual framework defined population education as an education in the interrelationships among population, development, resources, environment and quality of life.

All concepts having an interactive relationship with social environment require reconsideration particularly after a perceptible change takes place in the context in which they were formulated. Sometimes, it is the odd fate of a concept to have too successful a rein. After it secures scientific acceptance, it may become so popular and fashionable that it is applied indiscriminately, leading to the dilution of its essential characteristics, generating a need to resuscitate it. The concept of population education has also undergone such a process.

The need to reorient the conceptual framework of population education was reflected in the Istanbul Declaration and the Plan of Action adopted by the International Conference on Population Education and Development, 1993, which brought forth the limitations of the existing concept and recommended the inclusion of a number of emerging concerns in it.

But the reconceptualization of population education was necessitated by the latest and most striking development of a global consensus on population and development. In course of Population Debate since Malthus initiated it, population phenomenon has been analyzed in view of perceptions of its interrelationships with other variables of development and social environment.

The present perceptions of the patterns of these interrelationships reflected in the Programme of Action (POA) adopted by the International Conference on Population and Development, (ICPD) held in Cairo inl994, made it an imperative requirement for planned interventions addressed to population phenomenon to reorient, revitalize and rejuvenate themselves to realise the vision of the new paradigm of population and development.

The ICPD Programme of Action has effected what is being described as "Paradigm Shift" from number to conditions for population stabilization. It is considered essential now to focus on the individual needs instead of demographic targets and to integrate population concerns into development strategies rather than pursuing and providing sustenance to population control approach.

Moreover, the ICPD for the first time has explicated two distinct roles of education:

(a) education as a key factor in population stabilization; and

(b) education as a means to promote greater responsibility and awareness of the interrelationships between population and sustainable development.

The need to shift from purely demographic or population control approach to a broader sustainable development approach has been advocated in other international conferences also. The United Nations Conference on Environment and Development, Rio De Janeiro, 1992 focused on the linkages between population, natural resources, environment, development and quality of life in the Agenda-21 : The Global Plan of Action adopted by it. The International Conference on Population Education and Development, 1993 and the Fourth World Conference on Women held in Beijing, 1995 that adopted Beijing Declaration and Platform for Action also emphasized these linkages.

NATIONAL POPULATION EDUCATION PROJECT (NPEP)

The experiences gained during the implementation of NPEP have also suggested the need to reconceptualise population education again. The Population Education Framework even after the first reconceptualisation did not include elements relating to the process of growing up and HIV/AIDS, as these elements had been regarded very sensitive.

But without these elements the Population Education Framework remained incomplete. In view of the problems that adolescents have been confronting for lack of authentic knowledge about the process of growing up from childhood to adulthood and the recently realized urgency to impart HIV/AIDS education, it was felt that the Population Education Framework must incorporate all the elements that had been considered crucial for attaining the objectives of population education.

Moreover, the Framework of Population Education being primarily influenced by the IEC approach had not been in consonance with the existing school curriculum framework, and hence the gaps in effective integration. Population education tended to be didactic making efforts to convey messages. But the existing school framework is open-ended and is considered a process during which messages are caught.

Population education, therefore, needed to be reconceptualised as an educational endeavour that would make the learners aware of all possible dimensions of population - development inter-relationships, promoting a general approach of supporting and empowering learners to take rational decisions regarding population and development issues; and also making them aware of the social consequences of their individual decisions. Accordingly, the population education framework was once again reconceptualised. It makes an attempt to focus on all possible variables that interact with population and development phenomena and to bring the concept of population education in tune with the existing school curriculum.

RECONCEPTUALISED FRAMEWORK

The reconceptualised framework provides a broader definition to the concept of population education, which mirrors the basic tenets of the ICPD Programme of Action. Population Education is defined as an educational process which develops among learners an understanding of interrelationships between population and development, causes and consequences of population change, and the criticality of the conditions for population stabilization. It inculcates in them rational attitude and responsible behaviour towards population and development issues, so that they may make informed decisions.

The definition of population education given above seeks to delineate the major strands of the conceptual framework: objectives, basic themes, scheme of content, strategies of integration into school curriculum, methods of curriculum transaction and modalities of evaluation.

Objectives

The objectives of population education as delineated in the Reconceptualised Framework are as follows:

Population education aims at:

— Making learners aware of the interrelationships between population and sustainable development;

— Developing in them an understanding of the criticality of essential conditions of population stabilization for better quality of life of present and future generations;

— Inculcating in them rational attitude and responsible behaviour towards population and development issues;

— Making them understand the crucial aspects of adolescent reproductive health, focusing on the elements of process of growing up, and implications of HIV/AIDS and drug abuse.

— Inculcating in them rational attitude towards sex and drugs and promoting respect for the opposite sex; and

— Empowering them to take informed decsions on issues of population and development including those of reproductive health.

With a view to attaining these objectives a scheme of content contained in the Framework has been developed around the following six basic themes covering all the concerns delineated in the Programme of Action of ICPD, 1994:

— Population and Sustainable Development;

— Gender Equality and Equity for Empowerment of Women;

— Adolescent Reproductive Health;

— Family, Socio-Economic Factors and Quality of Life;

— Health and Education - Key Determinants of Population Change; and

— Population Distribution, Urbanization and Migration.

Broad content outline

Population education does not have its own content; it draws contents from the existing disciplines and attempts at providing the needed focus to those contents. Only such contents are borrowed from concerned disciplines as have the potential to help this educational intervention attain its objectives. The scheme of content of the Reconceptualised Framework, therefore, contains those contents that have been selected from the existing disciplines and that meet the requirements reflected in the ICPD Programme of Action. These contents have been placed under the six basic themes in the following manner.

I. Population and sustainable development

— *Population growth and structure: Implications for population stabilisation:* Population Growth, Fertility, Mortality, Age and

Sex Structure—Implications in terms of the interrelationships between population change and the pace and quality of economic and social development, patterns and levels of use of natural resources and the state of environment; Infants, Children and Youth - Need to promote to the fullest extent the health and well-being of infants, children and youth in the context of attaining the goal of population stabilisation; Elderly People - Increasing rate of life expectancy, need for health care and social and economic security and enhancement of their self-reliance; Persons with disabilities - Conditions for the realisation of the rights of persons with disabilities, valuing their capabilities and dignity, promotion of their self-reliance.

— *Population, Sustained Economic Growth and Poverty:* Integration of population issues in the development strategies—Planning, decision-making and resource allocation for meeting the needs of all, promoting social justice and eradication of poverty; Interrelationship between eradication of poverty and population stabilisation; Sustainable patterns and levels of resource utilisation, production and consumption; Sustained economic growth and status of women; Creation of job opportunities in the industrial, agricultural and service sectors, promoting self-employment.

— *Population and environment :* Interrelationship between population, development, natural resources, use of technology and quality of life - Socio-economic dimensions of sustainable development, such as poverty, consumption style, human health and human settlement; Sustainable management of resources - Unsustainable consumption and production patterns and their impact on environment, need for fostering sustainable resource use and prevention of environmental degradation; Environmental Pollution Air, Water, Land and Noise: impact on health and quality of life; Use of technology in agriculture, industry and other aspects of life styles - Impact on the sustainability of resources and environmental degradation; Interrelations between women and environmental issues; Future increases in population numbers and changes in concentration and distribution, particularly in ecologically vulnerable and urban agglomerations.

II. Gender Equality and Equity for Empowerment of Women

— Gender equality and *equity:* Equality and equity based on harmonious partnership between man and woman in different spheres of life; Promoting the fulfillment of women's potential through health care, education, skill development, ability to earn beyond traditional occupations, employment opportunities outside the household, and making them self-reliant; Empowerment and autonomy of women and improvement of their social, economic and political status; participation in the decision making process at various levels; Participation in all aspects of production, employment, income generating activities, science and technology, sports, culture, political processes and public life, and population related activities; Need to redefine the role-stereotypes and the social worth of women; Discriminations against women; Need to eliminate violence against women.

— *The girl child* : Need for change in the perception of the social worth of the girl child; Equal treatment of girls and boys; Elimination of discrimination; Adequate health care and nutrition, education and opportunities for realisation of the full potential of the girl child; Role-stereotypes and discrimination within the family; Impact of prenatal sex selection, female infanticide and higher rate of girl child mortality; Trafficking in girl children; Need to strengthen self-image, self-esteem and status of the girl child; recognition of the special needs of girls.

— *Male responsibilities* : Need for change in their knowledge, attitude and behaviour as necessary condition for achieving the harmonious partnership of men and women; appreciation of the key role of males in bringing about gender equality; Participation in all areas of family and household activities; Shared responsibilities of responsible parenthood; Parental care of child health, education; Equal treatment to daughter and son; Care for mother and elimination of violence against women and children.

III. Adolescent Reproductive Health (Adolescence Education)

— *Process of growing up* : Physical change and development during adolescence Phases of adolescence, male and female body clock, conception and pregnancy, pre and post-natal care, adolescent pregnancy; Socio-cultural development - Emotional development, identity development,, body image, self-esteem and self-concept, social relationships, changing relationships with parents, peer groups and the opposite sex; Gender Roles-Stereotyped gender role development, proper gender role development.

— *HIV/AIDS:* Basic information - Meaning of HIV/AIDS, routes of transmission, effects of HIV infection, how HIV is not transmitted, STDs and AIDS; HIV/AIDS. Prevention and control - Sexual relationships, blood, mother to child, no risk behaviour, risky behaviour, sexually transmitted diseases.

— *Drug abuse:* What is drug and drug abuse, factors promoting drug abuse, symptoms of drug addiction, drug dependence, effects of drug abuse, myths and misconceptions about drug intake, prevention and responsibility.

IV. Family : Socio-cultural Factors and Quality of Life

— *Family as basic unit of society* : Importance of institutions of marriage and family; Process of rapid demographic change and socioeconomic development - their impact on patterns of family composition and traditional notions of gender-based division of parental and domestic functions; Shared role and responsibilities of the members; equality of opportunities for all in the family, ensuring especially the rights of women and children; Participation of women in decision-making in the family; Female contribution to family income and welfare; Equal opportunities to female members for working outside the household and traditional occupation; Status of the girl child: Elimination of stereotyping and discrimination against her in the family; appropriate opportunities to girls for education; Care for health and nutrition and overall development of girls.

— *Socio-economic support to the family:* Basic needs: housing, food, clothes, health, education, social security and work; Need to promote social environment against domestic and sexual violence, dowry, drug dependence, child abuse, neglecting or abandoning women, old and handicapped members, extreme poverty and chronic unemployment.

V. Health and Education : Key Determinants of population Change

— *Health, morbidity and mortality:* Interrelationship between health, morbidity and mortality, population change and quality of life; Need for universal availability, accessibility and affordability of primary health care, including reproductive health care; need to reduce morbidity and mortality differentials between males and females as well as among geographical regions and social classes; Support to the role of women as primary custodians of family health and their access to basic health care, including reproductive health care services.

— *Child survival:* Linkages between child survival and timing, spacing, number of births and reproductive health of mothers; Reduction of disparities between male and female child care; Causes and consequences of infant and child mortality, and especially girl infant and girl child mortality; Need to, improve the health and nutritional status of infants and children.

— *Health of women and safe motherhood:* Health of women as a key factor for quality of life in a family and society; promotion of women's health through primary health care services; Improvement of the health and nutritional status of women, especially of pregnant and nursing women; Need to reduce the morbidity and mortality among women including maternal mortality.

VI. Population distribution, urbanization and Migration

— *Population distribution:* Interrelationship among patterns of population distribution, socioeconomic development, environment and quality of life; Factors influencing population distribution; need for adopting sustainable regional development strategies, particularly to promote a balanced spatial distribution of population.

— *Population growth in urban agglomerations*: Continued concentration of population in primate cities/mega-cities and economic, social, civic and environmental challenges; Problems of Urban agglomerations; overcrowding, increasing density and health hazards, acute pressure on civic amenities, growing slums and social problems.

— *Migration:* Causes of migration, especially related to poverty; Migration from rural to urban areas; Impact of migration on socioeconomic development of rural areas

STRATEGIES OF INSTITUTIONALISATION

Integration Strategy

Population education has been accepted as a critical curricular area and not as a separate subject, and hence efforts have been made to integrate its elements in the entire content and process of school education and teacher education. Since population education draws its contents from the existing disciplines of social sciences and sciences, it has been found more feasible and pragmatic to integrate its elements into the concerned subjects being taught at different school stages.

Population education elements have accordingly been integrated in the selected subjects being taught at different school stages, such as Environmental Studies and Languages at the primary stage; Geography, Economics, Civics/Social Studies, Science and Languages at the upper primary and secondary stages; and Economics, Geography, Sociology, Political Science, History, Psychology, Biology/Life Sciences, Home Science and Languages at the higher secondary stage.

Moreover, attempts have also been made to include a separate paper on population education, over and above integrating its elements in existing papers in the pre-service elementary and secondary teacher education courses. As regards in-service teacher training, while independent training programmes for teachers of all the school stages have been extensively organized, elements of population education have also been dovetailed with the general in-service teacher training programmes being conducted by different institutions.

Co-curricular Approach

Co-curricular activities have always been an integral part of the teaching-learning process. Their significance particularly for an educational area like population education, which aims primarily at influencing attitude and behaviour of the learners, can hardly be over emphasised. However, for population education co-curricular activities are considered important not only for reinforcing the classroom teaching but also for initiating the teaching-learning process without waiting for a number of its elements to become an integral part of school syllabi and textbooks.

The activities are expected to be organized in schools on such a scale and so frequently that both students and teachers, and in certain cases the parents also, are thoroughly exposed to the new population education contents.

Strategies for curriculum Transaction

Adoption of appropriate strategies for curriculum transaction is crucial for achievement of the objectives of population education. It is very often presumed that when there is teaching, learning takes place automatically, and that learners learn only because the teacher teaches them. But this is not always true. There can be no learning, in spite of teaching, and the learners can learn even without teaching. As a matter of fact whether learning takes place, whether things learnt are retained and whether the learning process leads to desirable attitude formation and behaviour change depend largely on the teacher and the teaching methods.

This is more so for educational areas like population education, the primary focus of which is on the inculcation of positive attitude and the development of responsible behaviour towards population and development issues. The expository method of teaching, the lecture method or 'chalk and talk' method has serious limitations. There is a series of "new" methods known as "participatory" methods which have been considered very effective because of their potential to induce students into taking active participation in the teaching-learning process. In this context problem solving/discovery approach and value clarification strategies are found to be more functional.

3

Population Dynamics

India is the second most populous country in the world after China. India supports 16.87 percent of the world's population on its meager 2.4 percent world surface area of 135.79 million square kms. At the time of independence country's population was 342 million. The country's population size had grown from 361 million in 1951 to around 846 million in 1991 and 1027 million in 2001. The population of India almost trippled during the period of 1951-2001.

The phenomenal increase in the population during the last fifty years has led to rapid industrialization and high rate of urbanization which have created tremendous pressure on natural resources like land, air and water.

The urban population has increased three and half times, from 62.4 million in 1951 to 217.6 million in 1991 and it again increased to 288 million in 2001. The percentage of urban population increased from 17.28 percent in 1951 to 23.33 percent in 1981, 25.71 percent in 1991 and which further increased to 28 percent in 2001.

The decadal growth rates of the population are irregular, as it increased from 13.31 percent in 1951 to 24.8 percent in 1971 and afterwards it marginally declined to 24.7 percent in 1981, 23.9 percent in 1991 and 21.34 percent in 2001.

The urban growth lead to an increase in the pollution levels and exposes population to serious environmental health hazards. Environmental pollution in urban areas is associated with excessive morbidity and mortality. Overcrowding and inadequate housing contribute to pollution related diseases such as respiratory diseases, acute water borne diseases, tuberculosis, meningitis and various other diseases.

Lack of opportunities for gainful employment in villages and the ecological stresses is leading to an everincreasing movement of poor families to towns. Mega cities are emerging and urban slums are expanding. There has been three and half times increase in urban population over 1951-1991. .

During the past two decades of 1971-91, India's urban population has doubled from 109 million to 218 million and is estimated to reach 300 million by 2000 AD. Such rapid and unplanned expansion of cities has resulted in degradation of urban environment. It has widened the gap between demand and supply of infrastructure services such as energy, housing, transport, communication, education, water supply and sewerage and recreational activities, thus depleted the precious scarce environmental resource base of the cities. The result is the growing trend in air and water quality, generation of wastes, and the proliferation of slums and undesirable land use changes, all of which contribute to urban poverty.

Poverty is said to be both cause and effect of environment degradation. The poor people, who rely on natural resources more than the rich, deplete natural resources faster as they have no real prospects of gaining access to other types of resources. Poorer people, who cannot meet their subsistence needs through purchase, are forced to use common property resources such as forests for food and fuel, pastures for fodder, and ponds and rivers for water.

Clean drinking water facility through taps is available to only 35 percent of urban households and 18 percent of rural households in India. Other residents use unsafe water sources like wells, ponds and rivers. Population pressure driven overexploitation of the surface and underground water resources by the poor has resulted into contamination and exhaustion of the water resources. Urban population is also using rivers to dispose of untreated sewage and industrial effluent.

The result is that health of those dependents on untreated water resources is increasing at risk. In the absence of capital resources, the poor are directly dependent on natural resources. Moreover degraded environment can accelerate the process of impoverishment, again because the poor depend directly on natural assets. Although there has been significant drop in the poverty ratio in the country from 55 percent in 1973 to 36 percent in 1993-94, the absolute number of poor have, however, remained constant at around 320 million over the years.

Acceleration in poverty alleviation is imperative to break this link between poverty and the environment. The poverty and rapid population growth are found to coexist and thus seems to reinforcing each other. It also contributes to environmental degradation through over exploitation of natural resources like land, air and water. The deterioration of natural resources and unsafe living conditions affects the environment and health of the poor people.

POPULATION IN INDIA: A PROFILE

The population of India as at 0:00 hours on 1st March 2001 stood at 1,027,015,247 persons. With this, India became only the second country in the world after China to cross the one billion mark. India's population rose by 21.34 % between 1991 - 2001.

Sex ratio

The sex ratio (i.e., number of females per thousand males) of population was 933, rising from 927 as at the 1991 Census. Total literacy rate in India was returned as 65.38%.

Table 1. Distribution of population, sex ratio, density and decadal growth rate of population : 2001

State/ UT	Total population Persons	Males	Females	Sex ratio (females per 1,000	Density (per sq.km)	Decadal growth rate males)
1	2	3	4	5	6	7
INDIA	1,027,015,247	531,277,078	495,738,169	933	324	21.34
1 Jammu&Kashmir	2,310,069,917	5,300,574	4,769,343	900	99	29.04
2 Himachal Pradesh	6,077,248	3,085,256	2,991,992	970	109	17.53
3 Punjab	24,289,296	12,963,362	11,325,934	874	482	19.76
4 Chandigarh	900,914	508,224	392,690	773	7,902	40.33
5 Uttaranchal	8,479,562	4,316,401	4,163,161	964	159	19.20
6 Haryana	21,082,989	11,327,658	9,755,331	861	477	28.06
7 Delhi	13,782,976	7,570,890	6,212,086	821	9,294	46.31
8 Rajasthan	56,473,122	29,381,657	27,091,465	922	165	28.33
9 Uttar Pradesh	166,052,859	87,466,301	78,586,558	898	689	25.80
10 Bihar	82,878,796	43,153,964	39,724,832	921	880	28.43
11 Sikkim	540,493	288,217	252,276	875	76	32.98

12 Arunachal Pradesh	1,091,117	573,951	517,166	901	13	26.21
13Nagaland	1,988,636	1,041,686	946,950	909	120	64.41
14Manipur	2,388,634	1,207,338	1,181,296	978	107	30.02
15Mizoram	891,058	459,783	431,275	938	42	29.18
16Tripura	3,191,168	1,636,138	1,555,030	950	304	15.74
17Meghalaya	2,306,069	1,167,840	1,138,229	975	103	29.94
18Assam	26,638,407	13,787,799	12,850,608	932	340	18.85
19West Bengal	80,221,171	41,487,694	38,733,477	934	904	17.84
20Jharkhand	26,909,428	13,861,277	13,048,151	941	338	23.19
21Orissa	36,706,920	18,612,340	18,094,580	972	236	15.94
22Chhatisgarh	20,795,956	10,452,426	10,343,530	990	154	18.06
23Madhya Pradesh	60,385,118	31,456,873	28,928,245	920	196	24.34
24Gujarat	50,596,992	26,344,053	24,252,939	921	258	22.48
25Daman & Diu	158,059	92,478	65,581	709	1,411	55.59
26Dadra &Nagar Haveli	220,451	121,731	98,720	811	449	59.20
27Maharashtra	96,752,247	50,334,270	46,417,977	922	314	22.57
28Andhra Pradesh	75,727,541	38,286,811	37,440,730	978	275	13.86

29Karnataka	52,733,958	26,856,343	25,877,615	964	275	17.25
30Goa	1,343,998	685,617	658,381	960	363	14.89
31Lakshadweep	60,595	31,118	29,477	947	1,894	17.19
32Kerala	31,838,619	15,468,664	16,369,955	1,058	819	9.42
33Tamil Nadu	62,110,839	31,268,654	30,842,185	986	478	11.19
34Pondicherry	973,829	486,705	487,124	1,001	2,029	20.56
35Andaman&Nicobars	356,265	192,985	163,280	846	43	26.94

Persons	1,027,015,247
Males	531,277,078
Females	495,738,169

Although India occupies only 2.4% of the world's land area, it supports over 15% of the world's population. Only China has a larger population. Almost 40% of Indians are younger than 15 years of age. About 70% of the people live in more than 550,000 villages, and the remainder in more than 200 towns and cities. Over thousands of years of its history, India has been invaded from the Iranian plateau, Central Asia, Arabia, Afghanistan, and the West; Indian people and culture have absorbed and changed these influences to produce a remarkable racial and cultural synthesis.

Religion, caste, and language are major determinants of social and political organization in India today. The government has recognized 18 languages as official; Hindi is the most widely spoken. Although 83% of the people are Hindu, India also is the home of more than 120 million Muslims—one of the world's largest Muslim populations. The population also includes Christians, Sikhs, Jains, Buddhists, and Parsis. The caste system reflects Indian occupational and religiously defined hierarchies. Traditionally, there are four broad categories of castes, including a category of outcastes, earlier called "untouchables" but now commonly referred to as "dalits." Within these broad categories there are thousands of castes and subcastes , whose relative status varies from region to region. Despite economic modernization and laws countering discrimination against the lower end of the class structure, the caste system remains an important source of social identification for most Hindus and a potent factor in the political life of the country.

Population Growth

The 1991 final census count gave India a total population of 846,302,688. However, estimates of India's population vary widely. According to the Population Division of the United Nations Department of International Economic and Social Affairs, the population had already reached 866 million in 1991.

The Population Division of the United Nations Economic and Social Commission for Asia and the Pacific (ESCAP) projected 896.5 million by mid-1993 with a 1.9 percent annual growth rate. The United States Bureau of the Census, assuming an annual population growth rate of 1.8 percent, put India's population in July 1995 at 936,545,814. These higher projections merit attention in light of the fact that the Planning Commission had estimated a figure of 844 million for 1991 while preparing the Eighth Five-Year Plan.

India accounts for some 2.4 percent of the world's landmass but is home to about 16 percent of the global population. The magnitude of the annual increase in population can be seen in the fact that India adds almost the total population of Australia or Sri Lanka every year. A 1992 study of India's population notes that India has more people than all of Africa and also more than North America and South America together. Between 1947 and 1991, India's population more than doubled.

Throughout the twentieth century, India has been in the midst of a demographic transition. At the beginning of the century, endemic disease, periodic epidemics, and famines kept the death rate high enough to balance out the high birth rate. Between 1911 and 1920, the birth and death rates were virtually equal—about forty-eight births and forty-eight deaths per 1,000 population. The increasing impact of curative and preventive medicine brought a steady decline in the death rate.

By the mid-1990s, the estimated birth rate had fallen to twenty-eight per 1,000, and the estimated death rate had fallen to ten per 1,000. Clearly, the future configuration of India's population (indeed the future of India itself) depends on what happens to the birth rate. Even the most optimistic projections do not suggest that the birth rate could drop below twenty per

1,000 before the year 2000. India's population is likely to exceed the 1 billion mark before the 2001 census.

The upward population in India spiral began in the 1920s and is reflected in intercensal growth increments. South Asia's population increased roughly 5 percent between 1901 and 1911 and actually declined slightly in the next decade. Population increased some 10 percent in the period from 1921 to 1931 and 13 to 14 percent in the 1930s and 1940s. Between 1951 and 1961, the population rose 21.5 percent. Between 1961 and 1971, the country's population increased by 24.8 percent. Thereafter a slight slowing of the increase was experienced: from 1971 to 1981, the population increased by 24.7 percent, and from 1981 to 1991, by 23.9 percent.

Population density

Population in India density has risen concomitantly with the massive increases in population. In 1901 India counted some seventy-seven persons per square kilometer; in 1981 there were 216 persons per square kilometer; by 1991 there were 267 persons per square kilometer—up almost 25 percent from the 1981 population density. India's average population density is higher than that of any other nation of comparable size. The highest densities are not only in heavily urbanized regions but also in areas that are mostly agricultural.

Population of India growth in the years between 1950 and 1970 centered on areas of new irrigation projects, areas subject to refugee resettlement, and regions of urban expansion. Areas where population did not increase at a rate approaching the national average were those facing the most severe economic hardships, overpopulated rural areas, and regions with low levels of urbanization.

The 1991 census, which was carried out under the direction of the Registrar General and Census Commissioner of India (part of the Ministry of Home Affairs), in keeping with the previous two censuses, used the term urban agglomerations. An urban agglomeration forms a continuous urban spread and consists of a city or town and its urban outgrowth outside the statutory limits. Or, an urban agglomerate may be two or more adjoining cities or towns and their outgrowths. A university campus or military base located on the outskirts of a city or town, which often increases the actual urban area of that city or town, is an example of an urban agglomeration.

In India urban agglomerations with a population of 1 million or more—there were twenty-four in 1991—are referred to as metropolitan areas. Places with a population of 100,000 or more are termed "cities" as compared with "towns," which have a population of less than 100,000. Including the metropolitan areas, there were 299 urban agglomerations with more than 100,000 population in 1991. These large urban agglomerations are designated as Class I urban units. There were five other classes of urban agglomerations, towns, and villages based on the size of their populations: Class II (50,000 to 99,999), Class III (20,000 to 49,999), Class IV (10,000 to 19,999), Class V (5,000 to 9,999), and Class VI.

The results of the 1991 census revealed that around 221 million, or 26.1 percent, of Indian's population lived in urban areas. Of this total, about 138 million people, or 16 percent, lived in the 299 urban agglomerations. In 1991 the twenty-four metropolitan cities accounted for 51 percent of India's total population living in Class I urban centers, with Bombay and Calcutta the largest at 12.6 million and 10.9 million, respectively.

In the early 1990s, growth was the most dramatic in the cities of central and southern India. About twenty cities in those two regions experienced a growth rate of more than 100 percent between 1981 and 1991. Areas subject to an influx of refugees also experienced noticeable demographic changes. Refugees from Bangladesh, Burma, and Sri Lanka contributed substantially to population growth in the regions in which they settled. Less dramatic population increases occurred in areas where Tibetan refugee settlements were founded after the Chinese annexation of Tibet in the 1950s.

The majority of districts had urban populations ranging on average from 15 to 40 percent in 1991. According to the 1991 census, urban clusters predominated in the upper part of the Indo-Gangetic Plain; in the Punjab and Haryana plains, and in part of western Uttar Pradesh. The lower part of the Indo-Gangetic Plain in southeastern Bihar, southern West Bengal, and northern Orissa also experienced increased urbanization. Similar increases occurred in the western coastal state of Gujarat and the union territory of Daman and Diu. In the Central Highlands in Madhya Pradesh and Maharashtra, urbanization was most noticeable in the river basins and adjacent plateau regions of the Mahanadi, Narmada, and Tapti rivers. The coastal plains and river deltas of the east and west coasts also showed increased levels of urbanization.

The hilly, inaccessible regions of the Peninsular Plateau, the northeast, and the Himalayas remain sparsely settled. As a general rule, the lower the population density and the more remote the region, the more likely it is to count a substantial portion of tribal people among its population. Urbanization in some sparsely settled regions is more developed than would seem warranted at first glance at their limited natural resources. Areas of western India that were formerly princely states (in Gujarat and the desert regions of Rajasthan) have substantial urban centers that originated as political-administrative centers and since independence have continued to exercise hegemony over their hinterlands.

The vast majority of Indians, nearly 625 million, or 73.9 percent, in 1991 lived in what are called villages of less than 5,000 people or in scattered hamlets and other rural settlements. The states with proportionately the greatest rural populations in 1991 were the states of Assam (88.9 percent), Sikkim (90.9 percent) and Himachal Pradesh (91.3 percent), and the tiny union territory of Dadra and Nagar Haveli (91.5 percent). Those with the smallest rural populations proportionately were the states of Gujarat (65.5 percent), Maharashtra (61.3 percent), Goa (58.9 percent), and Mizoram (53.9 percent). Most of the other states and the union territory of the Andaman and Nicobar Islands were near the national average.

Two other categories of India's population that are closely scrutinized by the national census are the Scheduled Castes and Scheduled Tribes. The greatest concentrations of Scheduled Caste members in 1991 lived in the states of Andhra Pradesh (10.5 million, or nearly 16 percent of the state's population), Tamil Nadu (10.7 million, or 19 percent), Bihar (12.5 million, or 14 percent), West Bengal (16 million, or 24 percent), and Uttar Pradesh (29.3 million, or 21 percent). Together, these and other Scheduled Caste members comprised about 139 million people, or more than 16 percent of the total population of India. Scheduled Tribe members represented only 8 percent of the total population (about 68 million). They were found in 1991 in the greatest numbers in Orissa (7 million, or 23 percent of the state's population), Maharashtra (7.3 million, or 9 percent), and Madhya Pradesh (15.3 million, or 23 percent). In proportion, however, the populations of states in the northeast had the greatest concentrations of Scheduled Tribe members. For example, 31 percent of the population of Tripura, 34 percent of Manipur, 64 percent of Arunachal Pradesh, 86 percent of Meghalaya, 88 percent of Nagaland, and 95 percent of Mizoram were Scheduled Tribe members. Other heavy concentrations were found in Dadra and Nagar Haveli, 79 percent of which was composed of Scheduled Tribe members, and Lakshadweep, with 94 percent of its population being Scheduled Tribe members.

LITERACY

Literacy is one of the important social characteristics on which information is obtained of every individual in the census. For the purposes of census a person aged seven and above, who can both read and write with understanding in any language, is treated as a literate. A person, who can only read but cannot write, is not a literate. Spread and diffusion of literacy are generally associated with essential traits of today's civilisation such as moder-nisation, urbanisation, industrialisation, communication and commerce. Higher levels of education and literacy lead to a greater awareness and also contributes to improvement of economic conditions. It acts as a catalyst for social upliftment enhancing the returns on investments made in almost every aspect of development effort, be it population control, health, hygiene, environmental degradation control, empowerment of women and weaker sections of the society. Improved levels of literacy also are prerequisites for acquiring various skills. In the censuses prior to 1991, children below five years of age were necessarily treated as illiterates.

The ability to read and write with understanding is not ordinarily achieved until one has some schooling or at least some time to develop these skills. Therefore, it was decided at the 1991 census that all children in the age group 0-6, will be treated as illiterate by definition and the population aged seven years and above only is to be classified as a literate or an illiterate. The same criterion has been retained at the census of India, 2001, also. It is not mandatory that to be treated as a literate, a person should have received any formal education or acquired any minimum educational standard.

Literacy status can be acquired through adult literacy classes or by attending any non-formal educational system. Persons who are unfortunately blind and read in Braille are also treated as literates. In censuses up to 1981, it was customary to work out the literacy rate taking into account the total population. Since literacy rate is more meaningful if the sub-population in the age group 0-6 is excluded from the total population, it was decided in 1991 to use the term literacy rate for the population relating to seven years and above. The same concept has been continued in 2001. The literacy rate taking into account the total population has now been termed as 'crude literacy rate'.

Table 2 presents the literacy rates for the country, states and union territories as reported at the census of India, 2001. Table 3 gives the number of literates and illiterates among the population aged seven years and above in absolute figures for India for the 1991 and 2001 censuses. It is important to take note of the changes in absolute numbers to observe their impact on the literacy trends in the country.

Of the 836,650,839 population recorded for the country at the Census of India, 1991 as many as 686,569,914 persons were aged seven years and above. Out of these 358,402,626 were literate and 328,167,288 illiterate. At the Census of India, 2001, out of the provisional total population of 1,014,651,658 the number of persons aged seven years and above is 858,219,695. Out of these 562,010,743 are literates and 296,208,952 illiterates. There has been an increase of 171,649,781 persons in the age group seven years and above during 1991-2001, while 203,608,117 additional persons have become literate during the decade.

Table 2. Literacy rates in India—2001: Figures at a glance

State/UT	*Persons*	*Males*	*Females*
India	65.38	75.85	54.16
Andhra Pradesh	61.11	70.85	51.17
Arunachal Pradesh	54.74	64.07	44.24
Assam	64.28	71.93	56.03
Bihar	47.53	60.32	33.57
Chhattisgarh	65.18	77.86	52.40
Goa	82.32	88.88	75.51
Gujarat	69.97	80.50	58.60
Haryana	68.59	79.25	56.31
Himachal Pradesh	77.13	86.02	68.08
Jammu & Kashmir	54.46	65.75	41.82
Jharkhand	54.13	67.94	39.38
Karnataka	67.04	76.29	57.45
Kerala	90.92	94.20	87.86
Madhya Pradesh	64.11	76.80	50.28

Maharastra	77.27	86.27	67.51
Manipur	68.87	77.87	59.70
Meghalaya	63.31	66.14	60.41
Mizoram	88.49	90.69	86.13
Nagaland	67.11	71.77	61.92
Orissa	63.61	75.95	50.97
Punjab	69.95	75.63	63.55
Rajasthan	61.03	76.46	44.34
Sikkim	69.68	76.73	61.46
Tamil Nadu	73.47	82.33	64.55
Tripura	73.66	81.47	65.41
Uttar Pradesh	57.36	70.13	42.98

The significant milestone reached in Census of India, 2001, is that the total number of illiterates has come down from 328,167,288 in 1991 to 296,208,952. Thus, for the first time since independence, there is a decline in the absolute number of illiterates during a decade. This is a major shift in improving the literacy status in India and the achievements of the decade 1991-2001 may permit us to label it as the 'Literacy Decade', if this trend can be made permanently irreversible from now onwards. Out of the 203,608,117 added to the literate population during 1991-2001, 107,986,561 were males and 95,621,556 were females.

Table 3. Number of literates and illiterates among population aged 7 years and above and their change—India: 1991 and 2001

Literates/Illiterates	*Persons*	*Males*	*Females*
Literates			
1991	358,402,626	228,983,134	129,419,492
2001	562,010,743	336,969,695	225,041,048
Increase in 2001 over 1991	203,608,117	107,986,561	95,621,556
Illiterates			
1991	328,167,288	128,099,211	200,068,077

2001	296,208,952	106,654,066	189,554,886
Increase in 2001 over 1991	-31,958,336	-21,445,145	-10,513,191

The projected population of those who attained the age of seven years and above after the conduct of the 1991 census, i.e., those who should have been enrolled in schools works out to 239.81 million as per the projections (including Jammu and Kashmir) made by the Office of the Registrar General, India (1996), while the increase in number of literates between 1991 and 2001 (excluding Jammu and Kashmir) is of 203.61 million. These figures possibly suggest that a majority of children who attained the age of seven years and above after 1991 attended school at one point of time or the other.

However, this preliminary trend can only be confirmed when age-wise data relating to literacy and children attending school is available. The number of literates have more than doubled in Dadra and Nagar Haveli and Rajasthan during the decade 1991-2001. The states and union territories, which have shown decadal percentage increase of more than 80 per cent, are Nagaland (85.60), Chhatisgarh (85.25), Madhya Pradesh (83.69), Daman and Diu (83.22) and Uttar Pradesh (81.75).

POPULATION PROJECTION

Population projection is a scientific attempt to peep into the future population scenario, conditioned by making certain assumptions, using data relating to the past available at that point of time. Assumptions used and their probability of adhering in future, forms a critical input in this mathematical effort. Predicting the future course of human fertility and mortality is not easy, especially when looking beyond much further in time. Medical and health intervention strategies, food production and its equitable availability, climatic variability, socio-cultural setting, politico-economic conditions and a host of other factors influence population dynamics, making it a somewhat unpredictable exercise. Therefore, much caution must be exercised when either making or using the population projections and the context of various conditions imposed, should not be lost sight of on the basis of past behaviour and the likely future scenario assumed.

Different population projections at the country level are made by the Government, National and International agencies from time to time. In addition, individual demographers make projections for the country as a whole and sometimes at the sub-national level also.

The international agencies who make projections for the world as a whole and also for individual countries are the United Nations Population Division, the World Bank, the United Nations Population Fund (UNFPA) etc. The need for population projection in India at various levels and by different components like age, sex, rural-urban etc., for the use by the official agencies uniformly, both at the center and the states was keenly felt in 1958 on the eve of the formulation of the third five year plan.

Beginning in 1958, it has been customary for the Office of the Registrar General and Census Commissioner, India to undertake the exercise of population projection on behalf of the Planning Commission of India. The first Expert Committee on Population Projections was set up by the Planning Commission in 1958 under the chairmanship of the Registrar General, India to provide a set of population projections for India and states.

The projections upto 1971 were then made available to the Planning Commission pending the release of 1961 Census data. Subsequently, with the release of the final population totals of the 1961 Census as well as taking into account the life table values of 1951-60, the Expert Committee was reactivated in 1963 for effecting a further revision of the projections and extending them up to 1981.The Committee gave its report in 1964. Out of the three sets of projections namely high, medium and low, the second one, that is, the medium one was recommended for official use.

Following the release of the 1971 Census provisional population totals, the Expert Committee was once again reconstituted to revise the existing official series of population projections of 1964. The Planning Commission again felt the need for another series of projections based on more recent data and subsequently constituted another Expert Committee in 1974, which submitted its report in 1978.

After the release of the five per cent sample data of the 1981 Census, Planning Commission reconstituted the Expert Committee on Population Projections in 1984. Population Projections for the period 1981-2001 were prepared under three assumptions on the basis of trends in fertility. This report was published in 1988 and the medium projections were recommended for official use.

In the light of the trends observed during 1980's in major demographic parameters, as revealed by the Sample Registration System (SRS), the Planning Commission apprehended that the future size of India's population might be higher than that projected by the Expert Committee. In order to have a fresh look at the projections, the Planning Commission set up a Standing Committee of Experts on Population Projections towards the end of October, 1988. This Committee reviewed the medium projections made by the Expert Committee of 1984, in light of the further data available on fertility, mortality and contraceptive prevalence (family planning) and submitted its report in 1989.

With the availability of age-sex distribution of population from the 1991 Census, the latest data relating to family planning performances and recent levels and trends in fertility and mortality as emerging from the SRS, a fresh need was felt by the Planning Commission for a new set of population projections. As such, the Planning Commission constituted a Technical Group on Population Projections in 1996 under the chairmanship of the Registrar General, India with the following objectives:

— To review the methodology of Population Projections adopted in the past

— To prepare fresh projections of mortality status and parameters of fertility conditions based on changed pattern of contraceptive use and proportion of married females (1991 Census) and other characteristics

— To make population projections afresh up to 2016

— To prepare projections of the possible period when NRR = 1 will be achieved by the States / UTs and the country as a whole.

The assumptions made to project the population of India up to 2016 are discussed below.

The Technical Group considered the Total Fertility Rate (TFR) as the overall indicator of fertility. The earlier approach of taking NRR=1 as the replacement level of fertility was changed to TFR =2.1. The TFR estimates based on the SRS data for India and major states were adopted. The lowest threshold of TFR was assumed to be 1.6. Two sets of TFR values from the SRS for India and major states for two time periods 1981-93 and 1985-93 were considered by the Group. On careful examination, the Group recommended the use of projected values of TFRs based on the period 1985-93 except for the states of Madhya Pradesh, Punjab, Rajasthan and Uttar Pradesh. For these four states, the projected levels of TFR based on the period 1981-93 were adopted. The projected levels of TFRs assumed for India for the initial period 1996-2001 and terminal period 2011-2016 were 3.13 and 2.52 respectively.

Although the SRS based sex ratio at birth of 110 for the period 1981-90, was found to be much higher than the internationally accepted conventional sex ratio at birth of 105-106, yet the Technical Group recommended the use of sex ratio at birth as obtained from the SRS in view of the overall broad consistency and reliability of the SRS data. ??For projecting the mortality levels, initially the Group considered two sets of mortality projections. The first one was based on five-yearly abridged life tables constructed from SRS Age Specific Death Rates (ASDR) for the periods 1981-85 to 1989-93. The second set of mortality projections were considered by utilizing the projected survival ratios based on the observed ASDR value from the SRS. After examining the merits of the two sets of mortality projections, the later one, that is, the survivorship ratio method was recommended for undertaking the population projections. An upper limit of 70 years for the expectation of life for males and females was recommended for all India and major states except for Kerala and Tamil Nadu. The projected levels of expectation of life at birth for males were 62.30 years for the period 1996-2001 and 67.04 years for the duration 2011-2016.Similarly, for females, these figures were 65.27 years and 69.18 years respectively.

In addition to considering the increase in the expectation of life at birth, the Group also considered the likely impact of AIDS on death rate. After considering the effect of likely deaths due to AIDS, it was found that future levels of the expectation of life at birth would have no significant impact of AIDS in the next 25 years.

Kingsley Davis, making a mathematical projection and assuming that mortality and fertility would behave as during the period 1921-41, estimated a population of 790 million for India and Pakistan combined. This obviously is much off the mark. On the other hand the term projection of Coale and Hoover with the assumption of sustained fertility until 1986 and for future years also estimated a population, which is higher by about one hundred and twenty millions from the provisional results of Census of India 2001.The additional impact of mortality decline notwithstanding, this projection possibly suggests that the minimum impact of family limitation programme is to the tune of about 120 million, since a sustained fertility was assumed right from the base year of projection and no mortality decline has been assumed after 1986.

Fertility in India has definitely declined in parts of the country though not at a pace as assumed in some of the earlier estimates made by this office for the Planning Commission. The population estimates made in 1980's have fallen short by 36 and 41 millions respectively. Possibly they reinforce the argument that fertility did not decline as rapidly or widely as was assumed. Even the more recent estimate of 1996 suggests a deficit of around 15 million. In effect this means that based on the assumptions used, the decline in growth of population may have fallen behind by about one year.

Registration System and fertility surveys on a stand-alone basis and for an external validation with a view to complement the other efforts. It is also important to take note that the perils of long term projections notwithstanding, it is felt that based on the medium term projection, India is all set to take over the population of China in possibly less than fifty years and continue to add to its population even beyond 2050. The writing on the wall is loud and clear and an acceptable way has to be found which fits into our socio-political system so that the dream of population stabilization becomes a reality in not too far a distant.

4

Factors Affecting Population Growth

India's population has always been connoted with some self explanatory evils like poverty, employment, economic backwardness, over crowding, low per capita income, environmental pollution, indebtedness etc. If population is taking its toll in India then why do we find so many countries like Japan, China, West Germany, Holland and Belgium surging radically and that too with a population density much higher than that of India? We always blame population as a cause of poverty. In our eyes, a newborn will certainly make our economy worse off. However, what if that child is being imparted good education and later provided with means of employment? Won't that child prove to be an asset to country in future course of time? Unfortunately, our government find itself incapable of providing that much-needed education to thousands of such children despite of spending lakhs and crores of rupees in provide free education, books and meals- thanks to the bureaucracy and corruption of Indian state.

Again, when we say that unemployment is caused by over population, we always forget that as the population increases demand for goods and services also increases. Consequently, to meet this ever-increasing demand, more and more people have to be employed. However, in India, despite of having this ever-increasing demand, we find thousands and lakhs of

Indians unemployed- thanks to government's irrational policies and myopic vision of trade. In our nation, even opening a paan corner or a rickshaw driving business can be as finicky as opening up a million dollar industry establishment. What more, a major proportion of a meagre income of 100 per day will have to be apparently divided among police, municipality, local goons and other parties.

One more reason why a substantial proportion of Indian population remain unemployed is lack of infrastructure like roads, railways, highways or lifelines like water, power provision etc. If our government starts building country's infrastructure, demand for workers will definitely increase and thus the employment. However, our state prefers to squander away taxpayer's money in providing subsidies that never reach to the needy, holding unconstrained and lavish parliamentary sessions and financing politicians' foreign visits. Even if it ventures into any infrastructure-building project, we end up witnessing frauds, leakages and other inefficient utilization of our hard-earned money causing a jet hole in tax payer's pocket. Ultimately, population is held responsible.

Now comes the problem of low per capita income which is actually the national income divided by total population. Per capita income can only be increased by two ways–increase the national income or decrease the population. As the government is not able to outwit the increase in proportion of population by increasing the national income, population is held as the scapegoat. A better way out would have been to use the increase in population in increasing the national income rather than blaming poulation to be the ultimate cause of low per capita income.

One more problem that surmounts is that of over crowding of cities leading to increase in slum areas and low standard of living. But saying that it is all because of over pouplation will not be logical statement. Why it is that in India, some states like Mumbai, Delhi and Chennai are densely populated and numerous others are scarcely populated. Definitely not because of population. Then what is the reason? It is fairly obvious that human beings are guided to do things that earn them more money– they are economically 'rational'. They prefer gains to losses. Thus, if many are choosing to shift from thinly populated countrysides to crowded towns, then surely there must be some economic rationale that explains this behaviour. It is glaringly evident, in this case, that urban areas generate prosperity and that people come flocking to them hoping for a share of that prosperity.

Now our government instead of concentrating on the magnitude of urbanization wastes its time in cursing population. If we want to embark upon the problem of poverty authentically, we must look upon urbanization as a way out. This, unfortunately, has never been considered by India. China, on the contrary, has a pronounced urban vision. China has made the connection between prosperity and urbanization to tackle the problem of overcrowding and poverty as a whole

Let alone all the problems, why is that India's population is being less fruitful. Sauvik Chatterji, a writer at Economic Times wrote about 'the more the merrier equation' in one of his articles in his regular columns "Antidote" which is as follows:

$$Pk + 3tc + F + S = \text{Prosperity}$$

Where:

Pk = Person with knowledge

3tc = Trade towns transport & communications tions

F = Freedom

S = Security

Pk refers to the person or human being with knowledge. The skills of the sweeper, the rag picker, the housemaid, the cab driver– all these are based on some 'knowledge'. Each kind of knowledge commands some price in the market. Trade is the basic economic activity of human beings that provides them with the means of living. Towns are where persons with knowledge are concentrated. You are more likely to strike a deal in a town than in the wide-open countryside. Transport & communications allow the economic pulse of the vast numbers of person with knowledge in them to inter-connect: "The More the Merrier". That is, they act as the vital auxiliaries to trade. "F" is freedom, the vital ingredient. Without economic freedom, the rest is useless. Each human being is looking out for his own economic benefit. He or she is the best judge of how that gain is to be obtained and should therefore be left free to get it. Indians possess very little economic freedom. In the 1999 world freedom index, India was ranked 120- "mostly unfree" is what we are. S is security, which our govt. has failed to provide to citizens even after 55 years of independence.

With this equation, we can judge why some Ps are poor. In our case, it is easy to see that many Ps are poor because all the other factors– K, the 3Ts, C, F and S – have been largely missing. We in India, don't have adequate modern knowledge. Transport and communications are rudimentary. Free trade is not practised. Economic freedom is in low supply. Security is likewise.

Now let us look at the various uncultivated advantages of Indian population. First, it's a mammoth population base of India that has made her an investment hub in the world. Similarly, there is a huge consumer base in India that can soak up the products of hundreds and thousands of companies without achieving the saturation. It's the demand for goods and services that is, why foreign direct investment is escalating drastically even with the presence of draconian FDI policy of our country. India has become a major source of revenue for many MNCs as well as native companies. It is all because of this edge that India has a say in world market. It is also evident from the fact that after Pokhran test, sanctions which were imposed by America became an error of judgment for her when its trade with India got hurt and she lost out a big target market in India and that is why America lifted up the sanctions very soon.

What more, India also has an incredible human resource base. It is not only providing human capital at cheap rates to various MNCs operating in India but also exporting brains to many countries and thus earning a lot of foreign exchange. It becomes evident from the very fact that many MNCs like GE Capital are wrapping up their call centres from many other countries so as to reduce their cost and started establishing their centres in India to get efficient human resources at cheap rates. Population itself is not a problem. It is the impotency of Indian govt and various concerned institutions in tapping the unbounded human resources of our country.

As in the "More the Merrier" equation, it was quite visible that persons with knowledge are increasing but the means by which they can become self-sufficient and not a burden on economy are missing. What we need to do is to build up those means at the first place.

The transportation links between surrounding towns and the metropolitans are grossly inadequate. For this, massive investments in transportation are essential. Once Indian population develops instant connectivity to all the surrounding as well as distant cities, trade will become easy and employment will also increase. Moreover, it will also counter the problem of overcrowding, lofty difference in real estate prices and unequal regional development. At the second place, we need to build up towns and trade through urbanization and introducing flexibility in trade norms. Thus providing the much-needed economic and personal freedom.

All said and done, more humans could have been more of a precious resource had we managed them efficiently. Population doomsday gives the impression that human beings are not a resource but a source of trouble. Statisticians who record an increase in the GDP when a calf is born, but reduce per capita income whenever a human infant is born seems to be assuming that human beings not worth anything. Should some discounted value of a human life not be added to GDP whenever a human child is born? Why do we look upon our children as a dead loss and not as future breadwinners? Whatever the reason may be one thing is for sure that it is not the people but their rulers who are the real problem.

FACORS DETERMINING POPULATION GROWTH

Until recently, birth rates and death rates were about the same, keeping the population stable. People had many children, but a large number of them died before age five. During the Industrial Revolution, a period of history in Europe and North America where there were great advances in science and technology, the success in reducing death rates was attributable to several factors:

(1) increases in food production and distribution,

(2) improvement in public health (water and sanitation), and

(3) medical technology (vaccines and antibiotics), along with gains in education and standards of living within many developing nations.

Without these attributes present in many children's lives, they could not have survived common diseases like measles or the flu. People were able to fight and cure deadly germs that once killed them. In addition, because of the technology, people could produce more and different kinds of food. Gradually, over a period of time, these discoveries and inventions spread throughout the world, lowering death rates and improving the quality of life for most people.

Food Production Distribution

The remarkable facts about the last 150 years has been the ability of farmers to increase food production geometrically in some places. Agricultural practices have improved in the India in the last two centuries. Much of the world experienced agricultural success, especially in the last 50 years. Between 1950 and 1984, for example, the amount of grain harvested worldwide increased from 631 million tons to 1.65 billion tons. This represents a gain of 2.6 times at a time when the world population increased by only 1.9 times.

In more recent years, the technology has produced a broader variety of techniques: new kinds of seed, chemical fertilizers, pesticides, and more sophisticated machinery. The use of technology has made possible the rapid expansion of agriculture in the United States and other MDCs and LDCs. The use of pesticides in LDCs, for example was expected to increased between 400 to 600% in the last 25 years of the twentieth century.

During the past 10 years, the world's food production has increased by 24 per cent, outpacing the rate of population growth. However, this increase was not evenly distributed throughout the world. For example, in Africa, food production decreased, while population increased. And world cereal production fell in 1993, according to the FAO, which predicted a food shortage in 20 countries during 1994. However, most experts agree that there is no shortage of food, and that equitable distribution should be sufficient to meet all needs for the future.

Lack of money to buy food is the problem of malnourishment. Poverty, in effect translates the world adequacy into national and local shortages. Within households, men and boys have priority for whatever food is available, while women and children, especially girl children are the first to suffer malnutrition. Few resources are available to women, even though they are often responsible the for food supply.

Improvement in Public Health

People have concerns about surviving daily living, such as meeting basic needs: food, water, and housing. First, access to safe drinking water was related to the incidence of epidemic diseases such as cholera and child survival. Less than 50% of the population had access to safe drinking water before 1990. By 1990, access to safe drinking water had increased by 75 per cent. But between 1990 and 2000 the numbers of people without access to safe water are projected to increase.

An increasing number of countries both developed and developing are approaching the limits of sustainable water use based on their own re-newable resources. Second, the pressure to provide adequate housing increases as the population grows. More than half of the developing world's population will be living in urban areas by the end of the century. This growth outstrips the capacity to provide housing and services for others. In some countries, finding a place to live is hard, especially for women. Some women and children are forced to live in the poorest community where they are open to exploitation and abuse.

The priorities for getting rid of poverty, improving food supply, ending malnutrition, and providing adequate housing coincide at all points with those required for balanced population growth.

Conquest of disease

The biggest population story of the last hundred years has been the conquest of disease. Scientists have learned a great deal about the ways to prevent and cure many types of disease. Thus, millions of people who would have died of disease a century ago are more likely to live to old age. The most effective tools in the conquest of disease have been improved knowledge about nutrition, vaccinations, better public health practices and the development of new medicines. In the late 80s, a baby born in Iceland was 32 times more likely to live to the age of one year as a baby born in Afghanistan.

The major reason for this large difference in survival rate is nutrition. When young children get enough of the right kinds of food, they are likely to live to be adults. In many nations the people know about proper nutrition for young children and adults. Unfortunately, in many LCDs the people lack the money and skills that would allow them to use the knowledge about nutrition they already have. As a result, infant death rates and therefore, overall death rates, remain high in many LDCs.

The second most important factor is vaccinations. As far back as 1800, scientists knew how to use vaccines to protect people from infectious disease. Use of that knowledge has reduced the rate of diseases like influenza, smallpox, polio and rubella in MDCs. Again, lack of resources has prevented many LDCs from making similar use of vaccinations to reduce the rate of infectious disease and death rates in their countries. Moreover, vaccines are still not available for some diseases-malaria is the most obvious example and the greatest concern in LDCs.

Third, better public health practices— the germ theory of disease, discovered by Louis Pasteur in the 1870s clearly demonstrated that a person's health was also a community problem. Sewage dumped into a public water supply could cause disease throughout the community. With this understanding, the science of public health was born.

Today, public health measures like waste treatment, water purification, vaccination, and nutritional education are well developed in MDCs. However, public health measures are still absent in many LDCs. As a result, disease continues to spread and cause high death rates. And finally, with the advent of new medicines, disease was less of a problem in MDCs because medical science has invented a whole range of new medicines with which to treat everything from infections to pneumonia.

In many LDCs, new drugs and medicines are simply not available. As stated earlier, death rates in MDCs have fallen largely because of improved health and medical knowledge and because of better health and medical practices based on that knowledge. Death rates in many LDCs remain high because the money, personnel and facilities needed to put that knowledge into practice are not available. Progress in medical science has, therefore, had a great effect on the population of most nations of the world. Nearly everywhere death rates have fallen.

At the same time, birth rates, at least in the LDCs, have remained high. This combination of high birth rates and low death rates have led to the population explosion in many countries throughout the world. The end of the population explosion worldwide will be determined by how much countries invest in family planning efforts to lower fertility and slow down population growth.

Different populations grow at different rates around the world. This depends on how many children families have and the number of years someone is expected to live. The population of many countries in Asia, Africa and Latin America are growing the fastest, especially where large families are still important. These poorer, less developed countries (LDCs) tend to have shorter lives and higher infant death rates. When couples know some of their children may die, they choose to have more. However, many couples wish to limit family size, but lack the information and means to make these choices.

Decreaced mortality rate

The average Indian male born in the 1990s can expect to live 58.5 years; women can expect to live only slightly longer (59.6 years), according to 1995 estimates. Life expectancy has risen dramatically throughout the century from a scant twenty years in the 1911-20 period. Although men enjoyed a slightly longer life expectancy throughout the first part of the twentieth century, by 1990 women had slightly surpassed men.

The death rate declined from 48.6 per 1,000 in the 1910-20 period to fifteen per 1,000 in the 1970s, and improved thereafter, reaching ten per 1,000 by 1990, a rate that held steady through the mid-1990s. India's high infant mortality rate was estimated to exceed 76 per 1,000 live births in 1995. Thirty percent of infants had low birth weights, and the death rate for children aged one to four years was around ten per 1,000 of the population.

According to a 1989 National Nutrition Monitoring Bureau report, less than 15 percent of the population was adequately nourished, although 96 percent received an adequate number of calories per day. In 1986 daily average intake was 2,238 calories as compared with 2,630 calories in China.

According to UN findings, caloric intake per day in India had fallen slightly to 2,229 in 1989, lending credence to the concerns of some experts who claimed that annual nutritional standards statistics cannot be relied on to show whether poverty is actually being reduced. Instead, such studies may actually pick up short-term amelioration of poverty as the result of a period of good crops rather than a long-term trend.

Official Indian estimates of the poverty level are based on a person's income and corresponding access to minimum nutritional needs. There were 332 million people at or below the poverty level in FY 1991, most of whom lived in rural areas.

Communicable and noncommunicable diseases

A number of endemic communicable diseases present a serious public health hazard in India. Over the years, the government has set up a variety of national programs aimed at controlling or eradicating these diseases. Other initiatives seek to limit the incidence of respiratory infections, cholera, diarrheal diseases, trachoma, goiter, and sexually transmitted diseases.

Smallpox, formerly a significant source of mortality, was eradicated as part of the worldwide effort to eliminate that disease. India was declared smallpox-free in 1975. Malaria remains a serious health hazard; although the incidence of the disease declined sharply in the postindependence period, India remains one of the most heavily malarial countries in the world.

Only the Himalaya region above 1,500 meters is spared. In 1965 government sources registered only 150,000 cases, a notable drop from the 75 million cases in the early postindependence years.

This success was short-lived, however, as the malarial parasites became increasingly resistant to the insecticides and drugs used to combat the disease. By the mid-1970s, there were nearly 6.5 million cases on record. The situation again improved because of more conscientious efforts; by 1982 the number of cases had fallen by roughly two-thirds. This downward trend continued, and in 1987 slightly fewer than 1.7 million cases of malaria were reported. In the early 1990s, about 389 million people were at risk of infection from filaria parasites; 19 million showed symptoms of filariasis, and 25 million were deemed to be hosts to the parasites.

Efforts at control, under the National Filaria Control Programme, which was established in 1955, have focused on eliminating the filaria larvae in urban locales, and by the early 1990s there were more than 200 filaria control units in operation. Leprosy, a major public health and social problem, is endemic, with all the states and union territories reporting cases. However, the prevalence of the disease varies. About 3 million leprosy cases are estimated to exist nationally, of which 15 to 20 percent are infectious.

The National Leprosy Control Programme was started in 1955, but it only received high priority after 1980. In FY 1982, it was redesignated as the National Leprosy Eradication Programme. Its goal was to achieve eradication of the disease by 2000. To that end, 758 leprosy control units, 900 urban leprosy centers, 291 temporary hospitalization wards, 285 district leprosy units, and some 6,000 lower-level centers had been established by March 1990. By March 1992, nearly 1.7 million patients were receiving regular multidrug treatment, which is more effective than the standard single drug therapy. India is subject to outbreaks of various diseases. Among them is pneumonic plague, an episode of which spread quickly throughout India in 1994 killing hundreds before being brought under control.

Tuberculosis, trachoma, and goiter are endemic. In the early 1980s, there were an estimated 10 million cases of tuberculosis, of which about 25 percent were infectious. During 1991 nearly 1.6 million new tuberculosis cases were detected. The functions of the Trachoma Control Programme, which started in 1968, have been subsumed by the National Programme for the Control of Blindness.

Approximately 45 million Indians are vision-impaired; roughly 12 million are blind. The incidence of goiter is dominant throughout the sub-Himalayan states from Jammu and Kashmir to the northeast. There are some 170 million people who are exposed to iodine deficiency disorders.

Starting in the late 1980s, the central government began a salt iodinization program for all edible salt, and by 1991 record production—2.5 million tons—of iodized salt had been achieved. There are as well anemias related to poor nutrition, a variety of diseases caused by vitamin and mineral deficiencies—beriberi, scurvy, osteomalacia, and rickets—and a high incidence of parasitic infection.

Diarrheal diseases, the primary cause of early childhood mortality, are linked to inadequate sewage disposal and lack of safe drinking water. Roughly 50 percent of all illness is attributed to poor sanitation; in rural areas, about 80 percent of all children are infected by parasitic worms. Estimates in the early 1980s suggested that although more than 80 percent of the urban population had access to reasonably safe water, fewer than 5 percent of rural dwellers did.

Waterborne sewage systems were woefully overburdened; only around 30 percent of urban populations had adequate sewage disposal, but scarcely any populations outside cities did. In 1990, according to United States sources, only 3 percent of the rural population and 44 percent of the urban population had access to sanitation services, a level relatively low by developing nation standards. There were better findings for access to potable water: 69 percent in the rural areas and 86 percent in urban areas, relatively high percentages by developing nation standards. In the mid-1990s, about 1 million people die each year of diseases associated with diarrhea.

India has an estimated 1.5 million to 2 million cases of cancer, with 500,000 new cases added each year. Annual deaths from cancer total around 300,000. The most common malignancies are cancer of the oral cavity, cervix, and breast. Cardiovascular diseases are a major health problem; men and women suffer from them in almost equal numbers.

World population grows as a result of net migration is the difference between the number of people entering a geographic area and those leaving. Over time, migration contributes more than just the initial number of people moving into an area, because the children and grandchildren born to the immigrant population add several times the original number to the population base. There is also an increase in the number of deaths as a result of in-migration.

Most Americans are immigrants or descendants of immigrants who arrived here over the past 200 years. Only a small fraction of the population is related to the American Indians who were here when the first European settlers arrived in the 1600s. Australia and Brazil are other countries whose current populations consist primarily of descendants of persons who immigrated there during the past two centuries.

International migration

International migration is at an all-time high in terms of absolute numbers. About 145 million people lived outside their native countries in the mid-1990s, and the number is increasing by anywhere from 2 million to 4 million each year. In the mid-1990s, the largest immigration flows were from Latin America and Asia into North America, and from Eastern Europe, the countries of the former Soviet Union, and North Africa into Northern and Western Europe. The Middle East draws migrants from Africa and Asia and hosts millions of refugees from within the region. There is considerable migration within Asia, Africa, and Latin America.

Most people move for economic reasons, but some migrate to escape political or religious persecution or simply to fulfill a personal dream. Some experts divide the many reasons people leave their homes for a new one into push and pull factors. Push factors might be widespread unemployment, lack of farmland, famine, or war at home. The Great Depression is a good example of a push factor, as hard times encouraged more residents to leave the United States than move in. In the 1980s and 1990s, hundreds of thousands of Africans were pushed out of their homelands to neighboring countries because of famine and civil war.

Factors that attract migrants include a booming economy, favourable immigration laws, or free agricultural land in the area to which the migrant is moving. The labour shortage in Japan is pulling record numbers of legal and illegal immigrants to fill the low-status, low-paying, or dangerous jobs that Japanese natives reject.

The United Nations estimates that to keep a working population of 87 million through 2050, Japan would have to accept 609,000 immigrants a year. Between 1990 and 1999, the number of legal foreigners increased from 1.1 million to 1.6 million. Estimates of illegal migrants in Japan range from 150,000 to 300,000.

The majority of migrants to the United States in the past 200 years were European. During the first decade of this century nearly 9 million immigrants entered this country, and more than 90 percent were from Europe. By mid-century, just half of the migrants were from Europe. The total number of immigrants fell to around 1 million in the 1940s. In the 1980s the number of migrants increased to levels similar to those at the turn of the century. But 84 percent of these migrants were from Latin America and Asia, and just 10 percent were from Europe. The volume of legal immigration and the prevalence of migrants from Asia and Latin America will continue in the new century.

The origins of immigrants change over time, as do their numbers and the effect that they have on U.S. population growth. According to one estimate, about 42 percent of the U.S. population in 1900 resulted from immigration during the preceding century.

Immigration was an even greater factor in growth between 1900 and 1950, when 20 million people entered the country. Natural increase added an average of 1 percent of the population increase per year during that period. At that rate the population would have doubled in about 70 years. But it took only 50 years to double. Migration stepped up the doubling by 20 years. The volume of legal migration has fluctuated since the 1930s. Immigration has accounted for an increasing portion of population growth as American women began having fewer children. Today one-third of the U.S. population growth is from net migration. The U.S. Census Bureau projects that the U.S. population will reach 403,687,000 by 2050. Of this projected growth, 36 percent may result from immigration, with 46,691,756 new immigrants being added in the next 50 years.

GOVERNMENT POLICIES

Of the three components of population change, migration is the most difficult component to predict and is most affected by government policies and government policies. Because nations can control their borders, they may regulate the flow of legal immigrants. The oil-producing countries in the Middle East offered financial incentives to attract immigrants, just as the United States and Australia once offered free land. In 1990, Japan permitted employment rights and residence for ethnic Japanese from Latin America.

In 1998, 660,477 immigrants were admitted legally to the United States. Many foreigners also enter the country illegally each year. The exact number of persons migrating illegally to the United States is unknown, but estimates range from 100,000 to 500,000 per year.

POPULATION & DEVELOPMENT

Rapid population growth is a major cause of poverty when population growth exceeds the rate of economic growth. In this situation, standards of living fall and greater demands are placed on limited resources. Rapid population growth has short and long run impacts:

— In the short run falling per capita income means fewer resources are available for education to develop human capital- a major factor in raising productivity

— In the long run more workers are available to help raise Gross Domestic Product (GDP) after a lead time of 15+ years

— Implications: Reduce family size through education, family planning, tax incentives' or legislation eg China one child programme

— Dependents are those supported by the economically active eg children, ill adults and the elderly. The dependency ratio measures the ratio of dependents to economically active. Cet par a high ratio reduces per capita incomes. A high dependency ratio places a high burden on government spending and is a cause of poverty.

The impact of Aids

AIDs is a tragedy that is affecting the size and structure of population. If AIDs is widespread amongst the economically active, the work force becomes ill and - where parents die - responsibility for dependents falls to the extended family or the state. AIDs damages economic growth through:

— Falls in productivity through substantial absenteeism

— Increased private sector costs for recruitment & training

— Lower disposable income as millions of workers lose income and only necessities can be afforded. A greater proportion of disposable income is used for medical and funeral expenses

Migration and development

Rural-to-urban migration is a common experience in less developed countries. Those who migrate in search of a better standard of living are usually younger, better educated, and less risk adverse. There are two main motive for migrating:

1) *Push factors:* These are generally negative and include: famine, loss of land, political persecution. Relatively few migrations occur solely for push factors alone

2) *Pull factors:* These are generally positive and include perceived improved job and social opportunities earnings in cities. Such workers are economic migrants.

Large scale rural-to-urban migration places a strain on city economic systems. For example:

— There is insufficient demand for labour to absorb newly arrived workers

— Squatter settlements and over-crowded slums strain the capacity of government to provide basic services such as water, electricity and sewerage

— The environment, natural resources, social cohesion and individual rights are at risk.

SPECIAL SITUATION IN LESS ECONOMICALLY DEVELOPED COUNTRIES

The populations of most less economically developed countries (LEDCs) are growing very rapidly. Most are at stage 2 and 3 of the Demographic Transition Model. They have declining deaths rates and high birth rates. Therefore, natural increase is high.

— Death rates are declining because of improvements in sanitation and healthcare.

— Birth rates are high for a number of reasons:

— Lack of family planning education or contraceptives

— In rural areas children are needed as labour on farms. In urban areas they are needed to work in the informal sector to earn money for their families.

— Women have a large number of children as there is a high level of infant mortality

— Culture/religion mean it is unacceptable to use contraception

India's population is estimated to be around one billion. India has one of the highest population growth rates in the world. In the last ten years its population has increased by 181 million. If this growth rate continues it could become the world's most populated country by 2020.

However, India's population growth rate is slowing. This is particularly the case in the southern state of Kerala. In Kerala there have been a number of initiatives to reduce population growth:

1. *Women are being educated*: Around half of all Indian women cannot read or write (illiterate). However, in Kerala 85% of women are literate. Better educated women are more likely to keep their children healthy. Therefore Infant mortality has dropped. This has led to a drop in birth rates. If children are surviving families no longer have to have a couple of extra children to replace those that die.

2. Contraception is more widely available

3. The status of women has improved significantly

   Women are no longer seen as a burden - they are regarded as an asset. Traditionally in India when a woman gets married the family have to pay money to the bridegroom's family. This is called a dowry. However, in Kerala it is the bridegroom's family who pay a dowry to the brides family.

POPULATION DISTRIBUTION

Population distribution means the pattern of where people live. World population distribution is uneven. Places which are sparsely populated contain few people. Places which are densely populated contain many people. Sparsely populated places tend to be difficult places to live. These are usually places with hostile environments e.g. Antarctica. Places which are densely populated are habitable environments e.g. Europe.

POPULATION DENSITY

Population density is a measurement of the number of people in an area. It is an average number. Population density is calculated by dividing the number of people by area. Population density is usually shown as the number of people per square kilometer. The map below is a choropleth (shading) map and illustrates population density. The darker the colour the greater the population density.

World population distribution is uneven. Some areas have a high population density while others have a low population density. Areas of high population density tend to be located between 20° and 60°N. This area contains a large land area and a relatively temperate climate.

POPULATION CHANGE

The world's population is growing very rapidly. In 1820 the world's population reached 1 billion. In 1990 it reached 6 billion

Table 1. Factors Affecting Population Density

Physical Factors	High Density	Low Density
Relief (shape and height of land)	Low land which is flat e.g. Ganges Valley in India	High land that is mountainous e.g. Himalayas
Resources	Areas rich in resources (e.g. coal, oil, wood, fishing etc.) tend to densely populated e.g. Western Europe	Areas with few resources tend to be sparsely populated e.g. The Sahel
Climate	Areas with temperate climates tend to be densely populated as there is enough rain and heat to grow crops e.g. UK	Areas with extreme climates of hot and cold tend to be sparsely populated e.g. the Sahara Desert
Human Factors	High Density	Low Density
Political	Countries with stable governments tend to have a high population density e.g. Singapore	Unstable countries tend to have lower population densities as people migrate e.g. Afghanistan.
Social	Groups of people want to live close to each other for security e.g. USA	Other groups of people prefer to be isolated e.g. Scandinavians
Economic	Good job opportunities encourage high population densities, particularly in large cities in MEDCs and LEDCs around the	Limited job opportunities cause some areas to be sparsely populated world. e.g. Amazon Rainforest

people. This rapid growth in population has been called a population explosion.

The major reason for population changes, whether in an individual country or for the whole world, is the change in birth and death rates. The birth rate is the number of live babies born in a year for every 1000 people in the total population. Death rates are number of people dying per 1000 people. When birth rates are higher than death rates the population of an area will increase.

Over the past 150 years improvements in health care and sanitation around the world have led to a drop in the death rate. While birth rates have dropped in MEDCs, birth rates are still high in LEDCs. Therefore the number of people in the world has grown rapidly.

LIFE EXPECTANCY

Life expectancy is the average age a person can expect to live to in a particular area. Life expectancy can be used as an indicator of the overall 'health' of a country. From this figure you can determine many features of a country e.g. standard of living. As a general rule the higher the life expectancy the more healthy (or developed) a country is.

THE DEMOGRAPHIC TRANSITION MODEL

The Demographic Transition Model attempts to show how population changes as a country develops. The model is divided into four stages.

— *Stage 1*: Birth rate and death rate are high - low natural increase - low total population

— *Stage 2*: Birth rate is high - death rate is falling - high natural increase (population growth)

— *Stage 3*: Falling birth rate - low death rate - high natural increase (population growth)

— *Stage 4*: Birth rate and death rate is low - low natural increase - high total population

The Demographic Transition Model does not take into account migration.

POPULATION STRUCTURE / POPULATION PYRAMIDS

The population structure for an area shows the number of males and females within different age groups in the population. This information is displayed as an age-sex or population pyramid. Population pyramids of LEDCs (Less Economically Developed Countries) typically have a wide base and a narrow top. This represents a high birth rate and high death rate. Population pyramids of MEDCs (More Economically Developed Countries) typically have a roughly equal distribution of population throughout the age groups. The top obviously gets narrower as a result of deaths. Population pyramids for every country in the world can be found here. Population pyramids are used to show the structure of the population according to age and sex.

5

POPULATION AND QUALITY OF LIFE

ECONOMIC TRENDS

Gross national product (GNP) per capita increased from Indian Rs. 6340 in 1991/92 to Rs. 13,193 in 1997/98. The annual growth rate of the GNP increased from 0.5% in 1991/92 to 7.0% in 1995/96, but declined to 4% in 2000/2001. The percentage of poor in rural areas increased from 20.5 in 1991/92 to 22.9 in 1992/93 and to 37.3% in 1993/94. Since the early 1990s, overall economic growth has been faster. The situation regarding balance of payments has strengthened considerably, and the central government's fiscal deficit as a proportion of the gross domestic product (GDP) has declined significantly.

DEMOGRAPHIC TRENDS

The crude birth rate (CBR) declined from 29.5 in 1991 to 26.1 in 1999, while the crude death rate (CDR) declined from 9.8 to 8.7 per 1000 population over the same period. The total fertility rate (TFR decreased from 3.6 in 1991 to 2.85 in 1996-98. The annual population growth rate declined from 1.97 in 1991 to 1.74 in 1999. The population, however, continues to grow, as the decline in the birth rate is not as rapid as the decline in the death rate. Due to the increase in life expectancy at birth, the number of elderly persons in the population is now increasing, for which specific health facilities will need to be provided. Urban migration over the last decade has resulted in the rapid growth of urban slums, with ad hoc provisions for health care if any. Within the 9th plan steps are proposed to improve urban primary health center (PHC).

SOCIAL TRENDS

From the 2001 population census, the literacy rate for males is 75.85% and for females is 54.16%. The changing economic situation created by urbanization, industrialization and new economic liberalization has transformed the Indian social structure and values from a traditionally agrarian economy to a modern industrial order. The emerging nuclear family is exposed to severe economic and social constraints and changes.

The traditional mechanisms for social security and adjustment in times of crisis and conflict are fast disappearing. This transformation has resulted in the creation of several social problems for individuals and groups such as older persons, the disabled, drug addicts, street children, child labor, HIV-infected populations, etc. There has also been increased violence - individually as well as collectively - especially towards women and young girls, which has assumed a national dimension.

The problem of drug abuse is no more confined to a particular section of society but has infiltrated all strata. The large uncontrolled influx of rural migrants to urban areas in search of better earnings and job opportunities leaves them totally vulnerable, particularly the children of these migrant families. The negative influence of the electronic media appears to have resulted in an increase in juvenile delinquency, vagrancy, robberies, murders and kidnappings. There is a plethora of social legislation to safeguard the interest of persons in distress and to deal with the various social problems. Many of the acts have been amended in recent years to give them more teeth in terms of their effectiveness.

However, there are wide gaps in the implementation of these acts with regard to coverage, quality and content, which affect social development and the well being of the people. The 9th Five year Plans (FYP) envisages a more holistic approach to these social problems, with strategies aimed at specific target groups and/or problems.

FOOD SUPPLY AND NUTRITIONAL STATUS

The proportion of newborns weighing less than 2500 grams at birth was reported as 23% in 1995/96. The proportion of children under 3 years whose weight-for-age was less than minus 2 SD below the median was 47% (1998/99). It is estimated that 200 million people are exposed to the risk of iodine deficiency disorders (IDDs) and that 63 million suffer from goitre. Surveys conducted in 275 districts have revealed that 235 districts are endemic for IDDs. In 1991, 87.5% of pregnant women were found to be anaemic. The National Institute of Nutrition in Hyderabad reported that 56% of children under five years of age had iron deficiency anaemia. The contribution of vitamin A deficiency to blindness was estimated to be 2% in 1975 and 0.04% in 1990.

A national IDD control programme was launched in 1992, which covers all states and union territories. The strategy is the use of iodated salt and all aspects of programme implementation are being addressed. Anaemia contributed to 20% of maternal deaths in 1991. An intervention programme that commenced in 1992 prioritized pregnant women for iron and folic acid administration.

During 1994/95, 85.8% of pregnant women were covered with the recommended daily dose of iron folate tablets. The most susceptible group for vitamin A deficiency blindness is preschool children. The child survival programme seeks to administer five doses of vitamin A to all children under three years. During 1994/95, 72.6% of infants and 54.8% of 1-2 year old children were administered vitamin A. Other actions include the Integrated Child Development Service (ICDS) programme that provides a package of services to 54 million beneficiaries comprising preschool children, pregnant women and lactating mothers, and the mid-day meal programme for primary school children.

The following goals have been set to be achieved by the year 2000: reduction by 50% of moderate and severe protein-energy malnutrition (PEM) in preschool children, reduction of low birth weight to less than 10%, elimination of blindness due to vitamin A, reduction of iron deficiency anaemia among pregnant women to 25%, and reduction of IDDs to less than 10% in endemic districts.

The proportion of males 15 years and over who were regular smokers in the 1980s has been estimated at 32-74% (rural) and 46-63% (urban), and females 20-50% (rural) and 2-16% (urban). Currently there is an increasing trend in smoking among youth. Other significant changes in lifestyles relate to lack of physical activity among the affluent, increased use of fast foods, substance abuse, and violence, particularly against young women and children. The government has taken action to promote healthy lifestyles through sports, health education, setting up of no smoking zones, legislation banning smoking in public places, and establishing drug detoxification centers. A major constraint is the government revenue derived from tobacco, sponsorship of activities, especially sports events by tobacco companies, and high-pressure advertising.

HEALTH AND ENVIRONMENT

General protection of the environment

Due to an increase in unplanned urbanization and industrialization, the environment has deteriorated significantly. Pollution from a wide variety of emissions, such as from automobiles and industrial activities, has reached critical levels in many urban and industrial areas, causing respiratory, ocular and other health problems. Monitoring of the urban environment in selected cities in recent years by the pollution control authority has identified 21 critically polluted areas in the country.

Agricultural activities including widespread use of fertilizers, pesticides and weed killers also alter the environment and create health hazards.

Water stagnation and the consequent multiplication of vectors has increased the risk of vector-borne diseases. The risk associated with disposal of hospital wastes has added to the overall unhealthy situation. India is a party to the UN Conference on Environment and Development (UNCED) held in 1992. In the same year, a national conservation strategy and a policy statement on environment were formulated. The policy addresses issues related to sustainable development including health. Thrust has also been given to management of hazardous waste, adoption of clean technologies by industries, establishment of effluent treatment plants, criteria for environmentally friendly products, phasing out of ozone depleting substances, and creating mass awareness programmes. A very far-reaching notification by the Ministry of Environment and Forests gazetted in 1994 makes it obligatory for almost all development projects to conduct an environmental impact assessment study which has to be evaluated by an impact assessment agency.

A Government constituted group at the highest level has identified six priority programme areas, namely urban low cost sanitation, urban waste water management, urban solid waste management including hospital waste management, rural environmental sanitation, industrial waste management and air pollution control, and strengthening of health surveillance and support services.

These areas have been addressed in the Dayal Committee Report that forms the basis for a comprehensive national programme on sanitation and environmental hygiene. There are many constitutional provisions and laws pertaining to the environment and its protection and improvement. However, the level of enforcement has been extremely poor. Besides, there is no comprehensive legislation on environment and health. In view of the current situation and the Dayal Committee Report, it was proposed that action be taken by the concerned ministries/departments to prioritize the areas and activities that should be included in the 9th plan. During the 9th FYP the Ministry has proposed the following actions:

Strengthen environmental health and health risk assessment in the country. A division of environmental health will be established in the Department of Health for this purpose.

— Establish a hospital waste management programme.

— Initiate drinking water quality surveillance as a part of disease surveillance.

Water supply and sanitation

The proportion of the population with safe drinking water available at home or with reasonable access was 92.6% in 1998/99 for urban areas and 72.3% for rural areas. The proportion of the population with adequate excreta disposal facilities was 80.7% in 1998/99 in urban areas and 18.9 in rural areas. At the time of formulation of the 8th plan, it was estimated that with regard to water there were about 3000 hard-core 'no source' villages out of a list of 'problem' villages numbering 162,000. Besides this, about 150,000 villages were only partially covered. Regarding urban water supply, the service levels are far below desired norms. During the mid 90s, an accelerated urban water supply programme was initiated for towns having less than 20,000 population.

The provision of hygienic sanitation facilities through conventional sewage and on-site low cost sanitation has not been given priority. Though the 8th plan envisaged conversion of all existing dry latrines, the final result is nowhere near the target. The main constraints with regard to water supply are inadequate maintenance of rural water systems, lack of finances and poor community involvement.

Most municipalities do not have any system for monitoring the quality of water, with contamination causing episodes of water-borne diseases even in metro cities like Delhi and Calcutta. Most of the people in rural areas are not aware of the health and environmental benefits of improved sanitation. Future actions include phasing of the rural water supply programme, more financial support from the state finance commissions, more responsibilities given to local bodies and village panchayats, water supply and sanitation agencies to have full autonomy in declaring tariffs, improving manpower and equipment support to municipal authorities, and creating public awareness regarding safe water and sanitation.

The available data regarding health personnel show a national total of 503,900 physicians giving a ratio of 5.2 per 10,000 population. The number of registered nurse/midwifes totaled 607,376. The number of medical colleges has increased significantly over the past decades with the standard of medical education of undergraduates and postgraduates maintained at a high level.

The National Institute of Health and Family Welfare (NIHFW) is involved in providing in-service training for all categories of health and family welfare personnel. The curriculum for graduate medical education has recently been revised to provide integrated teaching and more practical learning, as well as greater opportunities for acquisition of skills.

The importance of social factors in relation to problems of health and disease are emphasized and a community-based approach is also included in the training. The main constraints are the shortage of funds, particularly for government institutions imparting medical education, and the problem of deployment of medical personnel to rural areas due to inadequate facilities to meet personal and professional needs.

Vacancies continue to exist in the posts of laboratory technicians, radiographers and other paraprofessionals which have serious service implications, particularly for programmes like malaria and tuberculosis. The ratio of nurses to doctors is also below the optimum. Other constraints include the low priority given to in-service training, inadequate staffing of training institutions, quality concerns among trainers, and inadequate facilities in training institutions. As for future actions, the central council for Health and Family Welfare suggested in 1993 that an Educational Commission in Health Sciences be set up to oversee, coordinate and support activities in this area. An omnibus council was also proposed to cover a range of paramedical personnel.

Financial resources for health

For the period 1998, the total health expenditure as a percentage of the GDP was 5.1%. Public expenditure on health was 18% of the total expenditure on health. The total government health expenditure as a percentage of the total government expenditure was 5.6%. Though India was committed to achieve HFA by the year 2000, the range and complexities of health issues have also been substantial.

On the one hand the government has been struggling to combat communicable diseases while on the other having to cope with noncommunicable diseases like diabetes, cancer, cardiovascular diseases, etc. In the constitutional provisions, health is primarily a state subject. States/union territories account for 76.26% of the 8th plan health sector outlay as compared to 23.74% from the center. To augment the resources for health care, earmarked outlays are provided to state governments under the Minimum Needs Programme (MNP) with the explicit stipulation that these funds cannot be diverted elsewhere, and in case of diversion the central plan assistance to state governments will stand proportionately reduced. The family welfare/family-planning programme has been a 100% centrally sponsored scheme from its inception.

The financial outlay has also been increasing over the successive five-year plan periods. In the 1996/97 budget, the allocation for health was increased by 21.6%. Efforts have also been made to mobilize resources through various international organizations and UN agencies. The government has encouraged the involvement of private agencies in secondary and tertiary levels of health care. Financial resources have been a major constraint to developing the primary and secondary levels of health care which are mainly provided by the government.

Dependence solely an government resources has been another constraint. For the future, the possibility of moving from strictly government-administered institutions to autonomous institutions or even to joint sector enterprises are options that are being discussed.

Physical infrastructure

Since early 1990s, the emphasis has been towards consolidation and operationalization, rather than on major expansion of the infrastructure. For this purpose, the following targets have been set:

— One subcentre staffed by a trained female health worker and a male health worker for a population of 5000 in the plains and a population of 3000 in hilly and tribal areas. As of 1998, 137,006 subcentres had been established.

— One primary health center (PHC) staffed by a medical officer and other paramedical staff for a population of 30,000 in the plains and a population of 20,000 in hilly, tribal and backward areas. A PHC center supervises six subcentres. As of 1998, 23,179 PHCs had been established.

— One community health center (CHC) or an upgraded PHC with 30 beds and basic specialities covering a population of 80,000 to 120,000. The CHC acts as a referral center for four PHCs. Up to 1998, 2913 CHCs had been established.

Urban family welfare centres (FWCs) have been set up to provide family welfare/family planning services. In all, 1529 urban FWCs are functioning. The status of the infrastructure to deliver primary health care appears to be satisfactory but actual programme implementation needs a lot of improvement. Constraints include deficiency of skilled personnel, lack of basic facilities and simple equipment, etc. Also, staff shortages continue to plague the services at all levels. A substantial part of the physical infrastructure has still to be completed.

A major factor has been that approved estimates/norms for construction have not kept abreast with the rising estimates of actual construction costs. More than one-quarter of the population now live in urban areas, with about 40-50% of those in the metropolitan and large cities living in urban slums, with primary health care provided by health posts. Very often these health posts are outside slum areas, making access difficult. They also lack basic drugs, equipment and technical support. Consolidation, with attention to specific health needs of the community, will underpin future actions.

Essential drugs and other supplies

No study has been done to assess the availability of essential drugs in remote facilities. The government, in consultation with the states and relevant agencies, has developed a national essential drugs list comprising over 300 drugs classified for use at the different levels of health care. This list serves as a guide to procuring agencies in central and state governments.

The drugs available in India as compared to those in other countries are considered cost effective and there is a price control on 78 essential drugs. Budgetary constraints do come in the way of essential drug availability in the public sector. Work is in progress to bring out a compendium on the rational use of essential drugs.

International partnerships in health

Various international organizations and UN agencies have continued to provide significant technical and material assistance which has had a positive impact. The various agencies include WHO, World Bank, UNICEF, UNFPA, USAID, Japanese Assistance, ODA (UK), SIDA, NORAD, DANIDA and German assistance. A National Institute of Biologicals has been set up as an autonomous organization, with funding from the Government of India, the Japanese and USAID.

DEVELOPMENT OF THE HEALTH SYSTEM

Health policies and strategies

The health sector in India is characterized by:

— a government sector that provides publicly financed and managed curative and preventive health services from primary to tertiary level, throughout the country and free of cost to the consumer and

— a fee-levying private sector that plays a dominant role in the provision of individual curative care through ambulatory services and accounts for about 82% of the overall health expenditure and 4.2% of the GDP. Nationwide health care utilization rates show that private health services are directed mainly at providing primary health care and financed from private resources, which could place a disproportionate burden on the poor.

The provision of health care by the public sector is a responsibility shared by state, central and local governments, although it is effectively a state responsibility in terms of service delivery. State and local governments incur about three-quarters and the center about one-quarter of public spending on health. The responsibility for health is at three levels.

— Health is primarily a state responsibility.

— The center is responsible for health services in union territories without a legislature and is also responsible for developing and monitoring national standards and regulations, linking the states with funding agencies, and sponsoring numerous schemes for implementation by state governments.

— Both the center and the states have a joint responsibility for programmes listed under the concurrent list.

Goals and strategies for the public sector in health care are established through a consultative process involving all levels of government through the Central Council for Health and Family Welfare. The outcomes from meetings of the Central Council for Health and Family Welfare have provided a thrust to various sub sectors within the health sector.

The private and voluntary sectors have emerged as an important arm of the health sector. From 1 April 1996 a change has been effected in the family welfare services with targets for contraceptive methods being replaced by a target-free approach. A huge campaign to eradicate poliomyelitis through pulse polio immunization (PPI) was initiated in 1995.

The traditional system of medicine is now playing a more significant role due to escalating costs of health care. State health systems/projects have been formulated to improve efficiency in the allocation and use of health resources through policy and institutional development. Specific efforts have been made to consolidate and strengthen the PHC infrastructure, under the minimum needs programme, by providing enhanced assistance to regions with severe health problems, supporting voluntary organizations, improving information, education and communication (IEC) activities, etc.

The convergence of services to provide a holistic approach to population control has also been promoted. In March 1995 a separate Department of Indian System of Medicine and

Homeopathy (ISM & H) was created within the Ministry of Health and Family Welfare.

Intersectoral cooperation

In order to meet current needs and emerging challenges, a number of working groups were constituted in 1996 to comprehensively review the existing health situation in its totality. The following areas are included: communicable diseases, health systems and biomedical research development, ISM & H, child development, environmental health, health education and IEC, women's development, and requirements for supportive and diagnostic services in primary, secondary and tertiary care. Consultations have also been held with NGOs. Two other committees have been constituted, namely an expert committee to comprehensively review the public health system in the country and the National Mission on Environmental Health and Sanitation.

The recommendations of these consultations have been discussed by the concerned ministries and were to be submitted as proposals for the 9th FYP. The active promotion of the *panchayati raj* system from the village to the district is a measure directed towards ensuring intersectoral collaboration. Specific health areas that have effectively made use of intersectoral collaboration include malaria control, AIDS control programme, blindness control, nutrition, and water and sanitation to name a few.

Organization of the health system

The focus of the 8th plan has been to improve access to health care for the underserved and underprivileged segments of society, through consolidation and operationalization of the health infrastructure at all levels with emphasis on primary health care. In view of the high maternal mortality, upgrading of existing maternal health facilities and establishing first referral units (FRUs) have been prioritized.

Many states have initiated major projects to upgrade their health services with assistance from funding agencies. Andhra Pradesh is implementing a Health Systems Project with World Bank assistance, and the states of Karnataka, West Bengal and Punjab are to follow. In support of Safe Motherhood, priority central assistance has been provided to establish FRUs in all 213 districts in six states where the maternal mortality is two to three times more than the national average. States in India have only recently begun to address issues relating to the organization of their health systems. Their capacity to bring about key policy reforms is still lacking. A substantial proportion of specialist posts in CHCs are vacant, and thus affects the functioning of first referral units. Other constraints relate to shortage of paramedical staff, support staff and inadequate involvement of NGOs.

Managerial process has been initiated for decentralization of authority to the various levels to enable decision making at the right time. Besides this, the *panchayati raj* bodies are also being revitalized. Training facilities for health management are being augmented with the NIFHW playing a pivotal role. A consortium of institutions dealing with health management has also been formed. As a further step towards managerial process development, the NIFHW is making efforts to strengthen institutions all over the country, including State Institutes of Health and Family Welfare.

A postgraduate certificate course in hospital management through distance learning is in its second year. Through various fellowship programmes, health personnel are being oriented towards newer developments in the field of management and management processes.

Networking has also been established between the Nuffield Institute of Health in the UK and NIFHW towards strengthening managerial processes. A recurring constraint has been the appointment of officials to managerial positions who do not have any managerial training or experience.

Health information system

In pursuance of the national health policy for the establishment of an efficient and effective management information system, a computer-compatible health management information system has been designed in collaboration with participating states, the national information center (NIC) and WHO. The system is being implemented in phases. The first phase, involving 13 states/union territories (UTs) commenced in 1992-93 and is at present operational in two states with others in the process of implementation.

In addition, each of the disease control programmes has its independent MIS, e.g. the National Programme for Control of Blindness, the National Leprosy (CBHI) Eradication Programme, the AIDS programme, tuberculosis control programme, etc. Obligations under the International Health Regulations continue to be observed. Morbidity and mortality data in respect of internationally quarantinable diseases are received by CBHI each week. Based on information received, weekly epidemiological reports are prepared and sent to WHO.

Surveillance of the principal communicable diseases other than those covered by the international health regulations is also maintained and reported monthly. Health condition reports giving morbidity and mortality data are received annually from states and UTs according to the ICD-9 classification. At present, the states need to be helped to augment their infrastructure facilities for computerization of data.

Community action

The concept of community participation is contained in national health policy. The broad areas of community participation at grass roots level are seen in the village health services scheme, the *Anganwadi* scheme of ICDS, and the formation of village level committees. Community action has also been successfully used in disease control programmes such as malaria and in areas such as the provision and maintenance of drinking water schemes and sanitation. The main constraint to community action is the low priority given to health by the community in contrast to schemes that provide direct financial benefit.

Emergency preparedness

Floods in India affect about 30 million people annually and drought about 50 million. Coastal areas experience two or three tropical cyclones of varying intensity each year. The Himalayan regions are prone to earthquakes. A Health Sector Emergency Preparedness and Response Programme has been in place since 1980. Crisis management groups have been used since 1980 and are constituted at national, state and district levels. In the Ministry of Health and Family Welfare, the Emergency Medical Relief Division is the responsible technical unit. With world health organisations (WHO) collaboration, emergency preparedness and response programmes in the health sector have resulted in:

- — preparation of a comprehensive health sector contingency plan at national level,
- — institutionalization of health sector disaster preparedness in seven national institutes,
- — training activities at institutional and state levels,
- — surveys, case studies and research projects, and
- — publication of books relevant to emergency preparedness. Limited studies have shown the need to improve competencies of grass root level functionaries in disaster prone areas, as well as to strengthen monitoring of activities. From 1995 the following activities are envisaged: transfer of expertise from national to state level institutions, training of target groups including translation of materials into the local languages, strengthening local infrastructure including stockpiling of essential supplies, disease control monitoring and surveillance, and operational research.

Health research and technology

India has a long history of biomedical research including health systems research. In several instances research results have directly influenced programme policies or led to modifications in programme strategies. Among the many research institutions, the Indian Council of Medical Research (ICMR), established in 1911, is the lead agency. In the 8th FYP, ICMR attempted to consolidate significant leads in priority or "thrust" areas that were identified by various scientific expert groups. These areas included emerging health problems like HIV/AIDS, other important communicable diseases like tuberculosis, leprosy, diarrhoeal diseases, malaria, filariasis, Japanese encephalitis, etc., noncommunicable diseases like cancer, cardiovascular diseases, metabolic disorders, etc., contraception, MCH and nutrition. Efforts have been made to develop a bibliographic database on HSR. With WHO support, nearly 400 HSR studies have been abstracted and a database was developed by the NIHFW in 1996. It is important that research findings have an application in the community.

There is a need to sensitize policy makers and administrators about the importance of research and its managerial and programmatic uses Financial resources also need to be improved. Dissemination of research findings and their utilization for identifying strategies to solve problems have not been up to the desired level.

HEALTH SERVICES

Health education and promotion

Health education and promotion has been an integral component of all national health and family welfare programmes. The IEC approach uses a community-based strategy. Interpersonal communication at grass roots level is being strengthened by establishing women's health organizations (*Mahila Swasthya Sangh* - MSS) in villages. By 1995-96, 74,000 MSSs had been established.

Funds were earmarked for setting up IEC bureaus in eight states in 1995-96. Training of frontline workers and field functionaries in various departments is being strengthened. The sensitization of local leaders is implemented through orientation training camps. National health programmes are supported with health education and promotion strategies and activities specifically designed to suit programme needs. Such national programmes include those for leprosy eradication, tuberculosis control, malaria eradication, and HIV/AIDS control, as well as the national iodine deficiency disorder programme and the environmental health and sanitation programme.

Interministerial committees at central and state levels meet periodically to review the progress of health education activities. NGOs and other professional organizations have joined with government agencies all around the country to improve health education. The media division of the CHEB has been strengthened to support media promotion activities as well as materials production.

Maternal and child health/family planning

The proportion of pregnant women attended by trained personnel in 1995/96 was reported to be 65.1%. The proportion of deliveries in 1995/96 attended by trained personnel (including trained TBAs) in the urban sector was 73.5% and in the rural sector 33.5%. The proportion of women of childbearing age using family planning in 1998/99 was 48.2%. The crude birth rate (CBR) was 26.1 per 1000 population and the infant mortality rate (IMR) for were and 68.0 per 1000 live births. There are wide interstate differences in achievements of health and family planning indicators. Any change in these indicators is dependent on the performance of four states (Bihar, Rajasthan, Madhya Pradesh and Uttar Pradesh). With regard to population growth, unless these states improve their family planning performance, the national growth rate will not change significantly.

High priority has been given to MCH since 1985. The success achieved with EPI is likely to have made a significant contribution to the reduction in the infant mortality rate from 95 in 1987 to 68 per 1000 live births in 1994-98. Perinatal mortality and stillbirth rates remain high, with only a marginal decline in the last decade. Several socioeconomic variables as well as technical and operational shortcomings constitute the main constraints. Though services are being strengthened and community education promoted, there is a lack of complete involvement by the people. Better coordination with NGOs, professional health organizations, private practitioners and the like is needed if better results are to be achieved.

For future action, a result-oriented action plan has been evolved in consultation between the center, states and UTs. The key features are improving the quality of outreach services, having a differential strategy for poorly performing districts as based on CBR, increasing coverage of younger couples, introducing newer and better quality contraceptives, strengthening family welfare schemes in urban areas, especially slum pockets, revitalizing training for health staff, IEC to focus on quality of life issues and interpersonal communication, and improving intersectoral coordination at all levels. After four decades, the importance of a holistic multisectoral approach to population stabilization has been realized.

A draft revised National Population Policy based on a holistic approach was placed before parliament in 1996. With a view to regulate and prevent the misuse of modern prenatal diagnostic techniques, legislation was passed in parliament in 1994. To ensure strong political commitment to curbing population growth, the 79th Constitution Amendment Bill seeks to incorporate promotion of population control and a small family norm, with an added clause enjoining all citizens to promote and adopt a small family norm. The bill also proposes to add an additional schedule, under which a person shall be disqualified from being elected to hold office as a member of either house of parliament or in a state legislature if he/she has more than two children - but is not to take place with retrospective effect.

Immunization

The proportion of infants reaching their first birthday who were fully immunized according to national immunization policies in 2001 was 49.0%. By individual vaccines the coverage in 1998/99 was as follows: DPT3 52.1% OPV3 59.2%, measles vaccine 41.7%, and BCG 69.1%. Percentage of pregnant women who received two doses of TT was 66.8% (1995/96),. As a result of the immunization programme, the incidence of polio and neonatal tetanus have declined significantly.

The strategies to maintain and improve coverage include outreach immunization sessions, intensification in high risk areas, national immunization days (NIDs) and mop-up rounds, strengthening surveillance, intensifying IEC and training, maintaining vaccines and essential supplies, and improving supervision and monitoring. WHO recommended strategies are being followed with regard to achieving the goal of polio eradication, neonatal tetanus elimination and measles control.

Prevention and control of locally endemic diseases

The incidence of malaria remained around 2 million cases per year during 1984-1992. In 1997, 2.7 million and in 1999, 2.3 million cases were reported. The incidence of *P. falciparum* is increasing and reached to 50% in 1999. For filariasis, present estimates indicate that about 420 million people live in endemic areas. There are 206 control units, 198 clinics and 27 survey units. Visceral leishmaniasis, which reappeared in Bihar in the 1970s, is now endemic in 30 districts in Bihar and 9 districts in West Bengal.

In 1996 there were 20,466 cases and 260 deaths reported. Japanese encephalitis (JE), though not a major public health problem, has over time been reported from as many as 24 states/UTs during one year, with an estimated 378 million people at risk. Dengue, dengue haemorrhagic fever (DHF) and dengue shock syndrome, all caused by the dengue virus, have been prevalent in India in almost all major urban areas, with periodic outbreaks of dengue fever and DHF. All four serotypes have been detected, and guidelines for prevention and control have been issued to all states. An expert committee drew up a malaria action programme in 1995.

A key strategy is the implementation of short and long term measures in selected high risk areas, high powered boards to expedite intersectoral cooperation, community involvement in antimalarial activities with intensified IEC, and capacity building at the central and grass roots levels through training. The progress of filariasis control is constantly under review and a strategy of selective treatment, vector control and IEC is being implemented.

A revised strategy of mass drug administration has been initiated in some districts in Tamil Nadu and Maharashtra states. In view of the seriousness of visceral leishmaniasis, the government has accorded high priority for its control. Strategies involve early diagnosis and treatment of patients and interruption of transmission by DDT spraying.

Treatment of common diseases and injuries

The national tuberculosis control programme has not achieved the desired results. In 1992 the programme was reviewed and a revised control programme formulated with short term course chemotherapy using the DOTS strategy. The problem of protein-energy malnutrition (PEM) and micronutrient deficiency disorders are quite significant and are being dealt with through a number of national programmes with well defined goals.

Diarrhoeal diseases, which are still a major cause of morbidity and mortality in infants and children, are being addressed through the promotion of exclusive breast-feeding, good child feeding practices, and the timely use of ORT during episodes of diarrhoea. Acute respiratory infections (ARIs) are a leading cause of death due to pneumonia in children under five years.

A strategy aimed at early recognition of the signs of pneumonia and timely referral has been very effective in reducing mortality. HIV/AIDS is predicted to be a major problem in India. A total of 22,529 seropositive cases were reported up to March 1996, but this number does not convey the actual magnitude of the problem. Almost 4 million HIV cases are estimated as of June 2000. Of the noncommunicable diseases, cancer and cardiovascular diseases are emerging as major health concerns that will require considerable financial resources for case management.

TRENDS IN HEALTH STATUS

Life expectancy

For the period 1996-2001, the life expectancy at birth is estimated to be 62.36 years for males and 63.39 years for females. In 1991 the sex ratio was 927 females per 1000 males which increased to 933 in 2001. To ensure the continued improvement in life expectancy, the health care delivery infrastructure is being expanded, MCH care is being improved, specific programmes such as the expanded programme on immunization (EPI), introduction of oral rehydration therapy (ORT), etc. are being strengthened, and efforts are continuing to contain locally endemic diseases. There is also an increased thrust in other development and poverty alleviation programmes.

The main constraints are the diverse population groups, low literacy and income levels, and sociocultural beliefs and practices which adversely affect health.

Mortality

The infant mortality rate (IMR) was reported to be 68 per 1000 live births in 1994-98 and the maternal mortality ratio (MMR) for 1998 was estimated at 407 per 100,000 live births. Estimates for 1996 of the number of deaths per year in children under five years from diarrhoeal diseases was 840,000, from acute respiratory infections 600,000 and from measles 330,000. Deaths from malaria were reported to be 1061 and 1057, cardiovascular diseases 2,386,000, traffic accidents 45,670, and work accidents 543. Between 1986 and 1999 the crude death rate (CDR) declined from 11.1 to 8.7 per 1000 population. Between 1980 and 1998 the IMR declined from 114 to 68, the leading causes of death being diseases of circulatory system, infections and parasitic diseases, injury, poisoning, perinatal conditions, and diseases of respiratory system. The number of reported accidental deaths in 1993 was 11,125 and 80,000 in 1998. The main constraints are low literacy and income levels, sociocultural beliefs and practices, and suboptimal utilization of health facilities.

Morbidity

The number of reported cases of the following diseases were: leprosy 560,000, malaria 2,276,788, measles 26,986, neonatal tetanus 1896, polio 142, and tuberculosis 1,223,127. The vaccine-preventable diseases have declined significantly since implementation of the EPI.

In India about 14 million people are estimated to be suffering from active tuberculosis and about 0.5 million die of the disease each year. Currently, short term chemotherapy using DOTS has been introduced and accessibility to tuberculosis treatment centres improved. The prevalence of leprosy has declined from about 39 per 10,000 population in 1985 to about 7 per 10,000 in 1995 and further down to 3.7 in 2000. The spectacular reduction in this disease has been due to the new regimen of multidrug therapy. The number of new cases detected annually has, however, remained more or less the same, at about 0.5 million.

Disability

Disability prevalence rates per 100,000 population estimated in 1994 are as follows: physical disability 3574, visual disability 827, hearing 806, speech 510, and locomotor disability 2041. The incidence rates per 100,000 population of these disabilities are: physical 173, visual 45, hearing 27, speech 10 and locomotor disability 105 (national sample survey). The main cause of blindness is cataract (80.1%), with about 6.5 million (2000) persons blind due to cataract.

The national blindness control programme is centrally sponsored with a four-pronged strategy to strengthen service delivery, develop human resources, promote outreach activities and develop institutional capacity. Due to changing lifestyles, mental disorders are likely to increase in the future.

The total number of mental disorders treated in specialized mental hospitals was 48,396 in 1991 and 38,323 in 1992. The majority of cases have been diagnosed as suffering from psychosis (85.7%).

FUTURE

Overall assessment and strategic issues

Mortality rates, especially the CDR, IMR and to some extent the MMR, have shown a declining trend. There has been an improvement in the expectation of life at birth for both males and females.

The vaccine-preventable diseases have started to decline. Guinea-worm disease has been eradicated and leprosy shows a declining trend. Tuberculosis is still a persistent public health problem, but the new short term chemotherapy and DOTS strategy offer some promise. Together with the persistence of communicable diseases, noncommunicable diseases are also emerging as public health problems.

The population growth rate though declining, continues to be alarmingly high, with some very populous states continuing to have high birth rates. Socioeconomic and sociocultural factors, the diversity among states, and low literacy remain major constraints. With regard to health policy, there are well formulated policy guidelines for health, nutrition, education, children, etc. which provide an overall framework for health and development.

Health is a state subject and the decentralization envisaged under the Panchayat Raj Act may provide greater opportunities for community participation in development. The outlay in the health and health-related sectors has been increasing over the five year plan periods, but as a percentage of the total outlay has remained constant over the years.

The health care delivery system has expanded, but issues such as consolidation of existing infrastructure and quality need to be given more attention. Though there is an upward trend in economic growth, reducing the gap between the haves and the have-nots is a major challenge.

Various international organizations and UN agencies continue to provide significant material and technical assistance for health and family welfare programmes.

The goal is to achieve optimal health for the people, which would allow them to lead socially and economically productive lives and be in keeping with the principles of the HFA strategy. The health care system envisaged would have a public-private mix, with the latter encouraged to take a greater share of secondary and tertiary health care services.

The National Conservation Strategy and Policy Statement on Environment and Development aims at ensuring that the demands on the environment do not exceed its carrying capacity for the present as well as for future generations.

Proposed strategies

Enhancing equity for health: Making health services and facilities accessible and available to the people, especially the underprivileged, through the regionalization of health services, rational transfer policies, incentives and career development opportunities, and minimizing inter and intrastate differences. Strengthening of health promotion and protection: Development of an integrated education and health promotion programme with locally relevant content, implementation of an integrated noncommunicable disease control programme, strengthening of intersectoral coordination for implementing preventive and promotive health in an integrated and comprehensive manner, and strict and effective enforcement of available legislation relating to health and the environment.

Strengthening the health sector through partnerships in health development: This includes public and private sector involvement, better use of indigenous systems of medicine, etc.

— Developing and strengthening specific health programmes.

— Developing and using appropriate health technology.

— Strengthening international partnerships for health.

6

Effect of Uncheked Growth of Population on Natural Resources and Environment

India's ongoing population explosion has placed great strain on the country's environment. This rapidly growing population, along with a move toward urbanization and industrialization, has placed significant pressure on India's infrastructure and its natural resources. Deforestation, soil erosion, water pollution and land degradation continue to worsen and are hindering economic development in rural India, while the rapid industrialization and urbanization in India's booming metropolises are straining the limits of municipal services and causing serious air pollution problems.

Following the 1984 Bhopal disaster—in which a toxic leak from the city's Union Carbide chemical plant resulted in the deaths of more than 3,000 people — environmental awareness and activism in India increased significantly.

The Environment Protection Act was passed in 1986, creating the Ministry of Environment and Forests (MoEF) and strengthening India's commitment to the environment, which was enshrined in the 42nd amendment to country's constitution in 1976. Under the 1986 Environmental Protection Act, the MoEF is tasked with the overall responsibility for administering and enforcing environmental laws and policies. The MoEF established the importance of integrating environmental strategies into any development plan for the country. Nevertheless, despite a greater commitment by the Indian government to protect public health, forests, and wildlife, policies geared to develop the country's economy have taken precedence in the last 20 years.

While industrial development has contributed significantly to economic growth in India, it has done so at a price to the environment. Not only is industrial pollution increasing public health risks, but abatement efforts also are consuming a significant portion of India's gross domestic product (GDP). As such, one of MoEF's main responsibilities continues to be the reduction of industrial pollution.

Environmental pollution is one of the serious problems faced by the people in the country, especially in urban areas, which not only experiences a rapid growth of population due to high fertility, low mortality and increasing rural-urban migration, but also industrialization which is accompanied by growing number of vehicles. In India, the rapid increase of human numbers combines with desperate poverty to deplete and pollute local resource bases on which the livelihood of present and future generations depends. Though the relationship is complex, population size and growth tend to expand and accelerate these human impacts on the environment.

According to the World Development Indicators report in 1997, 1.5 billion people live exposed to dangerous levels of air pollution, 1 billion live without clean water and 2 billion live without sanitation. The increase of population has been tending towards alarming situation. The world's population was estimated to be 6.14 billion in mid 2001 and projected 7.82 billion and 9.04 billion in the year 2025 and 2050 respectively. Contribution of India alone to this population was estimated to be 1033 millions in mid 2001 which has been projected 1363 millions and 1628 millions in 2025 and 2050 respectively.

According to the provisional results of the Census of India 2001, the population of India on 1st March 2001 is 1027 millions. If the world population continues to multiply, the impact on environment could be devastating. Population impacts on the environment primarily through the use of natural resources and production of wastes and is associated with environmental stresses like biodiversity, air and water pollution and increased pressure on arable land. India is the world's sixth largest and second fastest growing producer of greenhouse gases.

Delhi, Mumbai and Chennai are three of the world's ten most populated cities. Two-thirds of city dwellers lack sewerage, one-third lack potable water. India grows equivalent of another New York City every year in its urban population. By the year 2000, more than 350 million Indians will live in cities. In 15 years, more than half of Indians will be urban dwellers; 1/3 will be slum dwellers and squatters.

India is one of the most degraded environment countries in the world and it is paying heavy health and economic price for it. According to a World Bank sponsored study, estimated environmental damage in the year 1992 amounted to about US $ 10 billion or Rs. 34,000 crores, which is 4.5 % of GDP. Urban air pollution costs India US $ 1.3 billion a year. Water degradation leads to health costs amounting to US $ 5.7 million every year, nearly 60 percent of the total environmental cost. Soil erosion affects 83 to 163 million hectares of land every year. Beside, land degradation leads to productivity loss equal to US $ 2.4 billion or 4 to 6.3 percent of the agricultural productivity every year.

The lack of services such as water supply, sanitation, drainage of storm water, treatment and disposal of waste water, management of solid and hazardous wastes, supply of safe food, water and housing are all unable to keep pace with urban growth. All these in turn lead to an increase in the pollution levels. Also the unplanned location of industries in urban and sub-urban areas followed by traffic congestion, poor housing, poor drainage and garbage accumulation causes serious pollution problems.

However, all these factors together not only lead to deteriorating environmental conditions but also have adverse effects on the health of people. The peoples in environment polluted areas are infected by pollution related diseases. Due to air pollution the incidence of respiratory diseases lead to increase and water pollution triggers the number of patients suffering from acute water borne diseases.

Hence it have been the main areas of concern for demographers, ecologists, planners and policy makers over the recent past.

DEFORESTATION

Forests are an important natural resource of India. They have moderate influence against floods and thus they protect the soil erosion. Forests also play an important role in enhancing the quality of environment by influencing the ecological balance and life support system (checking soil erosion, maintaining soil fertility, conserving water, regulating water cycles and floods, balancing carbon dioxide and oxygen content in atmosphere etc. India has a forest cover of 76.52 million square kms. of recorded forest area, while only 63.34 million square kms. can be classified as actual forest cover.

This accounts for 23.28 percent of total geographic area against 33 percent recommended by National Forest Policy of 1988. Per capita availability of forests in India is much lower than the world average. In the year 1997, as compared to 1993, the total forest cover has decreased by 6710 Sq. Kms. The states, which have shown significant decline in the forest covers, are Andhra Pradesh and Madhya Pradesh. Whereas the states of Gujrat, Maharashtra, Rajasthan and West Bengal have shown an increase in forest cover.

In 1981-83, only 11.2 percent of country's total land area, comprises dense forest with a crown density of more than 40 percent, thus reflecting a qualitative decline of forests in the country. The total forest area diverted for non-forestry purposes between 1950 and 1980 was 4.5 million hectares i.e. at an annual rate of 0.15 million hectare. To regulate unabated diversion of forestland for non-forestry purposes, Forest (Conservation) Act, 1980 was enacted. It has resulted in reduction of diversion of forest area for nonforestry purposes considerably and the present rate of diversion is 16,000 hectare annually. Continuing deforestation, therefore, has brought us face to face with a major ecological and socio-economic crisis.

LAND/SOIL DEGRADATION

Direct impacts of agricultural development on the environment arise from farming activities, which contribute to soil erosion, land salination and loss of nutrients. The spread of green revolution has been accompanied by over exploitation of land and water resources and use of fertilizers and pesticides and fertilizers have increased many folds. Shifting cultivation has also been an important cause of land degradation. Leaching from extensive use of pesticides and fertilizers is an important source of contamination of water bodies. Intensive agriculture and irrigation contribute to land degradation particularly salination, alkalization and water logging. It is evident that most of the land in the country is degrading, thus affecting the productive resource base of the economy. Out of the total geographical area of 328.7 million hectares, 175 million hectares are considered to be land-degraded area.

Water and wind erosion is the major contributor of 141.3 million hectares to soil erosion, with other factors like water logging 8.5 million hectares, alkali soil 3.6 million hectares, acid soil 4.5 million hectares, saline soil including coastal sandy areas 5.5 million hectares adding to the situ degradation. While soil erosion by rain and river in hill areas causes landslides and floods, deforestation, overgrazing, traditional agricultural practices, mining and incorrect siting of development projects in forest areas have resulted in opening up of these areas to heavy soil erosion. Ravines and gullies reported 4 million hectares, area subject to shifting cultivation reported 4.9 million hectares and riverine and torrents erosion due to floods and eutrophication due to agricultural run off reported 2.7 million hectares.

The increasing intensification and extensification also results in salination, alkalization and water logging in irrigated areas of the country. For achieving and maintaining food security, sustainable forestry agricultural and rural developments controlling of land/soil erosion is very much necessary.

ENVIRONMENTAL POLLUTION

The term Environmental Pollution refers to ways by which people pollute their surroundings, air with gases and smoke, poison the water with chemicals and other substances, and damage the soil with too many fertilizers and pesticides. Also pollute the surroundings in various other ways.

Environmental degradation is a result of the dynamic interplay of socio-economic, institutional and technological activities. Environmental changes may be driven by many factors including economic growth, population growth, urbanization, intensification of agriculture, rising energy use and transportation. Poverty still remains a problem at the root of several environmental problems.

The pollution is widespread in the country and can be broadly categorized as flux type of pollution and sink type of pollution. The former refers to the pollutants dumped into the environment, either to air or in water; while the later is caused by accumulation either in soil or riverbed or also in ground water.

Air Pollution

The World Health Organization (WHO) defines air pollution as "substances put into the air by the activity of mankind into concentrations sufficient to cause harmful effects to health, property, crop yield or to interfere with the enjoyment of property". Some of the most important air pollutants are suspended particulate matter (SPM), nitrogen oxides (NO_x), carbon monoxide (CO), lead, sulphur dioxide (SO_2) etc. The urban air pollution has grown across India in the last decade is alarming. The main factors accounts to urban air quality deterioration are growing industrialization and increasing vehicular pollution, industrial emissions, automobile exhaust and the burning of fossil fuels kills thousands and lives many more to suffer mainly from respiratory damage, heart and lung diseases. According to a pollution related studies in the community and patients at the K.E.M. Hospital, Mumbai over the last twenty years have evaluated the full extent of the correlation and damage to human health.

Industrialization and urbanization have resulted in a profound deterioration of India's air quality. India has more than 20 cities with populations of at least 1 million, and some of them—including New Delhi, Mumbai, Chennai, and Kolkata—are among the world's most polluted. Urban air quality ranks among the world's worst. Of the 3 million premature deaths in the world that occur each year due to outdoor and indoor air pollution, the highest number are assessed to occur in India. Sources of air pollution, India's most severe environmental problem, come in several forms, including vehicular emissions and untreated industrial smoke. Continued urbanization has exacerbated the problem of rapid industrialization, as more and more people are adversely affected and cities are unable to implement adequate pollution control mechanisms.

One of the most affected cities in New Delhi, where airborne particulate matter (PM) has been registered at levels more than 10 times India's legal limit. Vehicles are the major source of this pollution, with more than three million cars, trucks, buses, taxis, and rickshaws already on the roads. With vehicle ownership rising along with population and income, India's efforts to improve urban air quality have focused in this area. In New Delhi, emissions limits for gasoline- and diesel-powered vehicles came into effect in 1991 and 1992, respectively, and the city has prohibited the use of vehicle more than 15 years old.

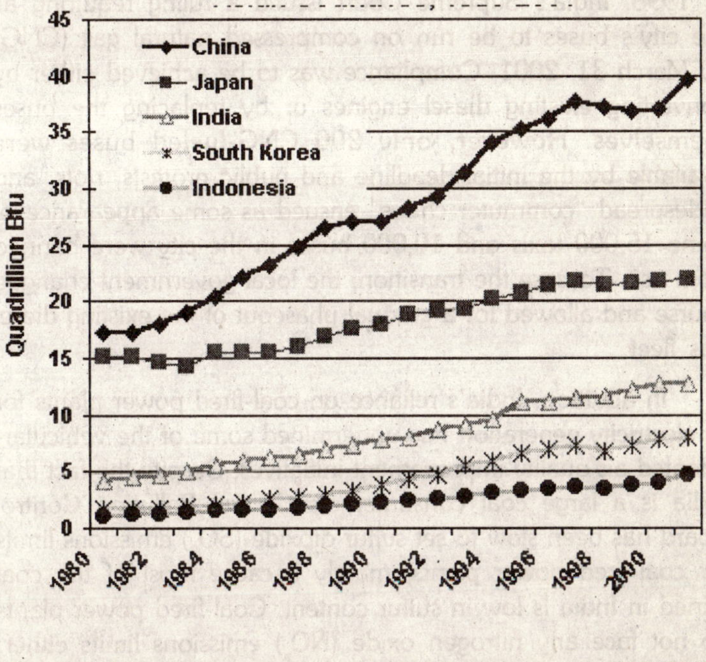

Figure 1. Energy consumption is selected Asian countries, 1980-2001

Emissions standards for passenger cars and commercial vehicles were tightened in 2000 at levels equivalent to the Euro-1 standards of the European Union, while the even-more-stringent Euro-2 standards have been in place for the metropolitan areas of Delhi, Mumbai, Chennai, and Kolkata since 2001.

Furthermore, the sulfur content of motor fuels sold in the four cities has been restricted to 500 parts per million (PPM) since 2001 in order to be compatible with tighter vehicle emissions standards. Motor fuel sulfur content in all other regions of India has been limited to 2,500 PPM since January 2000.

India's high concentration of pollution is not due to the absence of a sound environmental legal regime, however, but to a lack of environmental enforcement at the local level. Regulatory reforms aimed at improving the air pollution problem in cities such as New Delhi have been difficult to implement. In 1998, India's Supreme Court issued a ruling requiring all the city's buses to be run on compressed natural gas (CNG) by March 31, 2001. Compliance was to be achieved either by converting existing diesel engines or by replacing the buses themselves. However, only 200 CNG-fueled buses were available by the initial deadline and public protests, riots, and widespread "commuter chaos" ensued as some appearance of some 15,000 taxis and 10,000 buses in the city were banned from use. To ease the transition, the local government changed course and allowed for a gradual phaseout of the existing diesel bus fleet.

In addition, India's reliance on coal-fired power plants for its electricity generation has undermined some of the vehicular oriented air quality improvement initiatives. Despite the fact that India is a large coal consumer, its Central Pollution Control Board has been slow to set sulfur dioxide (SO_2) emissions limits for coal-fired power plants, mainly because most of the coal mined in India is low in sulfur content. Coal-fired power plants do not face any nitrogen oxide (NO_x) emissions limits either, although thermal plants fueled by other fossil fuels are subject to particulate matter emission standards. Again, however, the government's support for air quality standards has been undermined by the lack of enforcement of these standards.

According to a recent study, 84.000 deaths were directly attributable to outdoor air pollution in Indian cities. At the same time, indoor air pollution accounted for 496,000 deaths in villages and 93,000 deaths in cities. It is found that the area around RSP village, Jharia ranks fifth and FCI Hospital, Sindri ranks eighth among the top ten locations with highest annual mean concentrations of Nitrogen Oxides (NO_x), having 54 and 46 micro grams per cubic meters respectively. Apart from this, the suspended particulate matter (SPM) level in RSP College, Jharia is the fourth highest in India.

A study conducted by Center for Science and Environment from 1987 to 1998, to understand the trend of air pollution in Delhi based on three major pollutants: sulphur dioxide, nitrogen oxide and SPM. It shows an increasing trend, though fluctuations are noticed in terms of annual maximum levels. According to the studies conducted by Center for Science and Environment, total SPM levels are not only always above the standard but there are days when they have reached nearly seventeen times the standard. A World Bank study conducted in 1995 revealed that if the air pollution is controlled in Calcutta according to the guidelines of World Health Organization (WHO), lives of 5726 persons may be saved from premature death and of 30 lakhs people may also to be saved to be admitted to hospital.

Water pollution

Water is among the most essential requisites that nature has provided to sustain life on earth. About 80% of earth's surface are covered by water. The deteriorating quality of water is creating various problems for the mankind. The growth in population, about 90 percent of which will occur in urban areas, will also increase the demand for water for domestic and industrial use and treatment of. wastes. Water pollution from domestic and human wastewater is the main cause for much severe water borne diseases.

The industrial water pollution is due to inadequate measures adopted in the industry for the abatement of pollution. Inadequate disposal of urban waste and open dumping of garbage contaminates surface and ground water. Water and sanitation services are basic necessities of a community and are most essential conditions for development, as they play an important role in improving health and quality of life. Inadequate water and sanitation coverage is one of the most serious environmental problems. It has been estimated that 80 percent of the diseases in the world are associated with water usage or poor environmental hygiene).

In India, water pollution comes from three main sources: domestic sewage, industrial effluents and run-off from activities such as agriculture. The large scale use of pesticides may have revolutionized food production, but these chemicals are responsible for more than 2 million human poisonings every year with a resultant 20,000 deaths.

Polluting a river is dangerous because generally, rivers are the primary source of drinking water for towns and cities downstream of the point of pollution. Broadly, the causes of water pollution can be attributed to:

— Urbanization

— Industrialization

— Withdrawal of wastes

— Agricultural run-off and improper agricultural practices

— Religious and social practices

According to the scientists at the National Environmental Engineering and Research Institute, a staggering 70% of the available water in India is polluted. Only five states, Maharashtra, Gujrat, Delhi, Uttar Pradesh and West Bengal, generate more than 63% of the total waste water in India as they lack treatment facilities. Sewage generated from 25 heavy polluting cities and towns account for about 75 percent of the pollution load in the river. The Yamuna with 200 million litres of untreated muck being dumped in it everyday by Delhi's Sewerage System has become one of the most polluted rivers in the world. The increasing river water pollution is the biggest threat to public health. The diseases commonly caused due to polluted water are cholera, diarrhoea, hepatitis, typhoid amoebic and bacillary, dysentery, guineaworm, whereas scabies, leprosy, trachoma and conjucvitis are some of the diseases associated with water scarcity. All these could be attributed to the rapidly increasing population and lack of water resources.

Inadequate access to safe drinking water and sanitation facilities leads to higher infant mortality and intestinal diseases. More than one million children died due to diarrhoea and other gastrointestinal disorders in 1990s. In addition, around 90 lakh cases of acute diarrhoeal diseases have been reported in India, Uttar Pradesh reporting the highest number of cases. It is estimated that 73 million workdays are lost every year due to water related diseases. The cost of treating them and the loss in production amount to Rs. 600 crores a year.

Rapid population growth continues to be a matter of concern for the country as it has manifold effects, one of the most important being environment degradation. The outcomes of excessive population are industrialization and urbanization. The study reveals that rapid population growth has led to the overexploitation of natural resources. The deforestation has led to the shrinking of forest cover, which eventually affects human health. The considerable magnitude of air pollution in the country also pulls up the number of people suffering from respiratory diseases and many a times leading to deaths and serious health hazards. The situation is also similar for water pollution, as both ground water and surface water contamination leads to various water borne diseases.

From the various effects of environmental degradation on human beings, it appears that if human beings wants to exist on earth, there is now high time to give top priority to control pollution of all types for a healthy living. It can be said that even after fifty years of independence, India is unable to achieve the desirable standards of health for its population as consequences of environment degradation.

There is a need to control population growth in the country. Special efforts should be made for educating the general mass and local leaders about the adverse effects of large population through specially designed IEC activities. In order to increase green cover and to preserve the existing forests, afforestation and social forestry programmes should be implemented at the local level. Further, measures to control air pollution should be intensified throughout the country. Wastewater treatment plants be established in accordance with the need of time and its usage should be encouraged.

The heavy penalty should be imposed on industries disposing off the wastes into the river. Moreover, the landfills are to be properly managed to prevent ground water contamination. Since slums are one of the major sources of water pollution proper measures should be taken to facilitate the slums with water and sanitation facilities. More emphasis should be laid on compulsory environmental education at the school level in order to make people aware of the environment protection. The environment protection should not be a responsibility of government alone but mass and local leaders should be encouraged to make dedicated efforts to eradicate the environmental problems.

To sum up, it may be emphasized that the environment is neither a free gift of environmental goods and services, nor it can be thought of as just a sink for depositing of waste products from houses, industries and other sources. It is the need of time to protect environment for the present and future generation.

Pollution from high energy consumption

India's energy consumption is increasing rapidly, from 4.16 quadrillion Btu (quads) in 1980 to 12.8 quads in 2001. This 208% increase is largely the result of India's increasing population and the rapid urbanization of the country. Higher energy consumption in the industrial, transportation, and residential sectors continues to drive India's energy usage upwards at a faster rate even than China, which experienced a 130% increase in energy consumption from 1980 to 2001.

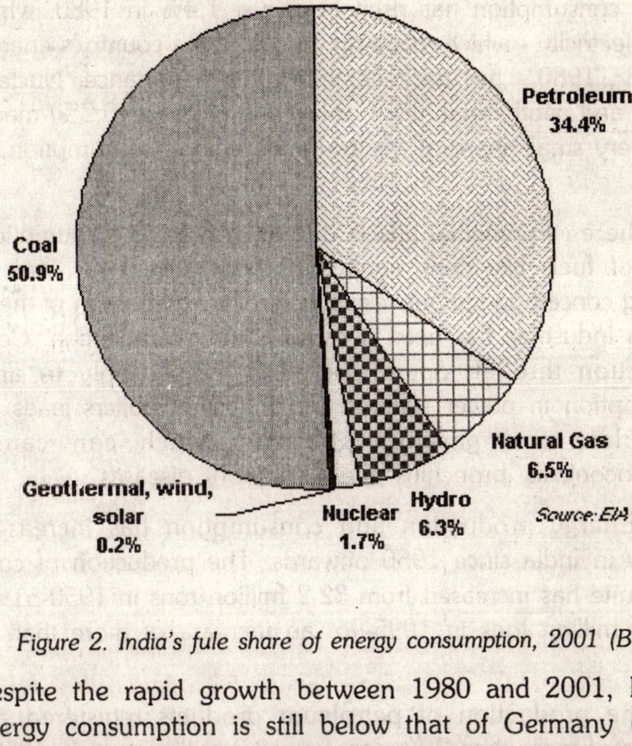

Figure 2. India's fule share of energy consumption, 2001 (Btu)

Despite the rapid growth between 1980 and 2001, India's energy consumption is still below that of Germany (14.35 quads), Japan (21.92 quads), China (39.67 quads), and the United States (97.05 quads). In addition, India's per capita energy consumption, which stood at 12.6 million Btu in 2001, is well below most of the rest of Asia and is one of the lowest in the world.

The 103% rise in India's per capita consumption between 1980, when per capita energy usage was just 6.2 million Btu, and 2001, is more problematic in the long-term, however. Coal accounts for just over 50% (6.5 quads) of India's energy consumption. The power generation sector uses the majority of this coal, with heavy industry a distant second. Petroleum (4.4 quads) makes up 34.4% of India's energy consumption, while natural gas (6.5%) and hydroelectricity (6.3%) account for much of the remainder.

Natural gas is growing in importance, as its share of India's energy consumption has risen from just 1.4% in 1980, while hydroelectricity - which made up 11.5% of the country's energy usage in 1980 - has declined in relative importance. Nuclear (1.7%) and geothermal, wind, solar, and biomass (0.2%) made up a very small share of the country's energy consumption in 2001.

The environmental effects due to increasing consumption levels of fuels like coal, lignite, oil and nuclear etc. are of growing concern to various researchers. The combustion of these fuels in industries has been a major source of pollution. Coal production through open cast mining; its supply to and consumption in power stations and industrial boilers leads to particulate and gaseous pollution which can cause pneumoconiosis, bronchitis and respiratory diseases.

Energy production and consumption has increased steadily in India since 1950 onwards. The production of coal and lignite has increased from 32.2 million tons in 1950-51 to 292.27 million tons in 1995-96, an increase of more than 9 times.

The production of petroleum products registered an increase of more than 22 times, from 3.3 million tons in 1950-51 to 74.7 million tons in 1995-96. The bulk of commercial energy comes from the burning of fossil fuels viz. coal and lignite in solid form, petroleum in liquid form and gas in gaseous form. In addition to emission of greenhouse gases, the burning of fossil fuels has led to several ecological problems and associated with health problems like cancer risk, respiratory diseases and other health problems. Burning of traditional fuel adds a large amount of carbon-di-oxide into atmosphere and increases air pollution.

The production of electricity has increased from 5 billion KWH in 1950-51 to about 380 billion KWH in 1995-96. The shares of thermal power and hydropower changed substantially. The share of thermal power has increased from 51 percent in 1950-51 to about 79 percent in 1995-96 whereas the share of hydropower declined from 49 percent in 1950-51 to 19 percent in 1995-96. The share of nuclear power is nominal. This clearly indicates that burning of fossil fuels, especially coals, emits lot of carbon di oxide in the atmosphere and leads to global warming.

The per capita commercial energy use in India has increased from 137 Kg of oil equivalent in 1980 to 248 Kg of oil equivalent in 1994 and it again increased to 476 Kg of oil equivalent in 1996. The energy consumption in India would be quite high and thus stricter commands and controls, technical innovations and application of efficient pollution abatement technology for vehicular and industrial air pollution could help in reduction of atmospheric pollution.

A considerable amount of air pollution results from burning of fossil fuels. Moreover the resources for fossil fuels are also limited thus exploration of alternate energy resources would provide the way out. Thus increased population and increased per capita commercial energy use would worsen the national as well as global atmospheric pollution.

An automobile exhaust accounts a sizable part of pollution. Their effect on human health is particularly of concern. There is a strong correlation between average blood lead levels and the lead content in gasoline. Hydrocarbons present in the exhaust, particularly, in vehicles with poor combustion cause respiratory problems. It can be inferred from the table that both, the illness and premature deaths have risen significantly in less than five years. About 15 to 18 million children in developing countries are affected by high levels of lead in their blood, which could be the result of emissions from vehicle exhaust and are likely to suffer from related illness.

Vehicular pollution

Transport activities have a wide variety of effects on the environment such as air pollution, noise from road traffic. Transport infrastructure in India has expanded considerably in terms of network and services. Thus road transport accounts for a major share of air pollution load in mega cities. In most urban areas of India, air pollution has worsened due to traffic congestion, poor housing, poor sanitation and drainage and garbage accumulation.

The environmental effects of fuels like oil and petroleum products are of growing concern owing to increasing consumption levels. The combustion of these fuels in vehicles has been a major source of pollution. With the increasing vehicles in country, the vehicular pollution has also increased and it accounts for a considerable share of vehicular pollution in India.

The different factors are the types of engines used, the age of the vehicles, poor road conditions and congested traffic. They add to air pollution in cities, which is a major cause of respiratory diseases. The principal vehicular pollutants are Carbon Monoxide, Oxides of Nitrogen, Hydrocarbons, suspended particulate matters, a varying amount of Sulphur Dioxide depending on the Sulphur content of the fuel and lead compounds.

The total number of registered vehicles in India has increased from 3 million in 1950-51 to more than 33 million in 1995-96, of which about 28 percent are concentrated in the 23 metropolitan cities of India. The number of registered two wheelers rose from just 0.27 million in 1950-51 to more than 231 million in 1991. The number of cars, jeeps and taxis also registered an increase from 1.59 million in 1950-51 to 41.89 million in 1991. The number of registered trucks and buses also registered an increase from 0.82 million in 1950-51 to 17.85 million in 1991 and 0.34 million in 1950-51 to more than 4.49 million in 1991 respectively.

The major share is contributed by metropolitan cities in all registered vehicles in the country. An increase in vehicular pollution is associated with a number of environmental problems like air pollution and global warming. Technical pollution parameters suggest that two wheelers are more polluting as compared to other motor vehicles. Carbon Monoxide, Oxides of Nitrogen, Hydrocarbons, suspended and particulate matters, a varying amount of Sulphur Dioxide depending on the Sulphur content of the fuel and lead compounds are the major vehicular pollutants. As a result of urbanization in India, pressure on urban transport is likely to increase substantially in this new millennium. It has been attempted to evaluate the future transport scenario to forecast the vehicle air pollution levels. Following are some of the points of due consideration:

— India is expected to have 31 metro cities by 2001 and 51 by 2021.

— The number of vehicles on Indian roads is estimated to increase by nine times by the tune of the century out of which 65 % to 70 % shall be two wheelers or three wheelers.

— Urban transport demand is expected to grow by 2.6 times by 2016 at the existing model split in larger medium sized cities.

— At the existing model split, the urban air quality is expected to deteriorate faster in the 21st century, as two-wheeler population would be as high as 86.13 % of the total vehicles used for passenger transportation.

— By the year 2001, CO emission levels are likely to rise seven times and that of hydrocarbons by nine times. The levels of other major pollutants are expected to go up five fold.

Carbon emissions

In 1992, India signed the United Nations Framework Convention on Climate Change as a non-Annex I country, meaning it is not obligated to reduce its emissions of carbon and greenhouse gases (GHG). India ratified the agreement in 1993. While India recognizes the importance of reducing these harmful emissions, the Indian government also places a high priority on economic development. As such, India is not a signatory to the Kyoto Protocol that mandates specific commitments by countries to reduce their emissions of greenhouse gases by an average of 5.2% below 1990 levels by the agreed 2008-2012 time frame. Nevertheless, India accepted the Kyoto Protocol on August 26, 2002. India's non-participation in the Kyoto Protocol has been cited as a major reason behind the opposition to implementing the Protocol by several signatories, including the United States.

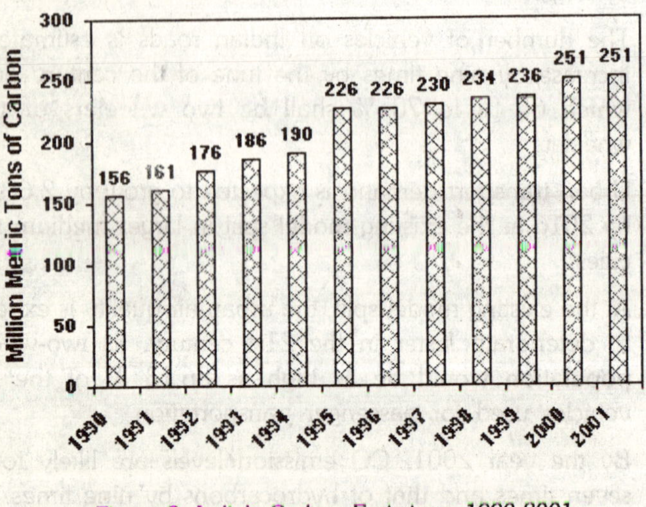

Figure 3. India's Carbon Emissions, 1990-2001

In 2001, India, with 251 million metric tons of carbon equivalent emitted, ranked fifth in the world in carbon emissions, behind the United States, China, Russia and Japan. Although India's carbon emissions stood at only 80% of Japan's (316 million metric tons of carbon equivalent) total and less than one-sixth of the United States' carbon emissions that same year, the rapid growth of India's carbon emissions - in combination with its exclusion from the Protocol - is the main point of controversy. Between 1990 and 2001, India's carbon emissions increased by an astonishing 61%, a rate surpassed only by China's 111% increase during the same time period.

India's carbon emissions are expected to continue to increase throughout the decade, offsetting the planned reduction in GHGs from the European Union and other countries that plan to implement the Protocol's emissions cut requirements.

The rise in India's carbon emissions has been exacerbated by the low energy efficiency of coal-fired power plants in the country. With the high capital costs associated with replacing existing coal-fired plants, a scarcity of capital, and the long lead time required to introduce advanced coal technologies, it stands to reason that many of India's highly-polluting coal-fired power plants will have to remain in operation for the next couple of decades.

As such, India's contribution to world carbon emissions is expected to increase in coming years, with an estimated average annual growth rate between 2001 and 2025 of 3.0% in the EIA International Energy Outlook 2003 reference case. The absolute increase in emissions will partially be a function of the degree to which coal is relied upon as a major energy source. If coal consumption is substituted by oil and natural gas consumption, India's overall carbon emissions would be reduced. India's per capita carbon emissions are relatively low - at 0.25 metric tons of carbon per person in 2001, India's per capita carbon emissions were less than one-quarter of the world average and 22 times less than the United States.

However, the country's per capita carbon emissions are expected to increase in the coming years due to the rapid pace of urbanization, a conversion away from noncommercial towards commercial fuels, increased vehicular usage and the continued use of older and more inefficient coal-fired plants. In fact, due to fast-paced industrialization, per capita emissions are expected to triple by 2020.

Energy and carbon intensity

In 2001, India's energy intensity (energy consumption per dollar of GDP) stood at 25,307 Btu per $1995. Although this figure is one of the highest in Asia, surpassed only by Pakistan (26,229 Btu per $1995) and China (35,619 Btu per $1995), India's carbon intensity has remained relatively flat over the past 20 years, even falling from a high in 1995 (30,459 Btu per $1995) back below 1980 level (25,861 Btu per $1995). By contrast, China's energy intensity level in 2001 was just one-third of its 1980 level of 105,632 Btu per $1995. India's still elevated energy intensity level is due in large part to the growth of energy-intensive industries that has taken place in the country during the course of its economic expansion, coupled with the virtual absence of energy efficiency and conservation measures in most industrial sectors. Carbon intensity (carbon emissions per dollar of GDP) in India also is relatively high compared to its neighbors. In 2001, India's carbon intensity measured 0.5 metric tons of carbon per thousand $1995.

In Asia, only China's carbon intensity (0.75 metric tons of carbon per thousand $1995) was higher than that of India, but whereas China has become less carbon intensive over the past 20 years, India's carbon intensity has remained at virtually the same level as in 1980.

India's heavy reliance on coal, much of it low-quality, goes a long way towards explaining the country's relatively high carbon intensity level. Indian economic policies such as high import tariffs on high-quality coal and subsidies on low-quality domestic coal also have contributed to increased use of low-quality coal, although initiatives to encourage the use of higher-quality coal, such as reducing the tariff on imported coal, may help in reducing the country's carbon intensity.

The introduction and adoption of technologies to reduce coal consumption and/or improve the efficiency of the coal that is combusted is an important government priority, given that the majority of India's power generation is coal-fired.

Renewable energy

Despite a trend towards urbanization, more than 70% of India's population still lives in rural areas. As the Indian economy develops, one of the greatest challenges that India's local and regional governments face is providing people in rural areas with access to energy. Renewable energy projects - in the form of solar-, wind-, and hydropower-generated electricity - are the key to providing rural areas with energy where power is in short supply. In addition, replacing coal- and other fossil fuel-generated electricity supplied to India's cities with energy from renewable energy sources could aid in reducing air pollution and help to meet the growing energy needs of the country's large metropolises as well.

India is the only country that has a separate government ministry exclusively for non-conventional energy sources, and India has one of the largest national programs to promote the use of solar energy. Whereas the majority of developed countries have turned to solar energy mainly out of concern about the environment and energy security, the use of solar power in India is being advocated as a way to provide energy to regions where there is a shortage of electricity.

Rather than build new, expensive generating capacity or connect rural areas to the existing power transmission infrastructure, India is turning to the use of solar energy. In many small villages and remote areas, solar photovoltaic systems are far more cost-effective than conventional energy.

Wind-generated energy is also an important component of India's strategy to boost the use of renewable energies. India is rich in wind energy potential, and the country has been adding installed wind power capacity at an impressive rate.

According to the Ministry of Non-Conventional Energy Sources, India now expects to exceed its target of installing 1,500 MW of wind power in the 2002-2007 period.

The improvement in grid connections, which have previously slowed the development of wind power in India, as well as an effort to provide incentives to wind-power producers, has spurred the growth of the wind energy industry in India.

Nevertheless, at the same time that small- and micro-level wind and solar energy projects are taking shape, the Indian government is looking to large-scale hydroelectric plants to meet its future energy needs. India has an estimated hydropower potential of 150,000 MW, but hydropower's share of India's energy consumption and production has declined in the past 20 years. Indeed, according to Former Indian Prime Minister Atal Bihari Vajpayee, the share of hydropower in the country's total installed generating capacity, which was over 40% about 20 years back, has fallen to 25%. Former Power Minister Anant Geete has said that only about 23% of India's hydropower potential has been exploited.

India's state-owned National Hydroelectric Power Corp. (NHPC) is planning to commission 1,090 MW of capacity by mid-2004, ending a protracted period of lackluster growth, and the government hopes that subsidies to support hydropower plant development will help it attain a goal of building 50,560 MW, almost tripling the country;'s current installed hydropower capacity.

INDIA'S ENVIRONMENTAL OUTLOOK

India faces significant challenges in balancing its increased demand for energy with the need to protect its environment from further damage. Sheer population growth and urbanization make the task all the more difficult for the Indian government, as increased vehicular ownership will contribute to existing air pollution problems and urbanization raises the health risks from that pollution.

A rapidly increasing population also will lead to an increase in electricity demand, taxing the already straining power generation, transmission and distribution infrastructure and putting pressure on the power sector to add new capacity to the system. Already, shortages of electricity have hampered India's industrial growth. As such, electricity is one of the keys to both India's economic development and its environmental protection efforts. The Indian government has introduced initiatives aimed to discourage firms from generating electricity using older, inefficient coal-fired plants, and it has reduced subsidies on low-quality coal.

The government has used fiscal incentives, in the form of customs waivers and soft loans, to encourage the installation of pollution abatement equipment, and market mechanisms such as user charges, deposit refund systems, marketable permits and taxes for implementing pollution measures also are being contemplated. In August 2003, India's Supreme Court laid down the principle of "polluter pays." India has made significant efforts in the field of environmental protection, developing environmental standards for both products and processes, requiring environmental impact statements in certain areas, and introducing environmental audits.

India's strong support of air quality and alternative fuel initiatives has brought progress as well as growing pains to the country. However, in the absence of coordinated government efforts, including stricter enforcement, air pollution is likely to continue to worsen in the coming years as urbanization picks up pace and vehicle ownership increases.

The Indian government's ability to safeguard the country's environment will depend on its success in promoting policies that keep the economy growing while providing adequate energy needs to satisfy the populace's growing energy consumption requirements in a sustainable manner.

POPULATION GROWTH AND ENVIRONMENTAL PROBLEM: THEORETICAL DISCUSSION

In the popular press, population growth is not often seen as an environmental problem. On a regular basis, we are warned about global warming, ozone depletion, rainforest destruction, groundwater contamination, toxic waste proliferation, shrinking animal habitat, endangered animal species, shrinking petroleum reserves, and a loss of biodiversity. Occasionally stories about these topics make connections with other topics, but usually they are dealt with singularly.

A host of responses have been proposed to combat these signs of man's impact on the natural world, but seemingly only those that are convenient are implemented. According to those who have studied the burgeoning population, all attempts to deal with environmental degradation will fail because they deal with the symptoms of the problem, not the problem itself.

The problem, they clearly state, is overpopulation. None would argue that the population is growing. Statistics show that for every person who was alive in 1830, there are now six people consuming the earth's resources. Where there were one billion mouths to feed, there are now six billion. The earth hasn't grown any larger, and many argue that it's capacity to sustain human life, through such developments as a decrease in topsoil, increase in desertification, pollution of groundwater and other factors, has actually decreased during this period.

Many have theorized what the actual carrying capacityof the earth is, with estimates ranging from less than the current population to as high as 50 billion. Such wide-ranging estimates, purported by experts, are one reason the population problem goes largely unnoticed.

Throughout history, there seems to have always been one or two people who were able to see and understand the effects of population growth on an environmental, social, and economic level. The first modern writer to deal with the idea of overpopulation was Robert Thomas Malthus, an Englishman who lived from 1766-1834. He was an ordained priest in the Church of England, as well as a professor of history and political economy at the East India College at Hertfordshire.

In 1798 Malthus wrote An Essay on the Principle of Population. In it he examined the future of mankind, and pondered whether expanding human numbers would eventually outstrip the capacity of the land to provide for them. At the time he wrote his famous essay, the prevailing ideas of the time reflected upon the perfectibility of mankind. It was believed that man had been progressing with the increasing population, and that rapid increases in population were not only desirable, but they would ensure that man would attain a state of perfection much sooner than if population grew more slowly.

Malthus had different ideas as to what such an increase in population would bring. First, he believed that human fertility could increase human numbers beyond the land's capacity to sustain them. The crossing of this threshold came to be known as the Malthusian Crunch.

Technological advances in the past two centuries, such as fertilizer, irrigation, hybrid crops, and others have extended the number of people the earth can feed. These advancements, which have enabled man to push back the limits placed on him by nature, have come to be known as the Malthusian Shuffle. Malthus also understood the geometric quality of population growth. Population growth is explained by a growth rate, symbolized by the percent the population is growing.

The geometric factor resides in a growing base. For example, two percent of a hundred is two, while two percent of six billion is one hundred twenty million. That one hundred twenty million would be added to the original six billion, and the base upon which the percentage of growth would be calculated the following year would be six billion, one hundred twenty million.

Eventually, Malthus wrote, the growing number of people would use up the available resources. This became known as the Malthusian Trap. Malthus wrote that it was inevitable that the human population would someday exceed those limits, and as a result the human population would be brought under control by vice and misery. As defined by Malthus, vice referred to human intervention, such as war, while misery referred to non-human intervention, such as starvation and/or disease.

While the validity of Malthus' essay has been argued by both sides since it was written, the lasting value of his work may be much more basic. He was the first to write that there were finite limits of material goods the earth could produce. Before his essay made its appearance, the earth and its resources were seen as inexhaustible. The belief was that man had been given the earth by divine providence, and that his duty was to "go forth and multiply". Even though that is what we, as a species, have done, Malthus' essay has given us a historical cause for thought regarding our future.

In 1968, Dr. Paul Ehrlich sounded the Malthusian horn to a new era with his book The Population Bomb. Like the earlier work of Malthus, Ehrlich's book received a mixed reaction from the public. For some, it served as an alert to the growing problems brought on by the expanding population. For others, it was criticized as an unprovable hypothesis generated by the new environmentalism movement. In the book, Dr. Ehrlich reasoned that the future of an overpopulated earth was soon to be a reality, and that future was grim. He prophesized great famines, resource wars, polluted oceans, the atmospheric greenhouse effect, and the general degradation of the natural environment. As a professor of population studies at Stanford University, Dr. Ehrlich has made the study of population his life's work.

In 1990 Dr. Ehrlich teamed up with his wife Anne, a senior research associate in the biological sciences at Stanford, to write a follow up to The Population Bomb titled The Population Explosion. In it, they discussed the predictions he had made in 1968 and compared them to what had actually transpired.

Similar to Malthus, a large number of his predictions had been accurate.

The Ehrlichs open their book with a discussion of the technological advances of the late twentieth century that have allowed the population to grow so large. They state clearly that this Malthusian Shuffle comes with a price; unsustainability. They document the increased productivity brought about by the green revolution, and show that the productivity for this type of industrialized agriculture peaked in the mid-80's. Since then, yields have fallen each year, while population has continued to grow.

They also explain how these types of farming practices, with their reliance on chemical fertilizers and by their monocropping ideology, have resulted in a net reduction of topsoil by as much as half. Also, they discuss the effects of over fishing on fish stocks, whose tattered remains are at the brink of being unable to reproduce their numbers due to younger, pre-breeding age fish being targeted as a result of the older fish having already been caught and sold.

Next the Ehrlichs examine the geometric properties of population growth. Similar to the arguments of Malthus, they state that it is a cycle that can not go on much longer. They discuss the lag time between action being taken to control the population and those actions having any real effects, and call this population momentum.

Simply put, barring any plunge in the birth rate that take family averages well below the reproduction rate of 2.1 children per female, and barring any substantial rises in the death rate, it will take between fifty or sixty years after a population reaches replacement reproduction to achieve zero population growth.

This is so because there is a high population of young people in the world right now. Births usually take place among the young, while deaths usually take place among the old. Thus if a population has a high percentage of young people, the average age of the population must increase before death rates catch up with birth rates. What this means is that if population were suddenly viewed as the specter it is in early December of 1998, and by January 1, 1999, all people of the world had no more than 2.1 children on average, the population would continue to rise until the middle of the next century before leveling off.

When discussing population growth, the argument is often made in industrialized nations that the problem lies in the third world, where the most explosive growth exists. Many of the populations of industrialized nations are at or near zero growth. If we had a pure population problem, where there were simply too many people, they would have a valid argument. But the population dilemma we face is as much a problem of resources and consumption as it is of population.

The Ehrlichs address this problem with possibly the most important idea of their book. They state that the impact of humans on the environment can be understood as the product of three separate factors. "The first is the number of people.

The second is some measure of the average person's consumption of resources (which is also an index of affluence). Finally, the product of those two factors-the population and its per-capita consumption-is multiplied by an index of the environmental disruptiveness of the technologies that provide the goods consumed.

The last factor can also be viewed as the environmental impact per quantity of consumption. In short, Impact = Population *x* Affluence *x* Technology, or I = PAT. "Using this equation, we can see that population does not act alone in its effect on the environment. Similarly, the argument of many in developed nations with low birth rates that they are not the problem is clearly bunk when it is understood that they use a much greater percentage of the world's resources. In effect, this equation levels the playing field between the first and third world, negating the validity of finger pointing by both sides. It clearly shows that both the developed and the developing world have contributed to the negative environmental impacts of the growing population.

The Ehrlichs expend considerable effort detailing the effects of population growth on agriculture, global ecosystems, and public health. In their lucid manner, they explain three possible futures for humanity: the bang, the whimper, and the alternative. The bang, they explain, is a nuclear war. Growing population will put an excessive strain on the world's resources, leading ultimately to increased tensions and a resource war. This possibility, they wrote in 1990, was becoming more unlikely due to the events of the time. But, they maintain, it is still a possibility.

The whimper would be a result of the life support systems of the earth ultimately becoming over stressed and ceasing to function in a way that could be manipulated by man to produce the mountains of food now being produced. Simply put, it would mean the end of the world as we know it, and possibly the end of civilization as we know it.

The specialization of labor would breakdown when food was no longer being supplied from somewhere else, and the results, in addition to widespread starvation, could be riots and/or epidemics. Economies would become localized, and food production would be the chief job of the much smaller population.

The alternative would be to simultaneously halt population growth and begin population shrinkage, convert the economic system from one of growthism to one of sustainability while decreasing percapita consumption, and convert to more environmentally friendly technologies. In short, simultaneously reduce the three multipliers in the I=PAT equation (population, affluence, technology). Interestingly, both the bang and the whimper are directly in line with what Malthus wrote two centuries prior, corresponding to vice and misery, respectively.

The Ehrlichs firmly believe that we are living on borrowed time, and that the population will decrease in the coming years. Whether that is by a voluntary decrease in the birth rate or by an involuntary rise in the death rate is the only question.

In his book Living Within Limits, Garrett Hardin, professor emeritus of human ecology at the University of California at Santa Barbara, addresses many of the same questions examined by the Ehrlichs. He also comes to many of the same conclusions. Early in the book Hardin quotes Herodotus, who reported that there had been a time when a person could walk across North Africa from the Atlantic to the Indian Ocean always in the shade of trees.

Next, he quotes a tenth century Samanid prince who identified the four earthly paradises as being the regions of Samakand, southern Persia, southern Iraq, and Damascus. Clearly these regions today are known for their sand, not for their similarity to earthly paradises. He uses this idea to introduce his theory that throughout human history man's trend of exploitation of the earth's resources has been colonize, destroy, then move on.

He makes a solid case for his theory, going so far as to introduce the plan of science (fiction) to colonize the stars once we have plundered the earth. Explaining this idea using real numbers, he quickly exposes it as a ludicrous dream ungrounded in reality. Hardin blames the ignorance about population issues on innumeracy. Innumeracy, he explains, is the numerical equivalent of illiteracy. It is the inability to read and comprehend numbers. The evidence, he states, is clear. It is the interpretation, or lack thereof, which constitutes the problem.

Economics, he states, is driven by the cowboy ideals of independence and inexhaustible resources stretching to the horizon. This line of reasoning is horribly outdated, explains Hardin. In reality, we are quickly diminishing the resources that drive our economy. Hardin uses the concept of a spaceship with clearly defined finite limits on its available resources to describe the earth.

While traditional economic theory describes the economy in terms of growth and GNP (gross national product), it ignores the basic realities of production. Economic theory recognizes the concepts of source (source of raw materials) and production, but ignores what happens after production. In the real world, there are three steps: Source - Production - Sink. Sink may be defined as that part of nature that has to absorb the unwanted, so-called by-products of production, or pollution. As ours is a growth-based economy which has been growing ever larger with the expanding population, the prognosis for the future when taking this type of oversight into account is grim. Essentially what he is saying is that economic theory ignores the T in the I=PAT equation, which as the Ehrlichs demonstrated is an important factor in environmental impact. With two such opposing ideologies, Hardin questions if there is any hope for reconciliation in the face of a growing population and increasing use of resources.

Hardin writes that Malthus was ninety five percent correct in his predictions. Throughout the book, he restates Malthus' ideas using modern facts and figures to support them. He shows that birth rates have not dramatically changed over the last few centuries, but death rates have decreased rapidly. Life expectancy, therefore, has grown considerably. Hardin predicts that this decrease in death rates, or rise in life expectancy, will be short lived. He believes that as a species we are out of equilibrium, and that equilibrium will be restored by a sharp increase in the death rate in the years to come.

In his book *A Bicentennial Malthusian Essay*, attorney and mechanical engineer John F. Rohe revisits principles found in Malthus' essay in order to determine whether their root causes are applicable in 1998. The book is broken up into five sections: Malthus himself, population growth, economic growth, the effects of population growth on the land, and the next two hundred years.

In the section on Malthus, Rohe biographies Malthus and explains how he came to write his famous essay as a reaction to the conventional optimism of the times. Rohe discusses the influence of Malthus' work on Charles Darwin, and how it helped Darwin to formulate his understanding of the results of excess reproduction contained in his theories of evolution and natural selection. Finally, we see how Malthus' divergent ideas ranged far from his Utopian peers of the late 18century.

In the section on population, Rohe looks at human evolution as a possible explanation for our inability to grasp large problems. He states that throughout man's evolution we have been concerned with small, localized problems in order to survive. When hungry, procure food; when cold, build a fire or a shelter. If the climate in the region we live changes, either adapt or move on in search of greener pastures. After all, prehistoric man had not the hubris to believe he could have been responsible for changes in the climate. It was too large, and he too small. There was no advantage to understanding large, slowly developing problems. Many believe that our nervous systems developed with this inability to grasp larger issues, being more focused on aiding us in the day to day survival activities we faced.

The section on economic growth is especially poignant. Like Hardin, Rohe points out innumeracy as a major problem. He writes that "during the 1996 presidential campaign, vice presidential candidate Jack Kemp professed he would like to see our GNP grow at a rate of five percent per year.

That's a doubling time of fourteen years. In a healthy lifetime of ninety-eight years, that's seven doublings! The progression of seven doublings is: 2, 4, 8, 16, 32, 64, 128. Does he really think the annual GNP can be 128 times as big in a single year sometime later in the lifetime of a child born today? In 98 years? That's 128 times as many new homes in a single year, 128 times as many new roads in a single year, 128 times as many new cars, planes, boats, skyscrapers, and televisions all in a single year... An affinity for growth reduces to an absurdity. Let's assume we maintain a steady growth rate of six percent per year. This is close to the U.S. rate of growth in the early 1980s and less than the present rate in some Asian countries. If we can maintain this rate of growth, the economy will be 339 times as big in a period of 100 years.

It is even more daunting to think that in just an additional fifty years we will be reproducing 100% of all items having economic value today in a single twenty-four hour period! In other words, every road, house, car, television, and other item of existing value today will then be manufactured in a single day!" Clearly, when growth is explained in such terms, it leaves little room for belief in sustained economic development. But, if the population is to continue growing at an exponential rate, such economic growth would be necessary in order to employ the masses. Any rational person can easily see that such growth simply isn't sustainable for anything but the short term, regardless of the rhetoric employed by politicians seeking office.

The effects of population growth on the environment could eventually bring about the implementation of policies which could be seen as anti-American. In addition to documenting the devastating effects population growth has had on the global ecosystem, Rohe states that continued population growth could spell disaster for that most cherished American ideal; private property.

As the environment continues to decay, public outcry will most likely turn the tide of lawmakers from that of protecting the individual's right to pollute to protecting the masses right to a clean environment. Although in direct conflict with entrenched American values, Rohe believes that the mystique of the American frontier, and the ability of the individual to live as an individual, will be usurped by a growing populace. Rohe sees the next two hundred years as being pivotal on whether man can change or not. If not, then the future is anything but rosy. If we are able to change, he lists three specifics which will need to be at the forefront of that change in order to forestall the demise of man. First, he feels that there needs to be a growth in numeracy, or an understanding of numbers. Not only in terms of human populations, but in understanding the problems we will face in the future. Second, he feels that a shift in values will be necessary.

The consumptive ways of late twentieth century man must go the way of the carrier pigeon, and as a species we must embrace an ethical and ecological balance that is in tune with nature and out of tune with merchandisers. Simply put, we must live our lives in recognition of the fact that there will be generations coming after us, and that we don't have the right to use all the resources and pollute the earth. Lastly, he believes that we must be willing to make ethical compromises. Somehow we must infuse in our collective mentality that the tenets of capitalism, such as maximizing profits at any cost, are not in the best interests of our species or our planet.

With the new millennium just over a year away, the popular press has been examining issues pertinent to our well being in the twenty-first century. Many articles have appeared of late on the topic of population, but few have made the connection between overpopulation and ecological crisis. Written in 1978, Bartlett's Forgotten Fundamentals of the Energy Crisis is one whose omission in a paper such as this would be conspicuous. The article itself is about energy use in relation to the lessons learned during the oil crisis of the early 1970s. With this as his impetus, Bartlett examined the future of oil as a commodity for energy production. He concluded that per-capita energy consumption was rising in 1978. To the layman, it would seem that percapita energy consumption continues to rise. Couple that with explosive growth in population and the result is a short future for oil and the plethora of products derived from it. Bartlett calculated how much oil the earth would hold were it completely hollow and full of oil, then using the concept of exponential growth figured out how long those hypothetical reserves would last.

After all, the grocery store is filled to the brim with food, never before in history have there been more goods available to so many people, and the standard of living for most of us here is high. But the problem remains. To the field of environmental history, these books add a definitive answer as to why the environment is breaking down. If one person has *x* impact, then six billion people have 6,000,000,000*x* impact.They serve to put the causes of the environmental problems of the era, often made out to be nebulous and ethereal, into a tangible equation that can be easily grasped and understood. Their main addition to the field, though, is to alert people to the impending consequences of our collective actions.

The core issue of overpopulation and its many negative effects on the earth, which are seen as individual environmental problems, is one of limits. Throughout nature, the evidence that actual limits exist regarding how many of a certain species a region can support is clear. For example, snowshoe hare populations in Alaska are on a twelve year cycle. Their population grows exponentially for twelve years, until there are too many hares for the limited food supply to feed.As a result, they die off in such large numbers that it takes them another twelve years to generate a population of similar numbers. But when they do, they face the same fate as their predecessors. Can we, as rational beings, recognize that we will face a similar fate if we allow our population to continue to grow unchecked? Edward O. Wilson, of Harvard University, points to a lily pond as an example of exponential growth: "At first there is only one lily pad in the pond, but the next day it doubles, and thereafter, each of its descendants doubles. The pond completely fills with lily pads in 30 days. When is the pond exactly half-full? Answer: On the twenty-ninth day."Had the lily pads been capable of rational thinking, would the majority of them have loudly proclaimed that there was no population problem at midnight on the twenty-ninth day? Two hundred years ago Malthus foresaw the demise of mankind, and the vehicle was the disregard of limits in the form of overpopulation.

7

POPULATION AND LITERACY CAMPAIGNS IN INDIA

A hundred years ago, education was not nearly so widely available as it is today. For this reason, illiteracy was very common. Today, education is almost universally available and illiteracy does not seem quite so common as it was a hundred years ago. Despite this perception, there are more nonliterate people in the world today than at any time in history, or at least in this century. A primary reason for this is the growth of population in those countries which have low literacy rates.

The world's population more than tripled in this century growing from about 1.6 billion in 1900 to about 5.75 billion in 1995. This is an increase of 4.15 billion people. During the same period, the number of nonliterates increased from about 300 million in 1900 to about 1 billion in 1995. While the nonliterate population has also tripled, the numerical growth is only about 700 million people.

At least 95 percent of the population growth has taken place in the developing countries. Since this is where we find most of the illiteracy, it is not surprising that the size of the nonliterate population is still growing. While UNESCO and many governments have launched campaigns to wipe out illiteracy by the year 2000, the best estimates indicate that the numbers of nonliterates will continue to grow for at least awhile. It is conceivable that the growth of illiteracy will be halted, but the elimination of illiteracy is not likely in the foreseeable future.

THE NATIONAL LITERACY MISSION

The Eradication of illiteracy from a nation that is set to become the most populated in the world is by no means easy. This was realised in eighties and the National Literacy Mission came into being on 5th May, 1988 to impart a new sense of urgency and seriousness to adult education. The first breakthrough came in Kerala, in Kottayam city followed by Ernakulam district where the literacy campaign was initiated in 1989 and completed within a year.

For the first time, an area-specific, time bound campaign approach had been implemented and the community become responsible for running its own development programmes and consequently determining its future.

During the last 10 years, 556 districts out of 588 in the country have already been covered under the total literacy campaign of which 259 districts have entered the post literacy phase and 85 in the continuing education phase.

The efforts of the mission have not gone in vain and it is evident from the latest figures available from the National Sample Survey Organisation. The literacy level in India has risen from 52% in 1991 to 62% in 1997. This is all the more creditable because of the countering factor of population growth.

The wide gap between male and female literacy rates at last seems to be narrowing as also the urban and rural difference. The creditable performance of the National Literacy Mission received international recognition when it was awarded the UNESCO's NOMA Literacy Prize for 1999.

The international jury while selecting National Literacy Mission (NLM) for the prize recognised its initiation of the total literacy campaigns which are now "accepted as the dominant strategy" for eradication of illiteracy in the country. It recognised

NLM efforts in "galvanising activities towards integration, conservation of the environment, promotion of women's equality and the preservation of family customs and traditions".

The international jury also appreciated the training imparted by NLM, the teaching learning materials produced by it, the setting up of autonomous education bodies, creating awareness for education and raising the demand for both the quality and quantity of primary education. The NLM in the meantime has been revitalised with the approval of the Union Cabinet on 30th September, 1999. The Mission's goal is to attain full literacy i.e. a sustainable threshold literacy rate of 75% by 2005.

The Mission seeks to achieve this by imparting functional literacy to non-literates in the 15-35 age group. To tackle the problem of residual illiteracy, now it has been decided to adopt an integrated approach to total literacy campaigns and post literacy programme. This means the TLCs and PLPs will be implemented under one literacy project to achieve continuity, efficiency and convergence and to minimise unnecessary time lag between the two. Post literacy programmes will be treated only as a preparatory phase for launching Continuing Education with the ultimate aim of creating a learning society.

Goals

The goals of the National Literacy Mission is to attain full literacy, i.e. a sustainable threshold level of 75 percent by 2005. The mission seeks to achieve this goal by imparting functional literacy to non-literates in the 15-35 age group. This age group has been the focus of attention because they are in the productive and reproductive period of life. The total literacy campaign offers them a seconds chance, in case they missed the opportunity or were denied access to mainstream formal education.

The scope of the programme has been enlarged to include people in the age group 9 to 14 years, in areas not covered by the non-formal education programme, to ensure that the benefits of TLCs are made available to out-of-school children as well.

Special care is taken to bring disadvantaged groups like women, scheduled castes and tribes and backward classes into the programme. The basic objective is to create a generation which will ensure that their children are educated, to realize the dream of Education For All.

In quantitative terms, the Mission seeks to impart functional literacy to all non-literate persons in 15-35 age group. In qualitative terms, functional literacy implies:

— Self-reliance in 3 R's
— Participation in the development process.
— Skill improvement to improve economic status and general well being.
— Imbibing values of national integration, conservation of environment, women's equality and observance of small family norms etc.

The NLM seeks to achieve these objectives through the following:

— by creating an environment conducive to teaching-learning process, provision of good and relevant teaching-learning materials and facilitating teaching-learning by good training, media and communication;
— by improving the pace of learning and injecting confidence among the learners about their potential to learn and by ensuring that the process is not drudgery;
— by integrating basic literacy with post-literacy and continuing education; and
— by developing the quality of human resources at all levels of functionaries through orientation and training.

LITERACY CAMPAIGN

The Government has decided that an integrated approach to literacy would be followed now. This means, the Total literacy Campaign and the Post Literacy Programme will now operate under one literacy Project. This approach would enable the enormous illiteracy problem to be tackled in a holistic manner. By treating the imparting of functional literacy as a continuum rather than as a one off benefit for the illiterate person, progress of literacy efforts would be made goal -directed.

Literacy campaigns would continue to run in those areas where there are large pools of residule illiteracy. At the same time, for those who have crossed the basic learning phase, programmes of consolidation, remediation, vocational skills, integration with life skills and such other aspects would be considered the basic unit. In effect, the task of making a person actually literate in a sustainable and meaningful way can be said to have been modesty discharged only after the Post Literacy Campaign actually constitute two operational stages on the learning continuum and now under the same scheme will operate in smooth progression, drawing there financial sustenance from one single and same budgetary provision.

It is proposed that a district, while submitting their intial project, would also submit their strategy for Post Literacy on the basis of there anticipated target and projections of achivements. The per learner financial norms of Total Literacy Campaign and Post Literacy Campaign would be the same as approved by the Expenditure Finance Committee the structures and strategies would also remain unaltered providing closer linkages. The integrated proposal seeks to effectively bring the activities of literacy campaigns under one 'Literacy Project' to achieve continuity, efficiency and convergence and to minimise unnecessary time lag between the two.

The existing funding pattern of literacy campaigns is proposed to be continued. The funding ratio between Center and State Government for normal districts is 2:1, whereas for districts under Tribal Sub-Plan the ratio is 4:1. The per learner cost for a Total Literacy Campaign will now be in the range of Rs 90-130. In many cases for reasons such as natural calamities, absence of political will, frequent tranfer of collectors, etc., a number of campaigns have stagnated. The restortation of such project would be continued as was approved by the cabinet in 1994. For this purpose, an additionally of 40-50% on the original project cost, will be admissible.

The impact of literacy and adult education programmes clearly shows that in the future, skill development and increased economic opportunity must form one of the major components of initiatives in this area. The challenge before the National Literacy Mission is to create a continuing education system where the effervescence of the mass upsurge of the literacy campaigns can be channelled into structuring a continuous and life-long learning process. The sheer complexity and contextual specificity of the concept of continuing education make any attempt to define it an extremely difficult exercise.

There is a multiplicity of views. This is because of two primary reasons. The first can be called normative, in as much as the area of continuing education is inchoate. Thinking in this relatively new field is flexible and open to several interpretations. The second is formal, in the sense that the content and style of the programme is determined by the context of its implementation. In the post literacy and continuing education stages, greater emphasis is being placed on skill development and acquisition of new learning. For those who have acquired basic literacy skills, we need to link these skills more intricately with their lives. This can only become a reality when they learn not only to practise these skills in their day-to-day life, but also clearly under stand that these skills will be of vital importance to them in order to improve the quality and the standard of their lives.

The continuing education scheme is postulated on the principles of:

— Treating basic literacy, post literacy and continuing education as one sustained, coherent learning process.

— Establishing a responsive and alternative structure for life-long learning.

— Responding to the needs of all sections of society.

— Learning not to be seen as a function of alphabets, but as all modes of human capacity building.

— Addressing the socio-economic situations of the community to provide infrastructure for larger development initiatives.

Thus, the scheme of continuing education, taken up in a district after it has completed the total literacy and post literacy phases, makes the learners aware of the power and significance of education. They realise that education is the agency for improving their lives and they tend to find ways to use their literacy skills in their everyday life to make it more meaningful and rewarding.

The continuing education scheme is, therefore, multi-faceted and enjoys supreme flexibility to allow grassroots community participation and managerial initiative. Establishment of Continuing Education Centres (CECs) and Nodal Continuing Education Centres (NCESs) is the principal mode of implementing continuing education programmes. The centres follow an area-specific, community-based approach.

The scheme envisages one CEC for each village to serve a population of about 1,500-2,000 people. About 10 such centres form a cluster with one more acting as the nodal CEC. The centres are run by full-time facilitators or preraks, and assistant preraks who are drawn from the community itself. The continuing education centre serves as:

— Library and reading room

— Teaching-learning centre for continuing education programmes

— Vocational training centre

— Extension centre for facilities of other development departments

— Discussion forum for sharing ideas and solving problems

— A composite information window for the community

— Cultural centre

— Sports and recreation centre

The CECs, including the nodal one, are set up in active consultation with the user community and its programme is designed to meet their demands. The stress on imparting literacy skills to non-literates is sustained. Teaching of primers, identification of target groups, environment-building activities, and other items of work if connected with basic literacy eradication continues unabated. Wide acceptance and local sustainability is achieved by involving NGOs, voluntary agencies, social workers, panchayati raj institutions in the planning and implementation of the scheme of continuing education.

Various development departments, technical institutions and professional groups provide inputs needed by the programme. State Resource Centres and Jan Shikshan Sansthans join hands by giving the necessary resource and training support. Apart from establishing CECs, the scheme also undertakes the following programmes:

— Equivalency programme designed as an alternative education programme equivalent to existing formal, general or vocational education.

— Income-generating programme where the participants acquire or upgrade their vocational skills and take up income-generating activities.

— Quality of life improvement programme which aims to equip learners and the community with essential knowledge, attitude, values and skills to raise their standard of living.

— Individual interest promotion programme to provide opportunities for learners to participate and learn about their individually chosen social, cultural, spiritual, health, physical and artistic interests.

The project for a continuing education programme is formulated by the Zila Saksharta Samiti taking the district as a unit. The proposal is submitted for approval to the State Literacy Mission Authorities of the concerned state or to the National Literacy Mission in case the district falls under a union territory. While the central government does provide financial assistance for initial establishment and running of CECs, in the long run all such CECs are expected to become self-sustaining.

The scheme, therefore, envisages provision of financial assistance from the central government and the state governments for the first five years. The central government provides 100 per cent financial assistance to a district for the first three years. In the fourth and fifth year, the cost is to be shared on a 50:50 basis by the central and state governments. Central support to the programme may be liberalised as more and more encouraging results are obtained. Clearly, the effectiveness of a CEC and the scope of its activities will be significantly determined by the extent of support it enjoys from the community. The CECs must be perceived by the people as arising from their own initiatives to meet their explicit needs. To achieve this objective, the ZSS will be expected to devise all possible ways to enlist community support and mobilise financial and material resources from the community itself so that the CECs and their programmes become self-sufficient in due course of time. In fact, some states such as Andhra Pradesh have achieved remarkable success in mobilising local resources through 'Corpus Funds' and 'Membership Fees'. The continuing education scheme is visualised as a mechanism for integrated human resource development. Well-organised and coordinated infrastructure for continuing education can advance the course of literacy in India leading to the rise of a learning society.

The structure of the continuing education programme, launched in 1995 as a fully funded centrally-sponsored scheme, will be retained and further strengthened and expanded in scope and content. A continuing education center will be set up for a population of 2,000-2,500 so that it caters to the need of at least 500-1000 neo-literates. A nodal continuing education will be set for a cluster of 10-15 continuing education centers.

The function of imparting basic literacy and transaction of literacy primers would be continued in the continuing education phase.The activity of teaching-learning for basic literacy would be available not only dropouts and left-outs but also to new illetrate entrantsin the age group 15-35.

The scheme will continue to be implemented by the Zilla Saksharata Samiti headed by the Collector. However, the Zilla Saksharta Samiti may also be headed by a democratically elected chairman of the Zilla Parishad in states where a full-fledged Panchayati Raj system has been established. The implementing agencies-voluntary agencies, mahila mandals, panchayati raj institutions, Nehru Yuvak Kendras, etc., for continuing education centres or nodal continuing education centres will be identified by the ZSS.

The scheme also envisages convergence with the programmes of Nehru Yuvak Kendras, National Service Scheme, National Service Volunteer scheme, etc., at the grassroots level. The infrastructure of these institutions will, as far as possible, be utilized to facilitate the functioning of the scheme.

DECENTRALISATION OF ADMINISTRATIVE AND FINANCIAL POWERS

In order to promote decentralization, the State Literacy Mission Authorities have been given the authority to sanction continuing education projects to Districts and literacy related projects to voluntary agencies in their States. The scheme of Jan Sikshan Sansthan, previously known as the Scheme of Shramik Vidyapeeth was initially evolved to respond to the educational and vocational training needs of adults and young people living in urban and industrial areas and for persons who have migrated from rural to urban settings. Now their activities have been enlarged and infrastructure strengthened to enable them to function as district repository of vocational and technical skills in both urban and rural areas.

Ever since its inception the National Literacy Mission has taken measures to strengthen its partnership with NGOs and to evolve both institutional and informal mechanisms to give voluntary organisations active promotional role in the literacy movement. Now under the scheme of support to NGOs they will be encouraged and provided with financial assistance to run post literacy and continuing education programmes in well defined areas.

In order to revitalise, re-energise and expand the role of State Resource Centres, not only their number is being increased but also their infrastructure and resource facilities are being strengthened to enable them to play the role of catalytic agents. The Directorate of Adult Education, a sub-ordinate office of the Department of Elementary Education and Literacy has been entrusted with the task of monitoring and evaluating the various literacy programmes being launched under the aegis of the National Literacy Mission. It also provides technical and resource support to the NLM including media support to enable it to achieve its objectives.

The National Literacy Mission is laying great stress on vigorous monitoring and systematic evaluation of adult education programmes launched under its aegis in the country. It has developed and circulated guidelines for concurrent and final evaluation of the total literacy campaigns and post literacy programmes.

A comprehensive set of guidelines on continuing education have also been prepared. So far final evaluation of TLCs have been undertaken in more than 210 districts. It is hoped that the new approach of evaluating literacy campaigns and post literacy programmes will ensure complete transparency and enhance the credibility of the results and impact assessments. The present approach is towards decentralization of financial and administrative powers to the State Literacy Mission Authorities (SLMAs).

The SLMAs - state level registered societies will have a 2 layer structure viz. Governing Council and Executive Council. The State Directorate of Adult Education will serve as Secretariat. The guidelines regarding the delegation of powers to the State Literacy Missions have already been issued, and some projects for continuing education have already been sanctioned by them. 18 States/UTs have set up SLMAs so far. Under the Ninth Plan, the release of grants to NGOs other than the State Resource Centres will be decentralized through the State Literacy Missions up to 50 percent of the total grant released during the financial year and the remaining will be disbursed by the National Literacy Mission.

Innovative projects in respect of all-India level NGOs will be considered by the grants-in-aid committee at the national level. They will be provided assistance for taking up continuing education programmes in addition to innovative programmes in all part of the country. Existing State Resources Centers will be strengthened and their annual maintenance grants suitably enhanced. Independent district resource units will now be subsumed in the State Resource Centres.

In August of 1999 India became the second country to have its population reach the one billion mark. Although certainly a landmark, a billion people in a country one third the size of the United States is more worthy of alarm than celebration. In any country, rapid population growth places a strain on the available resources, but in a developing country like India, many resources are already scarce (in 1960, 0.21 hectares of farmland was available to the average Indian, 0.10hectares in 1999, and it is thought to fall to 0.07 hectares in the next 50 years.

A quickly regenerating population exacerbates shortages of food and water and ensures that the nation's long-term growth will be hampered by a less healthy therefore less productive work force, a greater demand for natural resource consumption, and a higher level of environmental degradation resulting from such consumption.

Realizing these consequences, India has been implementing official family planning programs to curb population growth since the 1950's. However, India's population has more than doubled since those days (from 431,463,000 in 1960 to 1,014,003,800 in 2000) and current projections predict that India has a good chance of overtaking China as the most populated country in the world within the next half century. The graph below illustrates the possible projected exponential growth paths of both countries suggests that these programs fell short of the goals with which they were implemented.

In spite of these facts, India's rate of population growth is actually decreasing. In 1991 India's annual population growth rate was 2.15% and by 1997 this figure dropped to 1.7%, which indicates that India is indeed making some progress. While this may be true, most evidence would suggest that the country's policies have been largely ineffective and changes must be made to prevent further problems resulting from overpopulation. So where did India's efforts fall short? Throughout the decades following the implementation of India's Family Planning Program in the 1950s, the prevailing idea in dealing with overpopulation has been that drastic measures needed to be taken. Education regarding temporary methods of contraception was neglected in favor of encouraging sterilization. Government agencies would have sterilization quotas to fill among the employees, and the inability to meet them was sometimes met with withheld salaries. Workers were often rewarded with a radio or television if they successfully convinced enough people to opt for the surgery. At its worst, India's policy included declaring a state of emergency in 1976 and implementing forced sterilization in poor neighborhoods. When applying for government loans, or jobs people were told that their chances of receiving such aids would be increased if they could produce a certificate of sterilization.

The national focus on sterilization seems to have created an "all or nothing" mentality among Indians towards birth control especially since the awareness of other, temporary methods of contraception for much of the 20th century was minute. A 1993 study, India's National Family Health Survey, revealed that of all contraceptive use at the time, 67% was by female sterilization (compared to 9% male sterilization). The prominence of female sterilization indicates another flaw in the India population control strategies. By targeting women instead of men, the government inadvertently opts for the more hazardous means of birth control. The surgical procedure is more difficult and the rate of failure is high, not to mention the danger to the patient, which sometimes means death. Upon learning of these semi-forced, safety-negligent policies, we get what is likely to be a fairly accurate explanation why family planning efforts have failed to curb rampant population growth in India. When the only option available to many people is one that is irreversible, not to mention potentially life-threatening, people would probably be inclined to opt for no contraceptives at all. In such a scenario, the problem is not solved and the population keeps growing and resources per head keep dwindling.

Fortunately, in recent years, it appears that many Indians are aware of the negative effects of the traditional policies and are striving for a change in the system. Taking heed of the recommendations put forth in the 1994 UN Conference on Population and Development, India has shifted attention away from the strict promotion of contraceptive measures and is working on the development of women's economic, educational and social welfare which will give women more control over their own bodies and indirectly curb population growth.

In 1994, India put forth a "New Population Plan" (NPP), hoping that by the year 2010, the average total fertility rate will fall from the early 90's figure of 3.4 to around the replacement rate of 2.1. In order to achieve this goal, the NPP will make strides in improving reproductive health: it will allow universal access to contraceptives and promote greater education on contraception, train more people to safely aid in the birth of children, require a formal registration of all marriages and births, maintain and enforce the minimum age of marriage at 18, and strive to provide primary education for more citizens.

Other movements toward progress include the 2000 freezing of the population-proportional quota of representation for each state in the Lok Sabha. This means if a state effectively reduces its population it will not lose votes in the national government. Also, loans such as the $57 million from the World Bank affiliate, the International Development Association in 1989, have gone to rural and urban areas to successfully aid in the improvement of reproductive health and increasing the awareness of and access to temporary contraceptives.

RELATION BETWEEN FEMALE LITERACY AND POPULATION GROWTH: CASE STUDY FROM HIMALAYAN RURAL AREA

As about 80.29% of the total population of Indian Himalaya is residing in rural area, the literacy rate of females in rural areas has been taken as an index of demographic development. The index has a direct impact on the decadal growth rate, sex ratio of the population. The percentage literacy of females in rural area and decadal growth rate (1981-91) are plotted on X and Y axes respectively. Each point in the scatter diagram represents the data for one of the 62 districts for which data are available (excluding Assam Hills and Jammu & Kashmir). Regressing the rural female literacy on the decadal growth rate of population the study group get the regression equation Y = 35.46 - 0.32X. Thus, there exists a negative relationship between percentage female literacy and decadal growth rate for the entire Indian Himalaya. The negative slope indicates that the decadel growth rate is comparatively lesser in those districts which have higher female literacy, though the slope is very minimal (-0.32) and there exists a significant dispersion of few districts along the regression line. The confidence level 0,1, and -1 indicate the decadel growth of the concerned districts lie within estimated Y±1SE, >Y+1SE, and <Y-1SE values respectively as shown below:

Code	Districts	X	Y	SE
71	DIBANG VALLEY	0.00	39.03	0
73	WEST SIANG	0.00	31.64	0
68	TIRAP	4.50	28.70	0
76	EAST KAMENG	5.41	17.92	-1
78	TAWANG	6.14	30.14	0
75	LOWER SUBANSIRI	6.15	38.46	0
27	UTTARKASHI	7.50	25.54	0
57	THOUBAL	8.04	26.83	0
70	LOHIT	8.07	57.85	1
28	DEHRADUN	8.29	34.66	0
40	WEST GARO HILLS	8.82	29.80	0
15	CHAMBA	8.92	26.40	0
34	NAINITAL	9.49	35.52	0
72	EAST SIANG	9.50	30.60	0
67	MON	9.56	58.98	1
59	BISHNUPUR	9.87	28.07	0
74	UPPER SUBANSIRI	9.99	27.09	0
29	TEHRI GARHWAL	10.02	16.56	-1
77	WEST KAMENG	10.13	35.74	0
39	DARJILING	10.41	26.91	0
69	CHANGLANG	10.43	53.56	1
44	JAINTIA HILLS	10.60	40.97	0
43	EAST KHASI HILLS	11.09	30.07	0
26	SIRMAUR	11.73	23.72	0
54	CHANDEL	11.93	25.81	0
58	IMPHAL	12.82	27.89	0

17	KULLU	12.98	26.68	0
36	WEST DISTRICT	13.07	30.55	0
52	AIZWAL	13.40	40.38	0
33	PITHORAGARH	13.54	15.77	-1
35	NORTH DISTRICT	13.76	18.09	0
49	SOUTH TRIPURA	13.84	43.03	0
51	LUNGLEI	14.11	28.79	0
41	EAST GARO HILLS	14.13	38.29	0
48	WEST TRIPURA	14.13	32.53	0
53	CHURACHANDPUR	14.20	30.72	0
66	TUENSANG	14.20	69.87	1
23	SHIMLA	14.48	20.84	0
61	KOHIMA	14.53	62.34	1
16	LAHUL & SPITI	14.54	-2.51	-1
30	CHAMOLI	14.55	21.75	0
55	SENAPATI	14.70	34.09	0
50	CHHIMTUIPUI	15.10	50.37	1
32	ALMORA	15.18	10.46	-1
37	SOUTH DISTRICT	15.88	29.78	0
60	TAMENGLONG	15.94	38.51	0
42	WEST KHASI HILLS	15.96	36.26	0
25	KINNAUR	16.08	19.69	0
38	EAST DISTRICT	16.12	28.60	0
24	SOLAN	16.36	26.02	0
47	NORTH TRIPURA	16.83	28.84	0
62	PHEK	17.75	44.66	1
22	MANDI	18.38	20.40	0
31	PAURI GARHWAL	18.40	8.58	-1
63	ZUNHEBOTO	19.68	32.68	0
56	UKHRUL	19.83	31.74	0
64	WOKHA	20.34	42.34	1
21	BILASPUR	22.23	19.41	0

20	UNA	23.80	19.17	0
18	KANGRA	24.93	18.50	0
65	MOKOKCHUNG	25.74	52.67	1
19	HAMIRPUR	27.70	16.17	0

About 75.81% data (47 out of 62 districts) fall within the estimated Y±1SE, indicating that districts with high female literacy have a low decadal growth rate. The decadal growth rate of remaining 15 districts, which fall beyond estimated Y±1SE, are considered to be highly dispersed, indicating little impact of female literacy on the growth rate. Out of these 15 districts, the deviation of 9 (about 14.52% of total) are more than the estimated Y+1SE, indicating very high growth rate. These districts are Kohima, Phek, Wokha, Mokokchung, Tuensang, Mon (all in Nagaland), Changlang, Lohit (in Arunachal Pradesh), and Chhimtuipui (Mizoram) having a very small affect of female literacy on growth rate. The deviation of the remaining 6 districts falls below the estimated Y-1SE, and indicates a very low growth rate as compared to Indian Himalaya as a whole. These districts are Tehri and Pauri Garhwal, Pithoragarh, Almora (all in U.P. hills), East Kameng (Arunachal Pradesh), and Lahaul & Spiti (Himachal Pradesh) which represents a negative growth.

8

Population Education in Schools

The overall objective of India's Population Education Project, launched in 1980 with financial and technical support from United Nations' agencies, is to institutionalize such education in all the country's educational processes. As the Project begins its third phase, an emphasis is being placed on reaching the 60% of children who drop out of school between classes I-V through a variety of interventions in the nonformal education sector. Within the formal sector, integration of population education into school sylabi and textbooks at the secondary and plus-two levels will be pursued; such integration is now largely complete at the primary and upper primary levels.

Another focus will be to reach the estimated 60-70% of teachers who have not yet received the in-service training in population education and to integrate this subject into some courses taught at the pre-service teacher training level. To strengthen the attitude formation and value orientation aspects of population education, a greater emphasis will be placed on linking co-curricular activities in the community with the school curriculum.

Given the finding that students exposed to print, audio, and audiovisual media show higher levels of awareness of population themes, the use of the mass media in population education will be promoted. A weakness of the project to be addressed in the 1990s is inadequate coordination between the school and other sectors, especially at the grassroots level and in terms of development activities.

Another goal is to emphasize the links between family planning and population education. In the past, the population education project tended to differentiate itself from family planning to increase program acceptability. At present, however, there is awareness that a major purpose of population education is to create demands for family planning services.

POPULATION EDUCATION FOR SOCIAL BETTERMENT

In India primary education has increased 3 times in the last 30 years. Over this same period middle school education has increased 4 times, higher secondary education 5 times, and university level education over 6 times. The number of universities alone increased from 19 in 1950 to 118 by 1981.

The inconsistencies brought about by rapid population growth may be judged by the fact that while the number of institutions and the enrollment of students has expanded beyond measure, the number of illiterate persons has risen from 386 million in 1971 to 446 million in 1981. Clearly, education is vital for human resource development.

In political terms, human resource development prepares a population for adult participation in political processes. From social and cultural perspectives, the development of human resources helps people to lead fuller and richer lives. Population means people, and people need food, clothing, homes, education, transportation, health services, and jobs. As long as a country's resources can satisfy the essential needs of its population, there is no population problem. If the population grows faster than the rate at which the basic needs of each individual can be met, the buildup of such a situation produces a crisis of gigantic dimensions. To meet basic requirements, India needs to provide annually an additional 12 million tons of foodgrains, 188 million meters of cloth, 2.5 million houses, along with schools, teachers, and jobs over and above what is currently available.

Another need is for fresh air, pure water, and space to live in. The question is how is this need to be met when the earth is a finite sphere. What will happen when the world's 3.5 billion people double into a staggering 7 billion by the end of the 20th century. It is because of this concern for family well being and the betterment of human resources that the Family Planning Association of India has since 1969 undertaken innovative pilot programs in popultion education for the younger generation, for teachers, social workers, and other concerned groups. The government of India promotes population education for school and out-of-school youths through the 5-year national population education project for schools and through the adult education project for out-of-school youth.

Survey data from India consistently show that female education above the primary school-level is the most powerful determinant of lowered fertility. The Government of India's strategies of increasing accessibility to family planning methods and improving the population's quality of life have been impeded by low levels of female education. The finding that rural women experience 0.8 more live births than their urban counterparts is a reflection of the higher education of the latter group. Within Calcutta, females in slum areas had an average of 5.6 live births compared to 3.5 births among those from nonslum parts of the city, again reflecting the influence of education on fertility. In the high-fertility states of Uttar Pradesh, Rajasthan, Bihar, Madhyapradesh, Haryana, and Jammu and Kashmir, the percentage of females with an education above the primary level is under 5%.

The intermediate variable of education beyond primary school seems to exert its effect on fertility by both raising the age at marriage and promoting use of modern contraceptive methods. Women with 1-4 years of education comprise the majority of sterilization acceptors; however, this minimal amount of education is not sufficient to motivate women to delay marriage and to use family planning methods to space births. Given the critical importance of female education, authorities in India should design extension programs and door-to-door campaigns to motivate parents to send their daughters to school and keep them enrolled.

In 1981 India had a population of 683,810,051, representing a growth of 135 million over the preceding 10 years. An uneven sex ratio, rapid urbanization, a high dependency ratio, and a majority of the population in agriculture were other aspects of the population problem.

A goal of the Indian government is to reduce the net reproduction rate from its present 1.67 to 1 by 1996, which implies a reduction of family size from the present 4.2 children/couple to 2.3 children. The importance of population education in efforts to reduce growth was not realized until 1969, when the 1st National Seminar on Population Education recommended introduction of population content into the existing curriculum of schools and colleges. Following the seminar, the National Council of Educational Research and Training (NCERT) set up a population education cell in its Department of Education in Social Sciences and Humanities.

The population education cell developed curricula and instructional materials and worked out a model syllabus for population education for teacher training institutions. Promotional activities were later undertaken when it became apparent that the population education cell's efforts were not reaching the local schools. 4 regional workshops were organized in 1979, and a 3-year national population education project was designed to help students develop an insight into the relationship between population and economic problems and of India's population situation and policies, to institutionalize population education in the formal educational system, and to encourage rational family size decisions by students and the community at large. Two workshops were held for preparation of detailed state project proposals.

The state councils of Educational Research and Training or their equivalents were assigned the tasks of preparing the population education curricula, developing instructional materials, developing and implementing training programs for teachers and administrators, and monitoring the program. Workshops for curriculum and materials development were held in July 1980, and the NCERT Population Education Unit has published curriculum guidelines, draft syllabuses and reference materials. Several intensive workshops have been held for fulltime population education personnel. Five slide and tape presentations have been developed for teacher training. The project is still in too early a stage for evaluation of its impact on the target audience.

In China much attention has been paid since the 1970s, and particularly in the past 2 years, to implementing population education in the schools. The population education program in Chinese schools is an important aspect of the middle school teaching program. A teaching purpose, requirements, and content have been formulated.

The purpose of population education is to teach the students population science, to foster the students' correct outlook on population, and to promote a well rounded development of students morally, intellectually, and physically. The specific objectives of population education are outlined. To fulfill the program requirements, population education in schools is provided with rich content.

There are 2 ways of introducting the content into the curriculum: part of the knowledge is centralized in lectures on population education; and part is decentralized into physiology and hygiene, biology, geography, and other subjects. Fairly good results have been achieved using these 2 methods of population education. By way of centralization, the purpose of teaching is clear and the time concentrated, thus the teachers and the students pay more attention to it. It is also necessary to integrate population education with other subjects.

In addition to the national requirements, many schools have added the population state and development in their province, city or county to their teaching program so that the students can learn about the population situation of their native area. To improve the quality of population education, many provinces have held teaching training courses on population education to help them with the systematic knowledge of population science.

The task is primarily handled by the Educational Institutes of respective provinces and municipalities. By the end of 1981, 59 training courses had been conducted and 4900 teachers trained. To improve training quality the Educational Institutes have complied and printed teaching materials.

At this time population education is provided only in the ordinary schools and is unavailable in other kinds of schools. Leaders in some schools need to realize its importance. Much improvement could be made in the content and the quality of population education instruction.

SEXUAL AND REPRODUCTIVE HEALTH EDUCATION IN SCHOOLS

The Cairo International Conference on Population and Development (ICPD) in 1994, recommended that

> ". . . information and services should be made available to adolescents to help them understand their sexuality and protect themselves from unwanted pregnancies, sexually transmitted diseases and subsequent risk of infertility. This should be combined with the education of young men to respect women's self-determination and to share responsibility with women in matters of sexuality and reproduction."

Five years later, during the follow up meeting convened by the United Nations in The Hague, governments agreed that all school children should receive education about population and health issues, including reproductive health. They also agreed that by the year 2005, 90 percent of 15 to 24 year-olds should have access to information and services to prevent HIV infection, including female and male condoms, voluntary testing, counselling and follow-up. Yet progress has been slow. In only a few countries has young people's sexual and reproductive health become part of the public health agenda, with policies, standards, and services being adapted to address their specific needs.

While data suggest that early marriage and some harmful traditional practices against girls are declining in some parts of the world, there is still much to be done in providing information and youth-friendly services, and in raising awareness of young people's rights and needs. Part of the difficulty derives from the continuing 'sensitivity' of policy makers, parents, and teachers regarding young people's sexuality.

Many adults find it difficult to talk to young people about sex. Others show ambivalence over young people's sexual activity - encouraging it in boys, while discouraging it in girls. In many countries, laws and regulations prevent young people from receiving sexuality education and sexual and reproductive health services, in the mistaken belief that to talk openly about sex is to encourage sexual activity. Health workers sometimes refuse to provide services to young people, even where no legal or policy restrictions exist.

Information and education for young people are often unlinked to the provision of sexual and reproductive health services. As a result, many young people who receive information are not able to access the services they need or receive necessary care.

Even where sexual and reproductive health programmes for young people do exist, they rarely have the capacity to serve large numbers of young people, especially in rural areas. Few existing services are youngperson friendly, and many offer only a narrow range of options (e.g., by focusing only on abstinence) and do not engage young people in the design, management, and evaluation of services. This situation, lamentable as it is, has been exacerbated by HIV/AIDS. At the end of 2001, an estimated 40 million people globally were living with HIV/AIDS. About one-third of those currently living with HIV/AIDS are aged 15-24.

Most do not know they are infected. Many millions more know nothing or too little about HIV to protect themselves against infection. According to UNICEF, over 50 percent of young people aged 15-24 in more than a dozen countries, including Bolivia, Botswana, Côte d'Ivoire, the Dominican Republic, Ukraine, Uzbekhistan and Vietnam, have never heard of AIDS, or harbour serious misconceptions about how HIV is transmitted.

In mid-2001, a special session of the United Nations General Assembly took place. Its focus was on HIV/AIDS. The Declaration of Commitment issued after the meeting set the target of reducing levels of HIV infection among 15-24 year-olds by 25 percent in the most affected countries by the year 2005, and globally by 2010. It also called upon Governments to develop by 2003, and implement by 2005, national strategies to provide a supportive environment for orphans and children infected and affected by HIV/AIDS.

Education, both in schools and beyond, has a key role to play both in preventing HIV/AIDS and in mitigating its effects on individuals and communities. It can provide children and young people with knowledge and understanding to protect themselves and others, with skills to communicate and negotiate for safer sex and safer drug use, and with attitudes and values that foster respect and support for people living with HIV/AIDS. In the hands of good practitioners, education really can make a difference. It can provide hope for the future, unleashing the potential of young people themselves to alter the course of the pandemic. Yet in many parts of the world, the education system itself is under threat. Teachers and students are dying or leaving school early, reducing both the quality and efficiency of educational systems.

In 1999, an estimated 860,000 children lost their teachers to HIV/AIDS in sub-Saharan Africa. In the Central African Republic, AIDS was the cause of 85 percent of the 300 teacher deaths that occurred in 2000. Already, by the late 1990s, the toll had forced the closure of more than 100 educational establishments in that country.

In Zambia, teacher deaths caused by AIDS are equivalent to about half the total number of new teachers the country manages to train annually. Such events threaten the potential of education systems to change society for the better. They pose a major threat to the attainment of Education for All (EFA) goals, including action to promote literacy, to develop and harness scientific understanding, and to redress gender inequality.

Among its many provisions, the Dakar Framework for Action draws attention to the urgent need to combat HIV/AIDS if EFA goals are to be achieved. It calls on governments to ensure that by 2015, all children, particularly girls, children in difficult circumstances and those belonging to ethnic minorities, have access to and complete, free and compulsory primary education of good quality. But such an objective cannot be achieved unless urgent action is taken to protect the education system in the face of the pandemic.

It was against this backcloth that the Safe Passages to Adulthood expert meeting took place. Researchers, practitioners and policy makers from around the world came together to consider both the potential of education to protect against HIV/AIDS, and the changes that might need to take place to allow the education system to respond more adequately to present challenges. Three specific settings were focused upon: inschool settings, out-of-school contexts and higher education. The work of the following projects and activities was described and discussed.

In School work

— *The School-based HIV/AIDS Prevention Project in Sichuan Province, China:* This aims to enhance the capacity of the education system to promote HIV prevention and AIDS-related care and support among local school communities.

— *The School Health and Nutrition Project in Senegal:* This aims to embed work to promote young people's sexual and reproductive health within a wider programme of activities linked to school health improvement.

— *Life Skills Approach to HIV and AIDS Education in Schools in Vietnam:* This aims to improve the HIV/AIDS-related awareness and skills of school pupils.

— *The Regei DziveShiri Project.* This aims to explore the feasibility of carrying out a community-based randomised controlled trial of a new sexual and reproductive health programme for young people in Zimbabwe.

— The UNAIDS supported Sexual Health Education in South and South East Asia and the Pacific Project. This aimed to review and take stock of provision for sex and HIV/ AIDS education in selected Asia-Pacific countries.

Out-of-school work

— The Advocacy for Adolescent Reproductive Health Project in Kenya. This aims to strengthen the social and policy context within which sexual and reproductive health services are developed for, and provided to, young people.

— The K-REP Development Agency (KDA) and Population Council's Tap and Reposition Youth (TRY) Savings and Credit Scheme Project in Nairobi, Kenya. This aimed to improve the financial situation and the sexual and reproductive health of young women

— The Deepak Charitable Trust's Sexual Health Project in India. This aims to promote open discussion among policy makers, programme developers and service providers about young people's sexual health needs and concerns. Besides addressing the needs of young women, there was a particular focus on young men's concerns, including those related to semen loss.

— The Young People's Sexual and Reproductive Health Project in Malawi. This work aimed to strengthen the Department of Gender Youth and Community Service's capacity to promote sexual and reproductive healthrelated awareness and skills of young people

— The Youth Zone (YZ) Project in the Philippines. This aims to empower young people to make informed choices about their sexual and reproductive health Higher education

— The University of Botswana HIV/AIDS Project. This work aims to increase awareness and reduce STIs, unwanted pregnancies, and HIV/AIDS among the student population in higher education in Botswana.

— The Certificate Program in Adolescent Health, at Cayetano Heredia University in Lima, Peru. This has aimed to train professionals in adolescent sexual and reproductive health issues so that they can manage and contribute more successfully to health services addressing sexual and reproductive health-related needs

— Work by the Centre for the Study of AIDS in Africa (CSA) in Pretoria, South Africa. This aims to promote the AIDS- and HIV-related professional and personal awareness of staff and students in the University of Pretoria

— The Caribbean Community (CARICOM) Multi- Agency Health and Family Life Education (HFLE) Project. This regional initiative, which has involved work in Trinidad and Tobago, has aimed to train teachers to promote health and family life education in schools and colleges.

Although young people make up a significant proportion of the world's population, their sexual and reproductive health needs are often neglected. As mentioned earlier, even where sexual health services are available, young people may have difficulty accessing them, or may be actively discouraged from using them by parents and health service providers.

There are estimated to be around 14,000 new HIV infections every day, over 6,000 of which occur amongst 16-25 year-olds. Approximately 15 million women under 20 years of age give birth each year, and as many as half of these pregnancies are unintended.

Each year, 1 million to 4.4 million adolescents in developing countries undergo abortion, and most of these procedures are performed under unsafe conditions. An estimated two million girls are subject to harmful traditional practices such as female genital mutilation each year, which can be the precursor to recurrent and painful health problems later in life.

Substantial numbers of young people are the victims of sexual abuse and exploitation, and in some countries young people (both boys and girls) are traded or trafficked into sex work by their parents, families and local communities. This bleak situation of young people made vulnerable through silence, stigma, poverty and lack of access to services can be changed.

Since ICPD, some countries have put in place policies and programmes that have transformed the sexual lives of young people for the better. With effort and a sensitive approach, the attitudes of sexual health service providers can be changed through training so that young people are welcomed into services.

When provided with accurate information, and when offered the opportunities to discuss the personal relevance of this information, young people can change or reduce risky behaviours. They can act as educators in their local communities, raising and addressing sensitive topics. In short, when afforded the rights and means to address sexual and reproductive health, both young women's and young men's security and well-being can be enhanced.

Among the principles identified as central to the success of educational programmes to promote young people's sexual and reproductive health are:

— An accurate identification and understanding of the group(s) of young people to be served.

— The active involvement of young people in programme design and implementation.

— The removal of policy barriers to the communication of consistent and explicit messages.

— Action to change service providers' prejudices and attitudes.

— Efforts to help young people acquire the interpersonal skills needed to avoid risks as well as the confidence to use these skills in real life situations.

— Linking information and skills development to service provision.

— Investment in long-enough timeframes and resources to achieve change.

No single intervention is appropriate and relevant to all young people. Moreover, because young people are not an homogenous group, sensitivity to gender, sexual orientation, ethnic and cultural background is important in improving the quality of their educational experience.

No single policy maker, no single programme developer and no single service provider can hope to bring about the sorts of changes that are needed to improve the sexual and reproductive health of young people. Instead, polices and programmes should be developed with the involvement of numerous key players. Ministries and government departments, NGOs, educational and health services need to work together with young people if effective change is to come about. At a more local level,work must take place in school, out of school, with young people, with adults, and with the involvement of the local media.

Building on the experiences, goodwill and skills of young people themselves is an essential feature of successful approaches. As stated earlier, in many countries education systems are under threat as a result of HIV/AIDS. This poses major challenges for the use of education to effect improvement in young people's sexual and reproductive health. A range of interventions is needed to strengthen existing systems of educational provision and to develop new ones more attuned to changed circumstances.

Among the actions that should be taken are efforts to secure political commitment and leadership at the highest levels. Politicians, senior educational department officials and others must recognise that the situation is serious and that urgent action must be taken to plan for the future. This involves reaching shared understanding of the present and likely future impact of the epidemic on school systems, the teacher workforce, and teacher training.

Senior staff need to be trained and supported to manage HIV/AIDS education.Beyond steps to ensure that existing education systems can respond effectively are reforms to the kind of pedagogy most appropriate to the future. Under the impact of HIV/AIDS, and for other reasons, children and young people may be withdrawn from school to help in the home and to provide income for the family.

Young women are among those whose education suffers most. In these changed circumstances, urgent action is needed to provide education in more innovative and flexible ways - through community and distance education, for example, and through the radio, television and other electronic systems of communication. Without such action, the skills base of both rural and urban communities seems likely to be lost.

Action is therefore required on several fronts if education is to be able to play its role in promoting young people's sexual and reproductive health. Changes to the curriculum and nature of schooling; changes to out of school activities; greater synergy between formal and non-formal systems of education; and changes to the higher education system's capacity to prepare teachers and other adults for their future roles - all are urgently required.

The Safe Passages to Adulthood meeting provided an opportunity for many of these issues to be discussed, and for concrete actions in different parts of the world to be described.

Projects of school-based sex and health education

Participants from four countries, China, Senegal, Vietnam and Zimbabwe described their work with young people in schools. A fifth but related presentation described findings from the first major survey of school-based sex and health education in South and South East Asia and the Pacific.

In China, recent work has been undertaken as part of the School-based HIV/AIDS Prevention Project in Sichuan Province to train teachers to carry out school-based HIV/AIDS education. A 'cascade' model (whereby trainers train other trainers to then enable teachers) has been adopted. Efforts were made to enhance the quality and consistency of support through close monitoring of the different levels of training, and by providing awards for excellence in teaching about HIV/AIDS education at the school level. An important first step was consultation with senior officials in government ministries and departments. This facilitated political commitment and enabled resources to be identified to promote the involvement of teachers and, ultimately, young people themselves.

In many countries, HIV/AIDS is but one of several issues facing young people. Others may include food and shelter, employment, feeling safe, and being able to offer care to siblings, friends and family. To be meaningful to young people, health promotion programmes must engage with the priorities that they themselves identify.

For example, health promotion services are often divided into discrete topic areas, some agencies dealing with drugs, others with sexual and reproductive health, yet others with diet and nutrition. Accessing multiple health services can be a challenge for even the most motivated individual.

For young people who may come across professionals who are insensitive to their needs, this may be too great a challenge. It is far better to identify the health-related needs of a particular group, and organise services so that multiple concerns can be addressed together. Meeting basic entitlements, such as access to good quality education, can do much to improve the well-being of young people.

A basic education makes it easier for people to know what services can provide and how to access them. Life-skills education, with its emphasis on communication, problem solving and values clarification, can assist young people learn about the factors that enhance and compromise their health and well-being. Although information is an essential component of HIV/AIDS prevention, participatory and interactive educational activities enable young people to make sense of this information. This can help identify whether and in what ways HIV can affect them, and what steps they can take to protect themselves and others.

In Senegal, HIV/AIDS education and other sexual and reproductive health issues have been embedded within a wider programme of school health activities as part of the broader Focussing Resources on Effective School Health (FRESH) initiative is supported by WHO, UNESCO, the World Bank and UNICEF of education as it becomes integrated into the life of the school.

The role of good quality research in persuading government officials and others to take seriously young people's interests and concerns is often downplayed. Close focus evaluations of new school-based programmes and interventions can be valuable in helping identify what needs to be done, how best to do it, and whether and why success has come about. Such work has taken place as part of the development of new life skills approaches to working with young people in Vietnam.

Research is an essential underpinning for sexual health promotion. Initial contextual analysis can be used to identify whether there is a favourable policy environment, what issues young people are interested in, whether the workforce has the capacity to provide good quality education, whether local communities can be mobilised to tackle health issues, and whether services are in place to meet health needs. Once information of this kind is available, planners and educators can work together to develop programmes of work that build on the assessed, rather than the imagined, circumstances and needs of young people and local communities. Evaluation can help identify whether and why work has been successful. For funders, evaluation may show whether intended outcomes have been achieved, and whether money has been well spent.

For those more directly involved in programme implementation, evaluation may reveal how or why particular outcomes have been achieved. Providing information to young people and local communities about a programme's success (or indeed its failures) can help make planners and educators more accountable.

There are many ways of carrying out evaluations, particularly in the field of sexual and reproductive health. One approach assumes that the principles that guide clinical trials of a new drug are the most appropriate with which to judge the effectiveness of educational programmes. Although there has been debate about the usefulness of randomised controlled trials to evaluate educational activities, many SRH initiatives have been evaluated in this way.

The design of an evaluation may, on paper, appear ingenious. In practice, it might be a logistical nightmare.Many factors can disorient its implementation, from respondents' concerns about ethics, through difficulties in drawing a sample, to resistance to its findings.

In Zimbabwe, a feasibility study has recently been undertaken to identify whether a community-based randomised trial of sexual and reproductive health education might be acceptable and possible.

Research is not only valuable in finding out about whether and why success has come about, but also to find out what a situation is like before taking action. A recent UNAIDS assessment of the ways in which countries have responded to AIDS in their development of school-based education, conducted by the National Centre in HIV Social Research in Sydney, Australia has provided valuable information about policy and practice.

In the assessment, carried out across eleven countries in South East Asia, there were some surprising findings. For example, the Ottawa Charter for Health Promotion states that the presence of supportive policy is an essential component of effective health promotion. However, the study found that good policy was no guarantee that HIV/AIDS prevention activities in schools would take place. Furthermore, the absence of policy did not mean that HIV/AIDS prevention activities were not underway.

Sex Education and HIV Prevention in South East Asia Schools

Schools have long been identified as appropriate environments in which to undertake activities to promote HIV-related risk reduction among young people. However, relatively little is known about the ways in which education systems have responded to HIV/AIDS. To address this gap in knowledge, a research study was carried out covering 11 countries. This sought, among other things, to describe HIV-related school-based education, that is, to document how and in what manner such education is developed and practised. The eleven contrasting countries were: Brunei, Cambodia, China, Indonesia, Malaysia, Mongolia, Myanmar, Papua New Guinea, the Philippines, Thailand and Vietnam.

Information was collected via questionnaires and face-to-face interviews from Government officials, as well as national and international NGO representatives. Respondents were asked to provide information about schoolbased HIV/AIDS and sexual health in the following areas:

— The overall policy context

— The location within discipline/subject areas

— Age and class levels of students to whom it was delivered

— Content of the SRH curricula

— Training of teachers

— Perceived barriers to this kind of education

Findings highlighted that national policies generally described how HIV and AIDS should be incorporated into the curriculum, and many urged that school based education should go beyond the provision of information alone, to address health in its broader social context. However, there was little recognition of cultural differences in most countries' curricula. Rarely too, was there reference to specific risk practices. More often than not, it was suggested that 'healthy lifestyles' and 'appropriate values' simply needed to be taught. Mention of risk reduction strategies tended to be restricted to abstinence and fidelity.

The presence of a national policy did not necessarily mean that good school-based HIV/AIDS education was undertaken.And good education could be carried out in a country where there was little policy to guide practitioners. In relation to school curricula, there was generally found to be:

— An emphasis on the biological aspects of sexual and reproductive health, including HIV/AIDS

— An emphasis on marriage, fidelity and abstinence, with some reference to condom use, but where the relative risk of different sexual practices was not discussed

— A marked absence of reference to issues such as homosexuality

Mention of values was largely restricted to a focus on 'family values', whereby sex was considered as something that occurs only between husband and wife. Perhaps less surprisingly, in the HIV/AIDS curricula of many countries, there was a marked absence of reference to cultural differences, and to specific risky or protective sexual practices and behaviours. In many places it appears hard to raise issues of cultural diversity and difficult to talk candidly about the forms of sex that offer protection to young people.

Out-of-school work

Representatives of out-of-school projects and activities in Kenya, India, Malawi and the Philippines participated in the expert meeting. Between them, they described a wide variety of approaches to promoting young people's sexual health in out-of-school settings. Despite clear evidence to the contrary; there continue to be fears that teaching young people about sex will encourage sexual activity.

What can be done to facilitate a more realistic approach? Targeted advocacy can help raise the profile of sexual and reproductive health among senior decision makers. Such advocacy may be especially useful in promoting work with young people. It may encompass a variety of activities: highlighting health needs, identifying what can be done, marshalling resources, and ensuring that high quality programmes are provided.

However, advocacy is best planned with those who are to benefit. If this is not done, advocates may call for the wrong sorts of actions, at the wrong time and in the wrong place.

In Kenya, for example, where in recent years sex education books have been burned, family life education has been withdrawn from schools, and teenage mothers expelled from school, young people have been involved in the development of a new out of school programme of work.

They have acted as decision-makers about what, when and where activities should take place. In this particular context, the need for adults to work in partnership with young people is clear. However, advocacy involves more than simply working to promote young people's interests and needs. It also involves challenging dominant cultural values and understandings.

This can be successfully achieved by building a body of expert opinion, which values the importance of sexual and reproductive health work. In Kenya, by pursuing such a strategy, work with senior politicians has given rise to new and more inclusive education policies. Concurrent work with journalists has enabled ideas about the importance of young people's sexual health to be more widely disseminated. Here, advocacy has been as much about adults exemplifying values of equity and social justice, as it has been about working directly with young people.

Whether defined by income, living conditions or socio-economic status, poverty is the most important single determinant of ill health. Young women in poverty are especially vulnerable not only due to lack of income, but also through lack of control over day-to-day life. In Kenya, an innovative savings and credit scheme has assisted young women to create wealth and so take more control of their lives. Part of 'taking control' has been to provide women with informal opportunities to learn more about sexual and reproductive health.

There are a number of advantages and disadvantages to embedding sexual and reproductive health programming within a broader context such as this.A drawback can be that SRH-related issues are not prioritised, leaving young people vulnerable to, among other things, STIs or unwanted pregnancies.

More positively, young women (but also young men) may benefit by having access to a service that is not solely focussed on HIV/AIDS and so does not identify and stigmatise them as sexually 'in need'. Furthermore, professionals working in specialised services may only feel able to address one or another health-related need. They may feel unable to respond to the range of healthrelated needs that a young person may have.

Sexual and reproductive health matters can cause profound anxiety. For many young men in India, a particular concern relates to semen loss through masturbation or nocturnal emissions. Hard enough to discuss in many places in the world, workers from the Deepak Charitable Trust in India have found ways to address these sensitive topics so as to reduce men's anxieties and improve their feelings of sexual well-being. Such actions have also reportedly led to a greater openness about sexual and reproductive health, with benefits for the adoption of safer sex practices.

Beyond working with local men, the project has sought to raise the profile of men's semen loss anxieties with national agendas. Initially, project workers had to build and sustain partnerships with key opinion formers. A great deal of effort has been made to influence politicians, with as much attention being paid to involving local journalists in workshops and seminars. Via their newspaper columns, they were able to reach a greater number of people than the local project could itself involve.

In the rush to 'get things done', it is easy to set up projects without the adequate involvement of the people the work is meant to serve. Working in partnership requires time and attention to the details of how best to communicate with others. In Malawi, young people themselves have been consulted and then involved in the development of a range of sexual and reproductive health educational activities provided by the Ministry of Gender, Youth and Community Services, with the support of UNFPA. Building on the strengths and goodwill of young people themselves has resulted in noticeable benefits.

Finding sufficient resources to carry out work remains a challenge.Governments and politicians need to be alerted to the value of investing in education in general, and in sexual and reproductive health promotion in particular. Tackling these issues consistently and early is a cost-effective way of building healthy families, communities and societies.

Programmes and projects across the world have benefited from outside funding, be this provided by international agencies, international NGOs or private trusts. Important also is being able to access local sources of funding to assist projects' sustainability at the local level. In Manila in the Philippines, the Youth Zone Project has found ways of accessing resources from the private sector to directly benefit young people.

Higher education

University graduates are key in contributing to economic and social development. In the countries of Southern Africa, where upwards of 25 percent of the adult population may already be infected by HIV, it is important for future generations of university graduates to be knowledgeable about HIV/AIDS, especially in relation to their specialised areas of study.

Students and staff also require support in understanding how HIV/AIDS is personally relevant, and what they can do to protect themselves and others. By taking a campus-wide approach, the University of Botswana has been assisting people to address these concerns.

Working across a campus requires collaboration among a University's key players: those leading the HIV/AIDS programme, those concerned with student health and welfare and those who have a responsibility to ensure academic quality within the University. Drawing in representatives of external agencies (such as government ministries as well as national and international NGOs and donors) can inform the development and implementation of a programme and also release resources - whether financial or people's expertise and time.

Across the world, young people make up a significant proportion of the population. Too often, however, health professionals lack the insight and training to be able to respond effectively to young people's needs, especially those relating to sexual and reproductive health. By re-orienting existing training programmes, professionals can gain new expertise in working with young people.

As students, young people have much to give to others of similar ages. During a degree or other course, their small-scale research projects can generate new ideas about people's needs and how best to address them. As volunteers, they can be supported to work together to design, carry out and review new initiatives. The knowledge they have of student and campus life can help workers tailor programmes so that they build in the concerns, interests and capacities of their peers.

The Certificate Program in Adolescent Health at Cayetano Heredia University in Peru was reoriented to focus more on the SRH needs of young people. Concurrent with the involvement of young people and former students, a renewed political interest provided a supportive policy context for the development of the programme.

Focused action is needed across a higher education institution if the HIV/AIDS-related needs of students are to be addressed. At the University of Pretoria in South Africa, much has been achieved by staff in a specialist centre, who have brought together university colleagues and students to consider the professional and personal challenges that HIV/AIDS poses.

The work of the centre aims to build on the interests and capabilities of students. Given the changing economic and social climate in South Africa, there are new opportunities for young people to take a lead in commercial, government and NGO sectors. Entrepreneurial skills, as well as those associated with communication, project planning, training and facilitation are all potentially useful. It is these skills, as well as knowledge and understanding about HIV, that students can build through their involvement in HIV/AIDSrelated work.

The work of the Centre for the Study of AIDS is made possible because of the support of the senior management at the University. Much time and effort has been spent in bringing on board senior colleagues across the Faculties. With this support, addressing HIV/AIDS is increasingly seen as a priority across the whole of the University, and is not seen as an issue that only affects a few.

New initiatives in the field of sexual and reproductive health work best when they build upon the expressed needs of those who are expected to implement them, and when they have support from other key partners, whether these be governments, NGOs, community groups or faith based organisations. In the School of Education at the University of the West Indies in Trinidad and Tobago, a training programme on Health and Family Life Education has received such support, and teachers' new skills in undertaking such work have been recognised through accreditation.

The Caribbean Community (CARICOM) initiative, led by UNICEF, helped sensitise key policy-makers to young people's SRH-related needs and influenced them to take action to build the capacity of professionals across the region to meet these needs.

9

USE OF MASS MEDIA

The mass media have an important role in modern democratic society as the main channel of communication. The population relies on the news media as the main source of information and the basis on which they form their opinions and voting decisions. According to cultural selection theory, any selection of messages in the mass media will thus have a profound effect on the entire society.

The news media are the most important channels for the propagation of culture, ideas, and opinions. Most opinion formation takes place when people sit and watch news and debates on television. Analyzing the cultural selection in the electronic information society, we find that an important part of the selection lies in the choice between TV channels. Millions of lazy viewers sit in their comfortable arm-chairs with remote controls in their hands zapping between action films, revivalist preachers, and commercials for a new fragrance, hardly realizing that by choosing which cultural and political influences they expose themselves to, they also chose the cultural and political evolution of their country.

It is very important to analyze which selection criteria are in effect here. The electronic media are first and foremost pacifying. It is a relaxation machine, and the viewer wants to be entertained. The faces on the screen are not chosen for their opinions but for their entertainment value. TV stations do not compete on ideologies but on sense impressions. An extreme example is music videos, satiated with fast changing sense impressions in sound as well as in pictures.

Media scientists have often discussed how much influence the media have on people's opinions. People tend to selectively read what they already agree with and to rationalize their preformed opinions in the face of contrary arguments. Experimental evidence seems to indicate that the mass media have little power to change people's opinions on issues for which they already have formed a strong opinion, but they have a profound influence when it comes to setting the agenda and priming people on new issues. The way an issue is framed determines how it is discussed, which causes a social problem is blamed on, and which of the possible remedies are entered into the discussion.

The production of news often goes through several steps: informants and sources, press agents, reporters, news agencies, journalists, and editors. Many media are citing other media or opinion leaders so that the complete chain of information flow becomes quite long. Selection and distortion may take place at every link in this chain of information transmission.

The sources of news may be public institutions, politicians, private companies, police, courts, interviewees, etc. These all have an interest in providing information that portray themselves in a positive light and withhold compromising information. There is a trade going on between source and journalist. For example, the media rely heavily on the police for news about crimes and often report positively about the police in exchange for this information. Sources that are unsatisfied with the way they are portrayed in a certain newspaper or TV channel may retaliate by withholding information in the future.

Journalists may have political opinions that shape their selection and framing of news. They also have ethical principles about fairness and about reporting everything that is relevant, although they may depart from these principles when competition is fierce. Their selection of news is mostly based on the concept of *newsworthiness*, i.e. what they believe the audience finds interesting.

News media depend very much on their audience for economic reasons. They have to publish whatever makes people buy their newspapers, listen to their radio programs, or tune in to their TV shows and stay tuned through the commercial breaks. This is what newsworthiness really is about: catching the attention of the audience by presenting something spectacular, unusual, emotionally touching, and something that people can identify with. The concept of psychological buttons is really in place here. Topics like danger, food and sex make people pay attention.

Keeping informed about dangers in the environment was of vital importance to our ancestors in primeval society, which is the reason why we have a surveillance instinct that make us hunger for news about possible dangers. News about deviance, crime, and disaster are particularly salient. In fact, Ericson and coworkers found that stories about deviance and control constitute more than half of the news. The media have often been criticized for publishing too much bad news, but the fact is that the audience actually pay more attention to stories about crime and disaster than to good news.

The bad news are not always very relevant. Horrific stories about some bizarre and morbid crime that has happened in a far away place may be more button pushing than reports about well known and trivial dangers like traffic accidents or unhealthy eating habits. The average TV viewer may pay more attention to the story about a bizarre crime although (s)he is extremely unlikely to be affected by a similar crime, at the same time ignoring warnings about the immensely higher risks of traffic accidents or unhealthy life style.

Another pervasive psychological factor in the preferences of the audience is personal identification. A story is much more touching if presented in terms of personalities than if presented as abstract principles. A political conflict is perceived as much more interesting if it is framed as a personal battle between politicians than if framed as a clash between ideologies, and a crime story is more touching if vulnerable victims voice their anger and grief.

The owners and shareholders of news media may have political opinions that shape their decisions, but with increasing professionalism they often prefer their media to be politically neutral in order to cover as large an audience as possible. The present trend of concentration of business ownership means that many media owners also own other enterprises unrelated to news production. They may prevent their media from being too critical towards other firms that they own or towards business in general. The demand for economic efficiency and short time schedules means that journalists often have to print the messages from their sources with little or no editing. The thoroughgoing investigative journalism takes place more in myth than in reality.

Truth and relevance are not strong factors in the news selection process. Journalists work under a tight time schedule and have little time to verify their stories. Therefore, obviously, they sometimes make errors. These errors are seldom corrected because retractions and disclaimers are unfit. The media tend to stick to the interpretive frame originally assigned to a story, even in the face of strong contrary evidence. Misquoted sources and others who may be dissatisfied with inaccurate media stories have only very ineffective means for influencing the media to correct their stories.

MASS MEDIA'S ROLE IN POPULATION CONTROL

In Sri Lanka's population growth rate declined from 2.8% in 1953 to 1.7% in 1981. This achievement was a result of a political commitment on the part of the Sri Lankan Government to population control, a sound organizational and administrative structure, and socioeconomic changes that facilitated acceptance of small family size.

Communication and educational campaigns played a key supportive role in this effort. There was a strong mass media campaign aimed at motivating the population to practice family planning and population communication skills were taught to field workers. In the future, 5 areas of population communication will receive special attention:

1) development of communication programs closely linked to family planning service delivery;
2) development of training materials to improve the communication skills of development extension workers;
3) media research and evaluation;
4) integration of population communication with communication programs in areas such as agriculture; and
5) further development of all forms of mass media.

The major challenge facing family planning is the gap between awareness and practice. While support for the concept of fertility control has almost universal acceptance, the actual contraceptive prevalence rate is only about 50%. This contradiction requires highly creative communication programs that integrate the mass media with interpersonal channels of communication to promote the use of modern methods of contraception.

MASS MEDIA'S ROLE IN PROMOTING FAMILY PLANNING

In addition to their wide appeal and large audiences, television, video, and film have other advantages that make them suitable for health promotion. Of course, these advantages are balanced by some limitations. Family planning organizations need to develop strategic plans for using the media, considering their own needs and resources and balancing advantages and limitations. Important choices in such planning include the mixture of mass-media and interpersonal communication, which of the various media to use, and which services to promote.

Advantages

— *Attractive*. Moving images attract attention. Few people can walk past a television without stopping to look. Images are often remembered longer than verbal messages.

— *Agenda-setting*. The mass media bring certain issues to public attention while ignoring others. This agenda-setting can influence both public and private decisions by making certain issues seem more important than others.

— *Influential*. Television, video, and film are often seen by important audiences such as decision-makers. Usually the wealthy, who include those with political and economic power, are the first to own televisions and VCRs. They are accustomed to receiving information through these media and may pay more attention to messages from them than to messages from other sources. Political leaders consider these messages important partly because they know that many people are seeing them.

— *Acceptable*. Most viewers find family planning messages in the mass media acceptable. When women of reproductive age in 19 countries were asked, "Is it acceptable or not acceptable to you for family planning information to be provided on radio or television?" an average of 84% answered "yes." Over half of these women watched television at least once a week.

— *"Enter-educating."* Television, video, and film can educate while carrying out their usual role of entertaining. Everyone likes and wants to be entertained, and every culture uses some form of entertainment to teach social lessons. "Enter-educate," the term coined to describe this concept, means that entertainment can show people how they can improve their lives. Family planning messages can be incorporated into many forms of television and video entertainment.

— *Moving*. These media, especially when they entertain, can elicit emotions that may spur behavior change. Mass-media campaigns that arouse emotions can be extremely powerful, not only in influencing individual behavior but also in changing law and policy. The emotions aroused may be negative, such as fear, or positive, such as love, hope, or aspirations. Emotional appeals especially influence people who are already concerned and may attract the attention of people initially indifferent to the message.

— *Exemplary*. Television, video, and film can offer examples of behavior. Characters in drama, soap opera, and feature film often serve as role-models either to copy or to avoid. Also, by depicting characters and events, they can make abstract concepts such as family planning not only concrete, but also moving.

— *Cost-sharing*. High-quality products with commercial appeal can save family planning programs money and sometimes even generate income. Projects in Latin America, the Philippines, India, and Turkey have shown that, when organizations obtain corporate sponsorship, including donation of airtime and promotional materials, they increase the reach of the message at little cost to the organization.

— *Cost-effective*. Well-designed, high-quality TV, video, and film productions can reach large numbers of their intended audiences for very little cost per person. In Nigeria the songs and music videos "Wait for Me" and "Choices" cost an estimated 2.2 (US) for each person of reproductive age reached. In Turkey the estimated cost was 4 (US) for each married woman of reproductive age reached by a family planning message.

— *Educational*. Videotape, especially, is well-suited to training clients and providers and to other educational needs.

— *Illustrative*. In training films and videotapes the combination of sound and image can demonstrate and explain complicated messages and procedures.

— *Portable.* Portable film projectors and video players make it possible to take the message to the people, wherever they are. Films can be shown to larger audiences, but VCRs and monitors break down less often and are easier to repair than film projectors.

— *Replayable.* Films, videos, and television programs can be played over and over again. This is advantageous when many people, such as health workers, need to hear the same messages but cannot be brought together. Also, some people need to see and hear messages repeatedly.

Limitations

Using television, video, and film for family planning messages is not without problems, however. Productions for these media are often:

— *Costly.* The cost of television receivers and VCRs limits the audience in some areas. More commonly, the initial expense of production facilities, technicians, equipment, airtime, maintenance, repairs, and distribution limits production. Because of its cost, television production is often given the largest share of family planning communication budgets, leaving little for other media. Decisions about when to use television or video should be made objectively, not just because these media are glamorous and exciting to work with.

— *Less accessible.* Fewer people have access to television, video, and film than to radio. The people who need family planning information most—the urban poor and people in rural areas—often have the least access to television. Increasing satellite transmissions will give rural people better access to television, but only if they have receivers and electricity. Mobile play-back units, solar or gasoline-powered generators, and existing video parlors and other gathering places with TVs and VCRs also can help.

— *Restricted.* "Gatekeepers" may restrict content. Government often controls or closely monitors the broadcast media. Sometimes television, video, and film are scrutinized more closely than radio or print. Gatekeepers often think that audiences will object to family planning messages. As surveys show, these fears may be unfounded. Special-interest groups may be a greater problem, since broadcasters and government officials may fear their reactions. Involving the gatekeepers in project planning and consulting with special-interest groups may help avoid later objections.

— *Technical.* Trained technical personnel may be in short supply. Many people with different skills are needed to research, plan, produce, and implement a mass-media campaign or to produce a TV program or a film. In addition to project managers, talented and trained producers, directors, actors, technicians, and scriptwriters must be available to ensure a high-quality production.

— *Revenue-dependent.* Film-making has always been a commercial operation. So has television in some areas, and in others governments are beginning to require that television pay its own way. Dependence on advertising revenue may discourage TV stations from donating airtime and may influence program content. Also, there is little impetus for commercial stations to expand broadcast coverage beyond major urban areas, where the advertised products are readily available.

Airtime must be bought from commercial stations, and prime time—when the most people are watching—is expensive. Many countries require TV stations to broadcast free "public service announcements," but these are usually run when no one has bought the airtime—in other words, when few people are watching. Also, since many people regard television as strictly for entertainment, there may be little commercial support for "educational" programming.

Family planning programs can overcome this obstacle by making their messages more entertaining and by putting them into ongoing entertainment programs.

— *Unidirectional.* Lack of immediate feedback may limit behavior change in response to mass-media messages. Television and film, especially, provide little opportunity for viewers to participate. Many feature programs are shown only once, and the one-time presentation of material does not allow for different rates of learning, for people's varying needs for repetition, or for questions and clarification. Television, video, and film work better when messages are repeated as often as possible and combined with other forms of communication. Group viewing with discussion leaders can help.

— *Time-consuming.* Planning, researching, and producing television, video, or film projects can take months—or even years. In this time messages may become obsolete, or the people who deliver them, unpopular, requiring even more time for revisions. Careful planning and pre-testing in the early stages of project design can help keep projects on track and minimize delays.

Recognizing the potential of television, video, and film, a number of family planning organizations in the developing world, along with like-minded media professionals, are broadcasting family planning messages in a variety of formats. Many of these efforts have not been documented, and still fewer have been thoroughly evaluated. In every region, however, family planning programs are using television, video, and/or film to reach both potential and current clients. Evaluations, where available, show that these efforts can have a positive impact.

MASS MEDIA IN SEX/HIV/AIDS EDUCATION

Mass Media Programs for the General Public Mass media information and education programs for the general public are often the first step in national AIDS prevention efforts. In virtually every country where AIDS has been reported, the national government has undertaken some effort to make people aware of AIDS. The extent and timing of such efforts, the choice of media, and the content, style, and tone of messages have varied widely. Experience shows that mass media education programs can teach the public about AIDS. It is less clear how much they contribute to changing high-risk behavior.

Many early programs for the general began in a hurry. Thus they often skipped preliminary research, careful planning, and plans for evaluation.

The second generation of programs for the general public has benefited from more time to research, plan, and pre-test. In addition, a number of programs, including ongoing programs in Peru and the United Kingdom and the upcoming program in the Philippines, work with policy-makers, the news media, and health professionals. This helps to ensure more accurate press coverage and more services to meet the demand generated by communication programs.

Mass media news coverage is usually the way people first learn of AIDS. Coverage has ranged from massive to censored and from sensational to scientific. The illness and death of US actor Rock Hudson in 1985 first put AIDS on the front pages of newspapers around the world. But the often sensational coverage gave many the false impression that only homorsexual men could get AIDS. Scientific reports on AIDS research and statements by national leaders also are increasingly publicized. In the US, extensive news coverage of the 1986 report on AIDS by Surgeon General C. Everett Koop stressed the risks of heterosexual intercourse and the preventive benefits of condoms. This coverage may have contributed to a sudden surge in condom sales beginning in early 1987 and helped make the word "condom" usable in public discussion.

In some countries mass media entertainment also has dealth with AIDS—sometimes accurately, sometimes not. US television dramas, taken together, have presented a somewhat distorted view of AIDS and have seldom provided specific guidelines for avoiding AIDS.

Given the enormous power of the mass media to influence public attitudes, it is essential that AIDS programs planners work closely with print and broadcast jounalists and entertainment producers. While social constraints will always influence mass media treatment of issues involving sexual behavior, the media will be better able to provide accurate information, to correct misunderstandings, and to publicize lrevention practices if they have more help from health professionals.

Goals and Obstacles for Mass Media

Programs

Most AIDS education programs for general audiences have similar goals:

— To provide essential information,

— To encourage people to recognize and change behavior likely to spread infection,

— To maintain healthy behavior,

— To quiet groundless anxiety about transmission via casual contact,

— To prevent discrimination against those infected with HIV, and

— To mobilize public support for AIDS education and prevention programs.

Achieving these goals is not easy. Difficulties include:

— Developing messages for diverse audiences,

— Developing messages acceptable in the face of political, social, or begligious opposition, and

— Cost.

Diversity

The general public, by definition, encompasses people of diverse educational, economic, ethnic, and social backgrounds, often speaking different languages and at different levels of risk of HIV infection. Education programs, however, are most effective when designed specifically for well-defined audiences. Thus in broad campaigns the challenge is to develop messages that are attactive to many, understood by all, and yet personally relevant and persuasive to different people. To achieve greater impact, some national programs have focused on specific groups as well as the general public. For example, in 1988 the third phase of the British mass media campaign was designed to appeal to young people. Many more young people called telephone hotlines for information than during the first campaign, and many more remembered the ads and campaign slogan.

Acceptability

Government information programs for the general public are necessarily highly visible and so must be widely acceptable. In some areas fear of objections have prevented open discussion of sexual practices, use of explicit language, and particularly condom promition. In New York City, for example, with over 20 percent of AIDS cases in the US, the major television networks refuse to broadcast condom ads during prime time. Working directly with groups that might object can sometimes defuse potential controversies. In Peru, Proyector SIDA of the Ministry of Health Special Program on the Prevention of AIDS consulted representatives of the Catholic Church and reached a compromise to promote condoms for AIDS prevention and encourage marital fidelity at the same time.

Cost

Reaching most of the public with an educational campaign is expensive relative to other public health expenditures. In

Australia 97 percent of the population saw AIDS messages during the 1987 television campaign. Even though many television stations did not charge for air time, the campaign cost $3.4 million (US). During the second media campaign in the UK, just over 90 percent of all adults saw at least one television ad, but the campaign cost 3 million pounds (US$6.1 million). To limit costs, the UK AIDS program is now focusing on press advertising. Even if television is little used, the cost of printing large quantities of material and developing radio spots is beyond the resources of many programs.

Programs use various mass media to reach the general public. Developed countries have relied heavily on television and major newspapers and magazines because these reach the largest audiences. France, Poland, Sweden, Switzerland, the UK, the US, and West Germany also have mailed informational brochures to most or al households. Developing countries have emphasized radio and various print materials—brochures, leaflets, and posters.

The messages also vary. While promotion of monogomy or at least limiting the number of sexual partners is universal, emphasis on condoms differs greatly. Some countries, such as Sweden, Switzerland, and the Netherlands, promote condoms with public adverstising, open discussion in the mass media, and extensive distribution at bars, airports, resort areas, and schools as well as at health centers. In contrast, at least six countries in sub-Saharan Africa and four in southeast Asia have not promoted condoms at all.

Not surprisingly, fewer than one-forth of adults surveyed in some of these countries recognized that condoms block transmission of HIV, and condom use, whether for family planning or AIDS prevention, is rare. Midway between these two extremes, some countries, such as the US, cautiously endouse condoms, but only as less effective than fidelity and/ or abstinence.

Messages vary in tone as well as content. Early efforts often either provided information in a stright-forward, rational manner or else evoked strong negative emotions, particularly fear.

Now efforts are broadening in both approach and media used. More AIDS education campaigns evoke positive emotions such as humor or the sense of personal well-being that comes from making healthy choices. Also, attention is turning to approaches that blend education and entertainment to make information more appealing and persuasive. For example, in Cote d'Ivoire, Ghana, Tanzania, trinidad and Tobago, Uganda, Zambia, and Zimbabwe, traditional folk theater troupes are performing plays about AIDS. In Kinshasa, Zaire, 15-minute cassettes of popular music and AIDS prevention messages were played on 30 public buses, reaching an estimated 234,000 passengers in four weeks. Over 60 percent of 240 passengers syrveyed remembered the AIDS messages.

In South Africa and Thailand similar television play in taxis. In the Philippines a popular television soap opera aired an episode portraying the consequences for a businessman and his wife after he acquired HIV infection from a prostitute. The number of visits to sexually transmitted disease clinics in Manila doubled during the week after the broadcast. More campaigns now emphasize condom use and how to convince sexual partners to use condoms or other safer sexual practices. Condom social marketing, already underway in roughly two dozen countries elsewhere, is beginning in a number of African countries.

If programs for the general public are well-designed and carried out on a large enough scale, they can reach most of the population and may motivate some to adopt safer behavior. For the greatest impact, however, mass media campaigns must be combined with locally organized interpersonal and group approaches. Campaigns in Swizerland, Uganda, Zaire, and Mexico illustrate the strengths and weaknesses of general campaigns.

IMPORTANCE OF INFORMATION, EDUCATION AND COMMUNICATION (IEC)

IEC are critical for sustainable human development and pave the way for attitudinal and behavioral change (i.e., manifestations of a successful ZPG program). Indeed, this begins with the recognition that decisions must be made freely, responsibly and in an informed manner, on the number and spacing of children and in all other aspects of daily life, including sexual and reproductive behavior. Greater public knowledge and commitment in an already democratic Philippine setting should create a climate conducive to responsible and informed decisions and behavior. Most importantly, they also pave the way for democratic public discussion and thereby make possible strong political commitment and popular support for sustained ZPG efforts at the local and national levels.

Effective IEC activities include a range of communication channels, from the most intimate levels of interpersonal communication to formal school curricula, from traditional folk arts to modern mass entertainment, and from seminars for local community leaders to coverage of global issues by the national and international news media. Multi-channel approaches are usually more effective than any single communication channel. All these channels of communication have an important role to play in promoting an understanding of the interrelationships between population and sustainable development.

Schools and religious institutions, taking into account their values and teachings, are important vehicles for instilling gender sensitivity, respect, tolerance and equity, family responsibility and other important attitudes at all ages. Non-formal education on population and sustainable development issues may also be conveyed through the workplace, health facilities, trade unions, community centers, youth groups, religious institutions, women's organizations and other non-governmental organizations. Such issues may also be included in more structured adult education, vocational training and literacy programs, particularly for women. These networks are critical to reaching the entire population, especially men, adolescents and young couples. Legislators, teachers, religious and other community leaders, traditional healers, health professionals, parents and older relatives are influential in forming public opinion and should be consulted during the preparation of information, education and communication activities. All of forms of media, particularly role models in the local entertainment industry, also offer many potentially powerful tools in promoting national ZPG objectives.

Mothers Against Drunk Driving ("MADD"), the Milk Mustache Mania, and the Anti-Smoking Campaign in the United States are real life examples of effective and sustained information, education and communication campaigns. After more than twenty years, MADD is stronger than ever in advocating solutions to the problems of drunk driving and underage drinking. Similarly, the Anti-Smoking Campaign, which has taken root on many fronts, continues to aggressively discourage smoking, particularly by teenagers, young adults and the less educated sectors of the United States. Through the use of celebrities, the Milk Mustache Mania has encouraged milk drinking. Today, for the first time in six years, milk drinking among teenagers in the United States has increased. According to a new report by the National Family Opinion's Share of Intake Panel (SIP), while soft drinks remain the most dominant beverage among teenagers, 13 to 17 years of age, new data indicates that some teens are beginning to trade in their sodas for milk. These are but some examples of successful IEC campaigns that would surely present excellent case studies for an effective "ZPG Philippines" campaign.

10

AWARENESS AMONG COMMUNITY

In August of 1999 India became the second country to have its population reach the one billion mark. Although certainly a landmark, a billion people in a country one third the size of the United States is more worthy of alarm than celebration. In any country, rapid population growth places a strain on the available resources, but in a developing country like India, many resources are already scarce (in 1960, 0.21 hectares of farmland was available to the average Indian, 0.10hectares in 1999, and it is thought to fall to 0.07 hectares in the next 50 years). A quickly regenerating population exacerbates shortages of food and water and ensures that the nation's long-term growth will be hampered by a less healthy therefore less productive work force, a greater demand for natural resource consumption, and a higher level of environmental degradation resulting from such consumption.

Realizing these consequences, India has been implementing official family planning programs to curb population growth since the 1950's. However, India's population has more than doubled since those days (from 431,463,000 in 1960 to 1,014,003,800 in 2000 and current projections predict that India has a good chance of overtaking China as the most populated country in the world within the next half century. The graph below illustrates the possible projected exponential growth paths of both countries.

In spite of these facts, India's rate of population growth is actually decreasing. In 1991 India's annual population growth rate was 2.15% and by 1997 this figure dropped to 1.7%[4], which indicates that India is indeed making some progress. While this may be true, most evidence would suggest that the country's policies have been largely ineffective and changes must be made to prevent further problems resulting from overpopulation.

So where did India's efforts fall short? Throughout the decades following the implementation of India's Family Planning Program in the 1950s, the prevailing idea in dealing with overpopulation has been that drastic measures needed to be taken. Education regarding temporary methods of contraception was neglected in favor of encouraging sterilization. Government agencies would have sterilization quotas to fill among the employees, and the inability to meet them was sometimes met with withheld salaries. Workers were often rewarded with a radio or television if they successfully convinced enough people to opt for the surgery. At its worst, India's policy included declaring a state of emergency in 1976 and implementing forced sterilization in poor neighborhoods. When applying for government loans, or jobs people were told that their chances of receiving such aids would be increased if they could produce a certificate of sterilization.

The national focus on sterilization seems to have created an "all or nothing" mentality among Indians towards birth control especially since the awareness of other, temporary methods of contraception for much of the 20th century was minute. A 1993 study, India's National Family Health Survey, revealed that of all contraceptive use at the time, 67% was by female sterilization (compared to 9% male sterilization). The prominence of female sterilization indicates another flaw in the India population control strategies. By targeting women instead of men, the government inadvertently opts for the more hazardous means of birth control. The surgical procedure is more difficult and the rate of failure is high, not to mention the danger to the patient, which sometimes means death. Upon learning of these semi-forced, safety-negligent policies, we get what is likely to be a fairly accurate explanation why family planning efforts have failed to curb rampant population growth in India. When the only option available to many people is one that is irreversible, not to mention potentially life-threatening, people would probably be inclined to opt for no contraceptives at all. In such a scenario, the problem is not solved and the population keeps growing and resources per head keep dwindling.

Fortunately, in recent years, it appears that many Indians are aware of the negative effects of the traditional policies and are striving for a change in the system. Taking heed of the recommendations put forth in the 1994 UN Conference on Population and Development, India has shifted attention away from the strict promotion of contraceptive measures and is working on the development of women's economic, educational and social welfare which will give women more control over their own bodies and indirectly curb population growth.

In 1994, India put forth a "New Population Plan" (NPP), hoping that by the year 2010, the average total fertility rate will fall from the early 90's figure of 3.4 to around the replacement rate of 2.1. In order to achieve this goal, the NPP will make strides in improving reproductive health: it will allow universal access to contraceptives and promote greater education on contraception, train more people to safely aid in the birth of children, require a formal registration of all marriages and births, maintain and enforce the minimum age of marriage at 18, and strive to provide primary education for more citizens.[7]

Other movements toward progress include the 2000 freezing of the population-proportional quota of representation for each state in the Lok Sabha. This means if a state effectively reduces its population it will not lose votes in the national government. Also, loans such as the $57 million from the World Bank affiliate, the International Development Association in 1989, have gone to rural and urban areas to successfully aid in the improvement of reproductive health and increasing the awareness of and access to temporary contraceptives.

IMPORTANCE OF POPULATION CONTROL

Why should anyone be concerned with the idea of population control in today's increasingly crowded world? The earth will soon pass seven billion people and the number of people born into poverty is set to rise. Increasingly the idea of controlling the world's population through non-coercive means is a topic of debate in the world's capitals. Should we be concerned? Should anyone be concerned with the idea of population control as it is debated in our newspapers and magazines and TV shows?

Population control is any methodology used to control the type, location and number of people that inhabit the earth. Public debate is strictly limited however to non-coercive means in achieving any one of these goals; especially with regards to population reduction. An important example of this would be allowing people the free choice on procreative matters.

By using various methodologies both economic and administrative and educational to dissuade people from having more children than needed, a stable population base can be created. It should be noted here that the prevailing viewpoint of the world's decision makers is that Population control and environmental devastation are linked and the former contributes heavily to the latter. This view is foundational to understand the policies that are formulated to combat, what is viewed by policy makers as a runaway population explosion. Indeed, when the Nation Intelligence Councll (NIC) held their Global Trends Conference they identified seven key drivers that would shape the globe through the year 2015. The first was demographics; the second was natural resources and environment.

These trends are of the utmost importance to understand if we are to understand the motives and policies that are driving the population control agenda. Related terms and policy paradigms and nomenclature are 'Sustainable Development', 'Agenda 21', 'Rio Conference' 'Biodiversity Treaty', 'Bioshpere Reserves', 'World Heritage Treaty', 'Ecosystem Management', 'Desertification Treaty', Ecosystem Management etc. The idea that there are too many people inhabiting the earth is one that is ingrained in the world's leaders and one that, in their view, requires a solution.

The only socially and psychologically solution available to policy makers when discussing reducing the world's poplation is education. While other methods are debated they are rarely employed or even discussed with any real publicity. These include various methods of taxation, and other forms of financial disincentives. These methods are important to note because barring success of the educational solution track, the financial/ administrative disincentives administrative will probably become more likely as a method of reducing populations. However, this method is only really available where there is some degree of wealth and a fairly well developed governmental institutions capable of enforcing such a regimen. These are the regions that are the primary target of the so called population control agenda; remote, poor, economically underdeveloped regions of the world. Thus, if global policy makers are to have any success in their war on population (people), other methods must be employed.

MALTHUSIAN MANIACS

Many nations on Earth do not have enough food to feed their populations. However, recently the ability to increase food production is being hindered by bizarre weather patterns. In various regions on Earth, including in America, important food production areas are being challenged with floods. In other places, drought has been a problem. Unfortunately, though damaging as these natural disasters are, a more troubling danger contributing to world hunger is that of unequal distribution and shortages caused not by a lack of supply, but in unsold grain and food stocks that are kept off the market in order to keep the prices of grain high. Far from being a nefarious policy, this is done primarily to keep farmers in business.

Despite the many advances, technologically speaking, in agricultural production techniques, hunger on a massive scale still exists in many parts of the world. The intervention of the world's governments and by private institutions has been extensive and commendable. Nevertheless, large pockets of poverty and starvation remain in Portions of Asia, Africa, and Latin America.

Many of these trends have much of their roots in post-colonial economic and agricultural policies and others have their roots in mismanagement by many institutions that have ostensibly attempted to alleviate hunger and poverty in these regions. Falling commodity prices in the 1970's and 1980's did not help third world nations whose principle source of hard currency was through these same commodities.

Many of these nations also carried large a foreign debt load. These debts could only be repaid with the earnings collected from those commodities, which were increasingly worth less, in monetary terms. While most of these nations learned to manage their debt to some degree, it often meant decreased living standards for much of the rest of the population in these nations.

The lack of a coherent and successful policy in the 1970's and 1980's is leaving increasing problems in Africa in particular as it is one of the few region in the world where poverty, epidemics and ethnic violence are converging on a continent at the same time. Unfortunately where such misery exists there are always a few vile men who will attempt to exploit the situation for all its worth. Even using a starving means need to "influence" their "behavior". Such moral perversity can be found in the United Nations food program.

The idea in the minds of most people is that the UN is a benevolent organization who wishes only to help the helpless and bring peace to the world. We submit to you that it is not. While in the past the UN has helped some. It usually does so when the bright lights of publicity are shining and the CNN cameras are rolling. In reality, a review of the action of the World Bank and International Monetary Fund (IMF) and to a lesser degree, the Bank of International Settlements (BIS), all of which are associate agencies of the UN, have used their money creating authority to loan money to third world nations, at interest, ostensibly to help these countries with much needed development. Because these nations have only one thing the west wants, its natural resources (commodities), these nations once they default, become the economic vassals of the IMF and the World Bank.

This is one of the reasons there are so many problems in Africa today. Despite the veiled attempts by the national establishment media to portray to the American people that Africa cannot take care of itself, often the real problem is the austerity measures which frequently take the form of price controls and currency devaluation's which take an enormous toll on the general population in these struggling nations. Often the prognostications of the experts of these economic organizations deliberately overvalue the price of commodities produced by these developing nations thereby making them eligible for larger loan amounts. It has been argued back and forth by the banks supporters and detractors weather or not the World Bank is truly in business to help the poor nations out of their poverty, or simply an instrument for the rich nations to plunder the natural resources of the poor nations. It is a debate that will certainly continue, that is, until the remaining portions of that wealth is in the hands of the corporations and money-changers.

One of the first victims of this unseen war is the children of these nations. As living standards in these already poor nations' declines, the children are often forced to work to help make ends meet in these families. Food becomes scarce as social conditions deteriorate. This often adds fuel to the fire of already tense ethnic tensions with violence the frequent result. The World Bank and the IMF are very much part of the problem in this region of the World. The most important reason these nefarious policies can continue is that, first, the mainstream media simply don't report the facts to the American people and secondly, because most Americans are too busy to make more than a cursory look at these institutions and have no desire to look beyond the catch-all phrases to really care.

But today we do have some people who are attempting to sound the alarm bells. The turmoil in the Asian markets in late 1997 and 1998 showed an increasing debate as to the role of the international financial institutions. Hopefully, the debate will move into directions which will lead to reform of these institutions and a reduction in their role in profiting from human misery. It may also help alleviate the swirling mystery of how these institutions make some bizarre and at times abominable decisions, brought on by the World Bank's obsession with secrecy. What are they doing with our taxpayer money that they don't want anyone to know about? In this day and age, it would seem impossible to imagine a world without the likes of the money-changers. However, the use of debt to help out others is not a sound way to help thy neighbor.

The use of other peoples money to loan out to basket case economies for private profit, lends itself to a very, dangerous and immoral situation which the people accept all too willingly, mostly out of abject ignorance Unfortunately, there seems to be another purpose to the United Nations policy makers, which with a little investigation, reveals itself in the oft repeated slogan of population control. Population control is rooted in the idea that the world's population is increasing too rapidly and is outstripping natural resources.

"We must speak far more clearly about sexuality, contraception, about abortion, about values that control population, because the ecological crisis, in short, is the population crisis. Cut the population by 90 percent and there aren't enough people left to do a great deal of ecological damage." These remarks were spoken by Dr. Sam Keen, a new age writer, at the 1996 Gorbachev conference in San Francisco. His remarked were received with warm applause, by the new "Intellectuals".

This statement was made by Alexander King, president of the Club of Rome, a think tank for elitist and socialist ideas, which interlocks with the Council on Foreign Relations (CFR) and the Trilateral Commission. Now according to the National Academy of Sciences, DDT had prevented 500 million deaths. Consequently, the Globalists set out to ban the use of DDT, not because it wasn't effective or safe, but because it saved human lives. To these butchers, the preservation of human life is evil, letting hundreds of millions of people die is good.

Let us look at Africa, the Rwanda situation should have sent off alarm bells to the American people, unfortunately, during those massacres the WWF, and Bart Simpson were also on television, consequently, little attention was paid by the American masses. The Genocide first began in April of 1994. In the Early 1990's the Hutu led military issued decrees disarming the largely Christian Tutsi's. After the Tutsi's were disarmed, the Hutu's, using machetes massacred 800,000 Tutsi's. Please take note, Madeline Albright insisted the word Genocide *not be used*. This is because such a word must call for trials.

American foreign policy did not want that to happen. One must wonder if the American foreign policy establishment *really wanted the murder to come to an end* before any neighboring African troops intervened, as American troops prevented others form entering in to render medical assistance to the sick and dying. Now the Hutu's, after their faithful slaughter, has received millions of dollars in aid from no other source than the US Government. What is ignored is that fact the weapon of choice was the machete, a weapon easily outclassed by a simple machine gun.

The argument that the safety of any intervening troops, the primary consideration for denying entry in to the ravaged areas, simply lacks credibility. The press, course, as the faithful and diligent defender of the elite, took its pre-scripted role of mute silence, was remiss in not explaining who and why no help was sent. Whether you believe AIDS is man made or naturally occurring, the effects on population has been the same. Let us ask this question? Since when has having an incurable, contagious disease which just so happens to be transmitted through the act of reproduction been treated like a protected status, where some have even called for special rights?

Has this helped curtail or spread the disease? Since when has our society shown such kindness on people whose illness is always fatal? Since when have our leaders been so quick to move to protect the homosexual population, while largely understating the effects of AIDS in Africa? One factor seems to be increasing clear, it is Africa that is the target. Resource rich, beautiful Africa, populated with what Margeret Sanger, *the Founder of Planned Parenthood* called, 'human weeds', that is, Black people.

The Infamous Tuskeegee study is another interesting scene in the panorama of America's medical experiments. Here black men were, after, being told they were being treated for their illness, (syphilis) were deliberately kept from medicines which would cure them, so that doctors could observe the effects of syphilis on men. One must wonder when we will see crematoriums and gas chambers in America.

Let us consider the Abortion issue, once again it coincides completely with the population control agenda; the less people born the better. This form of murder seems far less objectionable to many Americans because the human life killed has no one to mourn for it, especially when its own mother is the butcher. When the abortion issue is raised, it is almost invariably raised in conjunction with the poor and yes, we have it again, black's. The implication here is that 'these people', according to much of what we hear from many quarters, cannot control themselves, and if more of "them" are born it will just add to the burden of welfare and crime to our societies.

As you can see Planned Parenthood has some interesting beginnings that are not generally known, for obvious reasons. Ms. Sanger also intended to hire some black ministers to propagandize for birth control.

> "The most successful educational approach to the Negro is through Religious appeal. We do not want word to get out that we want to exterminate the Negro population, and the minister is the man who can straighten out the idea if it ever occurs to any of their more rebellious members."

Yes, the Ghost of Adolph Hitler is alive and well. It has been living in America for 50 some years, in the person of our Presidents, who support organizations such as Planned Parenthood and their Cabinets, many of our Doctors and Senators, in our corporate board rooms and in our living rooms, in our news rooms and in our schools.

The American people are just like the Germans so many years ago, *in denial*. Until the stench of rotting corpses was unmistakable, most Germans were also in denial. Even then, most simply shut their eyes from seeing. Those that do see are cowering in the dark, knowing full well what awaits them if they speak out. A few are speaking out, but only a few, Americans may be able to hear them during a commercial break, while watching another inane sitcom or perhaps another sports extravaganza. That is provided, they aren't doped up or drunk.

Of course the infantile refrain is 'you know, it can't happen here, this is America!' Of course 'America' is the magic word and all corruption and evil magically disappear when you say America!! And if you, as an American, really believe that, then you have definitely been watching too much T.V.!

Blood is crying from the ground, the desire of those who are formulating UN population policy have all made target estimates of 500 million to 3 billion people as the ideal population of Earth. Some have stated that it is imperative that this be accomplished, soon, by any available means.

> "At present the population of the world is increasing ... War so far has had no great effect on this increase ... I do not pretend that birth control is the only way in which population can be kept from increasing. There are others ... If a Black Death could be spread throughout the world once in every generation, survivors could procreate freely without making the world too full ... the state of affairs might be somewhat unpleasant, but what of it? Really high-minded people are indifferent to suffering, especially that of others."

Population control is a integral part of the Globalist agenda. One point that should be made here is that the Nazi's own population control agenda was formulated and executed with extreme secrecy. While the Jews of Germany were horribly persecuted and demonized by the state, the systematic extermination of the Jews was not a publicly announced policy. All notes of the Wannsee Conference, where the policy of extermination was planned and discussed, were to be burned and the topic of the conference was held in extreme secrecy. So consider this dear reader, while all the signs were present that this is what Hitler had planned for the Jews, the actual policy was carried out secretly. History is repeating itself today. Far too many suspicions diseases are being discovered and the deaths of far too many micro-biologists who work in genetics are happening to all be a just a 'coincidence'. Coincidence theorists are the ones who would stand by and watch the holocaust happen all over again while they cling to their religion of 'coincidental denial.

Today or at least very soon, it will be possible to create viruses that only kill certain races of people, thus using science (just like the Nazi's) to exterminate people with a high degree of secrecy. This will be a possibility that no one really will consider until great swaths of the human family have been wiped out by a few powerful and satanically inspired people.

Secrecy will work greatly to the advantage of these evil men because anyone who speaks about it can be labeled a 'conspiracy nut' while the body bags are being filled. This is working now as a successful tact, as many much of the population of Africa has been decimated by.AIDS and any who questions the suspicious causes of the disease, the extremely ineffective methods employed in combating it and the extreme pricing in medications is labeled a 'conspiracy nut' or a 'right wing wacko'. If indeed our policy makers wanted to solve the AIDS crisis, serious debate as to the causes of this dreadful disease should be explored without scientific or political prejudices. This has not only *not* happened, but woe to any suggest such a 'unproductive' course of action.

MIGRATION

Another method of population control is through controlled migration. This is a method whereby large swaths of people are uprooted to new locations. This can be done by a variety of methods.

— *Economic*: providing jobs and economic assistance to areas desirable for human migration.

— *War:* Causing large scale military unrest where it is desired to have people migrate from such as regions rich in natural resources

— *Disease:* Using disease or the fear of disease to encourage migration

— *Famine:* Using famine as a means to induce people to migrate.

These and other methods can be used to control populations, not so much in a quantitative sense, but at least in terms of location. Highly concentrated populations are easier to control than widely dispersed ones and those with a rudimentary access to various forms of controlled media (electronic or print) tend to be somewhat more docile. The CIA states clearly that the there are two forms of migration that will be most prevent in the coming years

— *Urbanization* – people moving to cities to find work, health and/or educational opportunities.

— *Cross border migration* – Moving from one nation-state to another.

It should be noted here that when the National Intelligence Council presented its Global Trends 2015, they noted that State actors would play a dormant role in many of the emerging changes and that other non-state actors would be more important in shaping the globe. This will be true in many respects as the international corporation, the terrorist and the banker are far more important to today's global changes than Governments. The report went on to say that in the absence of a clear and overriding national security threat, "United States will have difficulty drawing on its economic prowess to advance its foreign policy agenda. The top priority of the American private sector, which will be central to maintaining the US economic and technological lead, will be financial profitability, not foreign policy objectives."

Here notice that the NIC realized the importance of the so-called 'private sector' (Corporations). So let it be noted here that these things are being discussed in antiseptically clean board rooms where the average American is not allowed entry or even invited to attend. While this report certainly does not provide any solutions to these problems rest assured that if the problem has been identified, someone somewhere will be tasked to come up with solutions.

What these solutions are or even the fact that they have been decided upon is rarely made public, though the funding for it will be footed by the taxpayer. Such a solution was sought by the US government back in the 1970's. The Nixon administration with then secretary of State Henry Kissinger formulated a truly Malthusian policy of depopulation in National Security Action Memorandum 200.

The US Government at the time considered the growing populations of the developing world as a grave threat to US national security. From then on a curious pattern begins to take shape. Indeed in the recent past, the deaths of many microbiologists is one that needs to be understood in light of the above memorandum and statements by our elite.

Something most suspicious is going on and no one is speaking about it... at all. It is not unreasonable, despite how many talking heads on TV say it is, to question and follow up with more questions regarding these suspicious deaths. What is going on? Who is responsible and what is the ultimate aim?

USE OF TECHNOLOGY TO POPULATION CONTROL

Another more prevalent method of population control is through the use of technology. This is used for a variety of purposes, from crime prevention, monitoring and tracking and ultimately the total control of society. The American Total Information Awareness Office (TIA) is such an agency spawned out of the pit of hell. Headed by the convicted Felon, Admiral John Poindexter, who was later forced to resign over his 'terrorism casino' proposal (which provide a place where people could bet on future terrorist attacks), this office is bent on collecting, tracking and analyzing as much information of Americans as is technologically possible.

The legal framework for the use of these new technologies has been codified in the US Patriot act. Ostensibly the act was to be used to stop terrorism, in reality in is becoming increasingly clear that the act was formulated long before the

911 attacks and was lying in wait just for such an attack to occur. Undermining the foundation principles of American Constitutional government is of extreme necessity in order to control populations.

Using the technological advances of the recent past, controlling populations is front page news in most newspapers, from spy camera's to microscopic electronic tags in clothing, from smart highways to computer spyware. These are all part of American life now, weather one is aware of these daily intrusions or not. Centralized planning for future population control technologies was imperative, the Soviet Union did it, the Nazi's did it and now America is doing it, using as a catalyst, the TIA office. Such planning and the psychological preparations that go with it are necessary for a totalitarian state.

Thus the preparatory psychological and legal frameworks have been set in order to provide our government and intelligentsia with the tools needed to control populations through technological means. At present these are conducted usually for the so called war on terrorism, a quaint euphemism that is increasingly seen as a war on all kinds of political and economic dissent.

The danger here for the intelligentsia is, that once their usefulness is complete, they too become victims of the system that they helped create. This was true of Stalin's regime and to a lesser degree, Hitler's. Those at the pinnacle of such power historically have never been able to maintain that power without succumbing to varying degrees of paranoia. This paranoia dispenses with the 'threat', real, perceived and delusional with extreme methods. This is true today of in America, John Ashcroft and George Bush and Donald Rumsfeld have succumbed to this paranoia and are using every means at their disposal to counter the 'threat', as they perceive it. That threat is terrorism. However, just like in Stalin's Russia, such a pathological view coupled with violent actions invariably breeds enemies that did not exist before, sowing the seeds of its own destruction.

Thus, these technological methods that are today being employed with increasingly less crudeness are creating a vast cadre of resistance not only in the political arena, but also in the scientific community. The Federation of American Scientists exposes much government corruption and misuse of technology and makes their information available to all. This is just one group of America's intelligentsia that have been useful to the system but are seeing the fruit of their labor used for purposes that are neither in the public interest nor in the long term interest of the nation.

Globalization has played an important role in population control insofar as this process is harmonizing legal, technological, economic and political frameworks for the coming global government. This process has neither been easy nor without major setbacks. Indeed it has been very difficult for global planners to get some of their agenda implemented because large segments of the population have become aware of the 'agenda' and are highly suspicious of the semi-secrecy with which these elitists work.

The world at large, unfortunately still has no clue as to the reasons and methods of the population control agenda and that it is one of the highest priorities of most of the world's governments. Not just the Malthusian aspect, but every aspect of this agenda is important when governments formulate their policies, be it domestic or foreign. The bad news is the Children of God are even more clueless than the average American and work desperately hard to remain that way.

The widest range of message inputs available giving information directly related to the needs and interests of potential users must be communicated in order to get people to change their contraceptive behavior. Both communication and clinical services are necessary for an adequate population and family planning program.

The communication aspect requires many diverse information and education activities. Public information activities include mass media use, advertising and promotion, public relations, and commerical marketing of nonmedical contraceptives. Education has been identified as population education, education for parenthood, and sex education, and it should be offered in the clinic, in community extension education programs, and as in-school education.

Some type of coordination of public information and education is needed. Possibly they could be combined under a program activity termed "Communications." A communications program which coordinates information and education should have a planning component which includes in its tasks research and evaluation. Each of the tasks in a communications program requires specific kinds of materials. Audiences need to be identified, messages and media selected, formats designed, and the material produced. The communicators require more job-specific training.

FAMILY PLANNING IN INDIA

The rapid growth of population is one of the major problems facing the country today. India is at the turning point in its population development. As early as 1970, the birth rate showed a distinct downward trend, and continued to fall further to its present lowest. Over and above this, it was possible for the first time since independence to slow down the population growth-rate as well. Considering the population of the country as is 845 million, and the annual surplus of births over deaths stands at 15 million, there is no doubt that the "population explosion" still continues. It is, therefore, necessary to slow down the population development even more in order to reduce the grave consequences of the "population explosion".

This section analyses the trend of population increase and to discuss the constraints as well as various family planning measures adopted to control the population growth. Some social factors like reluctance of minority groups towards adopting family planning programmes emerge as the major constraints.

With reference to family planning, the popular measures adopted in the country are sterilization, abortion IUD, conventional contraceptives, etc. Here it should be mentioned that family planning is not only concerned with limiting the number of children through preventive measures, but it is very much related with aspects of health-care and better standard of living.

From the first census the population of India has risen from 203 million to 685 million in 1981 and 845 million in 1991. India is thus the most heavily populated country after China ; through 16 percent of the world population is living there, it occupies only 2.4 percent the earth surface.

India's relative population increases since 1871 is remarkably low although the absolute increase is high. India's population development since 1871 may be split into phases. In the first phase, which is characterized by the British imperial health service, shows a strongly fluctuating course, indicating an altogether medium-sized population increases only.

The level of birth rates and death rates is decisive for this, the balance of which determined population development. The high values of both of these demographic indicators are perfectly in line with those of the Third World especially in the case of the death rate. The reasons of high death rate are famines diseases and epidemics with heavy tool of lives.

The two census periods 1891/1901 and 1911/1921 even had the effect of bringing about a population decrease amounting to no less than 41 million, i.e. 14.5 percent in the first case. The devastating influenza epidemic of 1918 cost 18.5 million lives. The British imperial government improvement in health services in India through medicine, hygiene, nutrition and education. The government improve public health services, controlled infectious tropical diseases and provided better access to medicine and medical care.

During the second phase, i.e. after independence, the rapid population growth led to the sudden increase in the population which became known as the "population explosion" on account of its very magnitude. This is expressed in the doubling of the population from 361 to 845 million between 1951 to 1991 India's relatively rapid population growth is thus identical to that of most developing countries.

The development of birth rates and death rates in India to date allows one to identify only two of the usual, phases of the demographic transition. Until 1920, India remained in the first phase of pre-industrial agrarian society, which was characterized by high values for natality and mortality; this resulted to significant population growth.

The early-industrial phase only set in during the 1920: it was characterized by a marked drop in mortality together with continuing high natality. Extending to the late 1960, this phase manifested a rapid increase in population. Only in the 1980 the demographic transformation process could enter in its third phase which brought with it a noticeable decrease in the birth rate, accompanied by a further drop in mortality.

In respect of further population developments, India finds itself only just at the beginning of the fully effective third phase, in which the regressive birth rate dominates in contrast to mortality. Attaining the following phases of the demographic transformation process is at present a merely hypothetical matter so far as Indian population development is concerned.

Indian population is increasing at the rate of 2.4%. The broad base, on the other hand, demonstrates the large proportion of children and young adults, the tapering apex shows the small proportion of old people (only 4.7 percent over 60 years of age). How young the Indian population really is, shown by the fact that every second Indian is under 18 years old. As a consequence of the large families the proportion of the population capable of employment (15-59 years) is only 53.2 percent, and hence comparatively low. Thus, the production potential dependent upon labour is more likely to be limited than indicated by the labour market. The Over young-age structure now poses insoluble problems for the Indian government with regard to education and employment; the 13 to 14 million excess of births per-year of the 1980 implies the construction of 1270 new schools annually, the training of 373,000 additional teachers if the demand is to be met. Added to this is the annual requirement of 4 million new work places.

India still has an alarmingly high proportion of illiterate people and a comparatively small number of literate ones. Although the 437 million illiterate persons include 60 million children below the school age, subtracting them from the total, still leaves every second Indian of school age, an illiterate. In 1991, there was a spatial amplitude in the literacy rate which varied between 69% (Kerala) and a depressing 20%. The grounds for this are to be found in the regionally varying number and upkeep of educational institutions.

The striking gradient also exists between urban and rural areas, with the large number and. better development of schools in town, resulting in a higher literacy rate (59.7% in 1971) than in the villages (only 27.4%). A comparison of the two sexes reveals a particularly low literacy rate among women. In 1981 the percentage of literate women was only 25 percent while in case of men it was 47 percent.

The population growth in India led as well to a rapid increase in the average density of population (1951:117 inhabitants/km^2 1981:221 inhabitants/km^2). The population density provides a graphic expression of the regionally very varied natural endowments as well as of the unequal agricultural potential of the Indian sub-continent. India is still regarded as a 'land of villages'. Proof of this is the large number of villages contrasting with the small number of towns.

Although in relation to the overall growth of the population, rural increase always exceeds urban growth, the substantial percentage increase in the proportion of urban population is very striking, especially since independence (i.e. from 16 percent to 24 percent). Evidence for this is found in the disproportionately high urban growth rates, i.e. 46 percent in 1971-81 in contrast to 25 percent for the overall population. Every fourth Indian is now living in a town, and further population developments in India are likely to follow a rural-urban population shift, a typical feature of developing countries.

The twin processes of urbanization and rural exodus are responsible for the rural-urban population development. The two phenomena are examined here on a quantitative basis. In India towns are classified into six classes on the basis of population number.

Class	*Number of inhabitants*
I	100,000 and more
II	50,000 - 100,000
III	20,000 - 50,000
IV	10,000 - 20,000
V	5,000 - 10,000
VI	5,000 above

The urban population development in India, already indicated by the large increase in the total number of towns from 1834 in 1901 to 3245 in 1991, receives emphatic documentation through the increase of urban population from 26 to 150 million (i.e. by 500%) A significant role in the rapid urban population development in India has been played by the 'metropolitan areas'. Their number has risen to 12 with a total of 42 million inhabitants, accounting for 27% of urban population.

The growth rate of million cities is altogether the highest in India. Every million city, with the exception of Calcutta, exceeds the growth rate of the urban population as a whole (1951-81:104 percent), and is for higher than the all-India growth rate (71%). Their rapid population increase is, therefore, only partly due to the surplus of births, partly and due to the gains through migration.

In the period 1971-81, million cities of India showed a population growth from 29.597 to 42.160 million inhabitants accounting for a rise of 12.563 million (42.4 percent), exactly twice as much as the natural growth rate (21.2 percent) of India. Migration plays an important role in the entire development of the urban population. From 1951 to 1991 the urban population increased by 47 percent, of which was 21.2 percent due to the surplus of births and 25.8% due to migration gains.

The considerable rural-urban migration, though effecting 27 million people during the period 1951-81, did not result at all in a regressive population development in rural areas. The considerable migration from rural areas and the disproportionally large increase in the urban population can be explained by push and pull factors, which operate in India in the same way as in other countries of the third world. The attraction of the large cities is concentrated in the hope a job and linked with it, upward social mobility.

Family Planning vs. population growth

Family planning vs. population growth was the motto of the national population policy in independent India since the introduction of the first five-year plan. Family planning programme is perhaps the most effective policy intervention to control fertility and stabilise population size. Since the effect of the programme varies from state to state, the fertility impact also varies from stage to state. Contraception is the need of the day to counteract the explosive increase in population.

After independence, family planning was stepped up. The sole aim was the lowering of the birth rate. There was no significant economic or social measure to accompany it. Religion plays a vital and important role in the life of the people of India. Muslim by and large does not adopt the family planning programme. Other factors responsible for the failure of family planning is illiteracy, poverty etc. Islam like other religions believes that children are the gift of god and advise a proper care to feed, love and educate them.

The family planning methods provided by the programme are vasectomy, tubectomy, the IUD, conventional contraceptives, (i.e. condoms, diaphragms, jelly/cream tubes, foam tables) and oral pills. In addition, induced abortion is available, free of charge, in institutions recognised by the government for this purpose.

Sterilisation is the main method for family planning programme in India. The number of annual acceptors of this method is far larger than for the IUD. The number of conventional contraceptive users relates to the prevalence of such use, rather than to number of new acceptors. During the emergency period, almost 11 million sterilization were performed but later on this programme witnessed virtual collapse.

Presently the sterilization programme is doing particularly well in Maharashtra, Andhra Pradesh, Gujarat, Kerala, Karnataka and Tamil Nadu. In Assam and the rest of the North-East, Bihar, Uttar Pradesh and Jammu & Kashmir performance on the increase, is but still it is very poor.

In a country like India where 76 percent population inhabit in rural areas higher fertility and natural increase in make it important to estimate family planning prevalence separately for rural and urban areas. In 1970-71 only 7.7 percent of rural couples were effectively protected by family planning against 22.5 percent of urban couples. By 1980-81, 18.5 percent of rural couples and 40.5 percent of urban couples were protected.

There was wide variation by state in the percentage of couples effectively protected by all methods in 1974-75. For instance, this percentage was as low as 6.8 in Bihar, 7.7 in Rajasthan and 8.4 in Uttar Pradesh. However, it was as high as 28.4 in Haryana, 26.0 in Maharashtra, and in Punjab. If sterilisation alone is considered, Maharashtra had the highest percentage of couples protected (23.6), followed by Tamil Nadu with 18.5 and Gujarat with 18.3.

It is worth to note the differential performance of the programme in rural and urban areas in each state. Over 20 percent rural couples were protected by 1980-81 in A.P., Gujarat, Haryana, Karnataka, Kerala, Madhya Pradesh, Maharashtra, Orissa, Punjab and West Bengal. And over 40% of urban couples were protected in Andhra Pradesh, Assam, Haryana Maharashtra and Tamil Nadu.

Percentage of eligible couples effectively protected in rural and urban areas by state and by method, 1980-81

The socio-economic characteristics of family planning acceptors are important in judging the demand for family planning and its differential effect on the fertility of various segments of the population.

In 1979-80, the mean number of living children at acceptance was 2.7 for the IUD, 3.5 for tubectomy and 3.7 for vasectomy. The percentage of couples accepting family planning with three or less living children was 75 for IUD, 60 for vasectomy and 52 for tubectomy.

During 1977-80 contraceptive failure was the reason given for termination in about 47% of cases at national level, although it was high as 90% in Himachal Pradesh and 66% in Maharashtra. An estimated four to six million abortions are criminally induced each year. These findings provide an insight to reorient the family planning strategy and fertility behaviour strategy and its fertility impact.

Social values and family institutions require that each couple should have at least one surviving son, particularly in rural areas. With high infant and child mortality a couple will not take risk of undergoing sterilisation before having at least two sons since, in practice, a sterilisation operation is irreversible off reversible methods such as the IUD, condom, and piller stage of family formation.

WOMEN AND POPULATION CONTROL

Social independence will bring women think independently. In present system prevailed in most of undeveloped and dense illiterate old thinking religious countries. Women are not entitled to decide their own for child birth control as it is a male who plays dominant role for want of male child. Special poor and illiterate families are more inclined to bigger families. Generally most of external contraceptives are meant for men. Cheaper and economical external contraceptive methods for women will help them to prevent them from unwanted birth of children.

— Child marriage should be totally discouraged, as even today it is practiced in many developing countries. Religious issue that plays to encourage child marriage. The daygirl child is borne to the parents she becomes burden to the parents and they get rid as soon as she attains puberty or in many cases before also. A strict penalty is very much required to arrest child marriage.

— Education of population control should be intensified in all rural population. Population control and methods should be a part of the courses in the educational institutions, especially in rural villages.

— Advantages and disadvantages should be introduced so that male and female, members are advantageous of lesser children.

— Holding higher and Government posts should have criteria of having respectable numbers of children as specified to bring down overpopulation.

— Religion should be updated according to present needs and all religions should discourage overpopulation.

— A woman bears no child is known as barren and is despised by society though is may be due to impotency of husband. Similarly, woman giving birth to only girl child is also seen as womans failure to bear boy. We still follow old religious fundamentalism. Selection of boy child accounts to increase of number of children in the family.

PRACTICAL SOLUTIONS

Not satisfied with the recent arrival of the one billionth baby, Indians are progressing ahead in the race for mass human production. Attempts have been made by different governments through several schemes to control the galloping population. But, obviously, something is going wrong somewhere. How else would one explain the protests from several politicians themselves against the family planning code involving them?

The immediate impact of gulping numbers is poverty, unemployment and illiteracy. Are funds posing problems? We do not think so. Take the example of Swarn Jayanthi Rojgar Yojna, a self employment scheme for urban poor, which is a direct fallout of over-population. The central government says that the implementation by states has been ``very poor" with Rs 510 crore out of the total Rs 540 crore earmarked for the scheme remaining unspent in the last three years. Unfortunately, all the money is lying with state governments.

Now let us shift the focus on practical solutions; Funds are crucial for such a gigantic mission. If funds are a problem, let the government divert funds unutilised for the other schemes towards this primary mission. Educating the masses is easier said than done. It involves lots of time, energy and money of several non-governmental and government agencies.

Many couples in India did not know that the local corporation offers cash incentives to those who settle for one girl child or two. Looking out for boy child, many couples end up having several girl children. "I would have settled for one daughter," confessed many women from the slum areas. One should note that the city of Mumbai with less than 10 lakh population boasts of below-poverty line families numbering 2,222, officially. And, such people who need their daily bread will rush for sterilisation at least to get the incentives, if informed by the civic authorities in time. A dozen gleaming couple received NSC certificates from the corporation officials recently for settling for one-daughters, but the event went uncovered by the media, thanks to poor publicity from the corporation. Hence, the need is to highlight the incentives already being offered by the authorities. Glorify the couples through simple functions, call the local leaders who will be too happy to take the lead. They get their publicity and India gets its numbers right.

Of course, the education process can continue. But involve all local community and political leaders. They need publicity. Let them take the lead. Give them the pamphlets and ask them to sponsor events. Just try it.

Now, there are many schemes under which condoms are distributed free to slum dwellers. There are many areas where the slum dwellers actually question the NGOs on how to `eat' condoms? So much for ignorance. There have been instances of such condoms being sold, instead of free distribution. There is need for a joint movement of NGOs and government agencies, with one authority taking control and making the participants accountable.

Slum-dwellers across the railway tracks are blissfully unaware of the schemes that can fetch them money in return for sterilisation. An helpline number can be publicised, targetting the illiterate and slum-dwellers. Counsellors can then convince them through local language. Condom vending machines are an excellent means. But they are still approached with a blushing face. There is also need to enforce a legislation. Such a democratic decision with majority votes will not be challenged by any sections. If there's a will there's a way.

NEW STRATEGIES

There is controversy over whether population growth is good or bad. Over-population and continuing population growth are making substantial contributions to the destruction of Earth's life support systems. In the past, human populations have rarely been subject to explosion. In numbers. The powerful long-term mo-mentum that is built into the human age structure means that the effects of fertility changes become apparent only in the future. For these reasons, it is now conven-tional practice to use the technology of population projection as a means of better understanding the implications of trends.

Population projections represent the playing out into the future of a set of as-sumptions about future fertility and mortality rates. More public education is needed to develop more awareness about population issues. Facts like the size or the growth rate of the human population should be in the head of every citizen. Schools should inform students about population issues in order for them to make projections about the future generations.

Action plans and strategies can be developed to increase public understanding of how rapid population growth limits chances for meeting basic needs. The spirit of open communication, and empowerment of individual women and men will be key to a successful solution to many population problems. Collective vision about health care, family planning and women's education at the community level build a basis for action. The creation of action plans help to meet challenges to find coop-erative solutions. Free and equal access to health care, family planning and educa-tion are desirable in their own right and will also help reduce unwanted fertility.

Individual choice, human rights and collective responsibility are key to al-lowing families to plan the size and spacing of their children. It is essential to achieve a balance between population and the available resources. Teachers, par-ents, community workers and other stakeholders should extend the range of choices about available resources to individuals, especially women, and by equal-izing opportunities between the genders from birth onwards. Teachers, parents, other educators, politicians and other concerned citizens can practice how to make good decisions in everyday life. Decisions about family size, and resource will affect the future generations. Through commu-nity forums, specific issues about the population growth can be discussed and possible action plans can be developed.

Teachers, as well as students can use the information super highway to gain knowledge about other countries' population and resources. Teachers can help students with problems and decision making on a daily basis. The investigation of world population will raise the level of awareness, so that we can learn to handle problems based on data. This data can help us to analyze our situations in a practical way. Teachers, students, parents and other stakeholders can look for trends in the population explosion. They can hold community meetings at school to discuss how this issue presents a challenge to the big picture of human population on the planet "Earth".

INDIA'S POPULATION POLICY AND CHALLENGES

Fifty years ago, when we achieved independence, India was considered to be an overpopulated country. India was the first country in the world to adopt family planning programme as an official program.

What does it mean? Does it mean that our population policy has failed? Does it mean our population policy has not grown over the years in the sense that it has not been able to capture the complexities of the issue and has not been able to attack the problem at its root effectively? There are two misconceptions in this type of a pessimistic stand. Firstly that nothing has been achieved on the population front and secondly that population policy means only family planning programme. To remove these misconceptions we must see what we have achieved on population front and how our population policy was adapted from time to time to meet the new challenges.

Complexity of Population Issue

It needs to be noted first that like all the countries undergoing socio-economic development, India also is undergoing the process of demographic transition. During the last five decades it has been successful in bringing down its crude death rate from about 22 per 1000 before independence to eight per 1000 by 1997 but the pace of fertility decline has not been keeping pace with this progress. Crude birth rate remained around 40 per 1000 even after three decades of independence and it has reached a level of only 27 by early 1997 which is much above the level of our crude death rate. As shown by this difference, our success in mortality control not accompanied by equal success on fertility front has been the main cause of population explosion in our country. Then the question arises why our efforts to bring down fertility were not equally effective.

It needs to be understood that fertility decline is much more complex than mortality decline. Everybody likes to live a long and healthy life, while there can be difference of opinion as to how many children one should have. Second, some of the decisions affecting mortality can be taken at macro level (e.g. provision of safe drinking water by chlorination at source itself) but, fertility is the result of micro-level decisions taken daily by millions of couples scattered all over the country. Lastly, couples do not accept small family norm unless they perceive the decline in mortality and that more children are surviving. In short fertility decline cannot be achieved unless we bring about a social change or change in attitude of couples, which is a slow process. The most important factor in this connection is that there is always discrepancy between micro level and macro level perceptions about desired family size. The issue is whether our population policy over the years has been able to address these complexities.

Major Landmarks

In fact if we look at the history of population policy it can be clearly seen that over the years our population policy has gone through many phases. At every stage we have learnt from our mistakes and accordingly we have changed the policy.

Immediately after independence, there was a feeling that most of our problems, including population problem, were due to neglect by British rulers and once we have our own government, the problem will be gradually solved. In fact, at the time of first five–year plan there was so much optimism that they did not visualise the population growth rate to increase beyond 2 percent per annum. Due to influence of Gandhian approach only natural methods of family planning were emphasised. It is no wonder that due to such passive attitude, during the first plan period even the budget which was provided for family planning could not be spent. The approach we adopted was a clinic approach. It meant family planning services were made available in the government clinics and it was expected that couples would avail of the services on their own. It did not happen and finally 1961 Census population figures was a big jolt, which opened the eyes of our policy makers.

It was only after 1965 that we switched over from clinic approach to extension approach. Instead of just making the services available in clinics, under this new approach, grass-root level functionaries were expected to go to the community and convince them about accepting small family norms and using family planning methods. During the late sixties and early seventies, the network of primary health centres and sub-centres was established all over the rural areas and family planning services were made available through them. It was during this period that sterilization and IUD camps were held. We started giving incentives to couples accepting family planning methods. It was during this period that maternal and child health services were integrated with the family planning services because it was realised that instead of talking about family planning in isolation, if the workers also provide services to mothers during pregnancy and delivery and after the delivery to both mothers and children, it would be helpful to generate the demand for family planning. It was during this period that targets were given to functionaries in terms of the number of sterilizations to be performed and IUDs to be fitted.

As a result of all these efforts we achieved substantial decline in fertility by seventies but we also realised certain harsh facts. Firstly, it was realised, that apart from efforts under family planning programme, other efforts beyond family planning were also crucial for fertility control. Women's status in general and women's education in particular, were found to be the crucial factors for accelerating fertility reduction. Raising the age at marriage was also identified as important policy dimension.

The policy announced in 1975 by Dr. Karan Singh, the then Health Minister tried to capture some of these dimensions. The decision to use even in future the 1971 population figures for determining the Lok Sabha seats and for grants to states to be determined by Finance Commission was one important feature of this policy and it has long-term political implications. Though our health minister gave a slogan, 'Development is the best contraceptive' in the 1974 World Population Conference, he made a complete about turn in his policy statement by suggesting the possibility of legislation for compulsory sterilization after two or three children, if the need is felt by a state.

As is well known, this finally took a very ugly turn during the emergency period and led to some atrocities committed in the name of family planning. Instead of bringing down the birth rate, it was partly instrumental in bringing down the government. Experiences during the emergency no doubt proved to be a big setback to family planning efforts.

During the late seventies and early eighties many changes were introduced to make our population policy more broad based. Over the years, the programme had become too bureaucratic.

To take care of this aspect, and to ensure community participation, government made efforts to involve NGOs (non-government organisations) in a big way by giving grants and by having a dialogue with them to chalk out a suitable role for them. Efforts were also made to link family planning efforts with the activities of NGOs which had good income-generating programmes for women. It was also realised that mass media plays important role in bringing about change in the attitude of couples and hence efforts were made to strengthen IEC activities. Another important landmark was the adoption of National Health Policy in 1983, which emphasised the goal of health for all by 2000 A.D.

Late eighties and early nineties witnessed many developments and challenges, which created the need for a really comprehensive population policy. Targets and monetary incentives came under a lot of criticism and it was felt that not only it had led to corruption in this field, but it was also responsible for a peculiar situation i.e., couple protection rate had increased substantially but birth rate was almost stagnant, because couples accepted sterilisation at late age or after 3-4 children, so it failed to produce desired impact on fertility.

Another new dimension was the demands on population policy made by the environmental degradation caused by population growth. In order to fit into the concept of sustainable development, it was essential to adapt a policy to prevent deforestation, soil erosion and other forms of pollution.

Over the years women's organisations had also become very vocal and they rightly pointed out that women are not just child producing machines. Excessive dependence on tubectomies for meeting family planning targets is a trend, which needs to be corrected. Family planning services need to be given not in isolation but in the total context of reproductive health of women from menarche to menopause. Then the question was also raised why only women? Men's involvement in the population control effects also needs to be emphasised. It was considered all the more essential due to the new challenges posed by STD and HIV positive, infections.

Further in the context of new economic reforms, globalisation and privatisation, a concern was expressed as to whether in this process to weaker sections in general and women in particular are likely to be marginalised. It was therefore essential to ensure adequate funding for social sectors and its proper utilisation by planning from grass-root level.

Swaminathan committee appointed by the government in 1993 considered all these views and, suggested a comprehensive population policy. It was visualised to be poor-friendly environment-friendly and woman-friendly. In order to ensure community participation, the committee suggested a greater role to decentralised structure of Panchayat Raj system in the effective implementation of this policy.

It also recommended removal of all targets and emphasis on quality rather than quantity. The committee also recommended the creation of two autonomous bodies viz., Population & Social Development Commission and Population & Social Development Fund to take over most of the tasks for which Ministry of Health and Family Welfare is at present responsible.

Accepting partially the recommendations of Swaminathan committee, government has adopted a new target free RCH approach instead of earlier MCH approach. It is the outcome of plan of action adopted at Cairo International Conference on Population and Development in 1995. In this approach women's health needs are to be catered to in totality and with greater involvement of men. In this approach targets are to be replaced by goals set by functionaries themselves after assessment of community needs.

Achievements and concerns

India has made the necessary policy changes from time to time, but effective implementation upto grass-root level has always been a problem. Even then as a result of these policy changes over the years and due to the modernising influence of overall socio-economic development, India's birth rate has declined from 36.9 in 1971 to 27.2 in 1997, while death rate has declined from 14.9 in 1971 to 8.9 in 1997. As a result of rapid decline in mortality not accompanied by the equally rapid decline in fertility, the exponential growth rate for the last three decades shows only a marginal decline (2.22 to 1961-71, 2.20 for 1971-81 and 2.14 for 1981-91).

Besides this is mostly the result of fertility decline in certain states like Kerala and other states in South India which are advanced in the process of demographic transition but the progress of four large North Indian states (Uttar Pradesh, Bihar, Rajasthan and Madhya Pradesh) has been very slow. Kerala has achieved below replacement fertility as indicated by total fertility rate of 1.7 (1994). Tamil Nadu, Andhra Pradesh, Maharashtra, Punjab have reached TFR below 3, but Uttar Pradesh, Bihar, Rajasthan and Madhya Pradesh all have TFR above 4 (i.e. 5.1, 4.5 and 4.2 respectively). Their death rates (9 to 11) are not much higher than the death rates of Kerala, Maharashtra and Tamil Nadu (6 to 8). But birth rates of Uttar Pradesh, Bihar, Madhya Pradesh are in the range of 32 to 35, while those of Kerala, Tamil Nadu and Maharashtra are in the range of 17 to 25.

It is important to note that the four large North Indian states contribute more than 40 percent of India's population growth.

In such a situation, the new population policy based on RCH approach has generated different types of reactions among all those concerned about the demographic future of India. Some groups are of the opinion that the new RCH approach is just old wine in new bottle and there is no paradigm shift except the change in the nomenclature from MCH to RCH. The other extreme is the group, which believes that in adopting RCH approach, India is on the right path. Delinking of fertility reduction goals and health programs has been due for a long time. If the new program is implemented in the true spirit with effective delivery of good quality care and wide gamut of reproductive health services, it will generate the demand for contraception even without any targets. The third group welcomes the spirit of the new RCH approach but finds that implementation of this approach is much more difficult than the earlier approach. It will require far more effective monitoring and supervision at each level.

Besides, skepticism is also expressed as to whether our grass-root level functionaries are well equipped to cater to the needs of wider reproductive health program. The limitations of infrastructure, especially in those states, which are slow in the process of demographic transition, is also pinpointed as a serious constraint. There is general agreement about the need to have effective reproductive health services including treatment of RTI and STD but there is also the concern as to whether we are spreading our resources too thin and losing focus on fertility reduction.

With the impending threat of AIDS, India does not have option of concentrating only on fertility reduction. The pragmatism lies in finding out the effective mechanism for implementing, the new RCH approach with better strategies for monitoring. The effective delivery of MCH and other health services will take care of the fertility goals.

In short, the facts and figures clearly indicate that India cannot afford to be self-complacent about population prospects by taking very optimistic view as some reputed researchers suggest. India certainly has achieved substantial decline in fertility in some state but unless there is a major break through in four large North Indian states, the problem will continue to be serious. It all depends on how effectively these states implement and monitor the new Reproductive and Child Health approach.

POPULATION AND SUSTAINABLE DEVELOPMENT

The goal is shared by millions: a better life, with a higher standard of living, education, health care and economic opportunity not only for themselves today, but also for their children in future.

Today, some 1.3 billion people are living in absolute poverty. Without higher standards of living, one fifth of the world's people and their children will continue to suffer malnutrition, disease and illiteracy.

Development that can be maintained or sustained would increase standards of living without destroying the environment. Yet more population will be generated, more habitats will be destroyed, and more natural resources will be used up as the world population continues to grow.

The 20 per cent of the world's people living in the highest income countries are responsible for 86 per cent of total private consumption compared with the poorest 20 per cent, who account for only 1.3 per cent.

The richest fifth account for 53 per cent of carbon dioxide emissions, the poorest fifth, 3 per cent.

A child born in the world adds more to consumption and pollution levels in one lifetime than do 30 to 50 children born in developing countries.

Slowing the world's population growth could take some pressure off natural resources and increase the ability of countries to conserve fresh water, introduce more sustainable farming methods and reduce emissions of greenhouse gases.

Local damage is easy to see: a tropical rain forest destroyed for cattle grazing, brown haze over a city, a huge lake drained by irrigation. Global impacts are less obvious: the build up of carbon dioxide in the atmosphere, declining fish catches, the health impacts of pesticides and other chemicals. More advanced research would help identify trends and impacts. Human impact on the environment is a function of population size, per capita consumption and the environmental damage caused by the technology used to produce what is consumed.

In Asia, up to 70 per cent of the power generating capacity and 90 per cent of the cars in use in 2010 will be added between 1998 and that time. Implications for air quality are profound. Globally, atmospheric concentrations of carbon dioxide are already 28 per cent higher than pre-industrial levels; experts worry that continued increases could raise sea levels and seriously disrupt agricultural production.

A sixth of the world's land area – nearly 2 billion hectares – is now degraded as a result of overgrazing and poor farming practices. Another 16 to 20 million hectares of tropical forests and woodlands are lost each year.

Rapid population growth and poverty intensify environmental health threats. Water contaminated by feces remains one of the biggest killers worldwide, and malaria kills millions every year. Overcrowding and smoky indoor air from cooking and heating contribute to respiratory infections that kill millions more, mostly children.

Of the estimated 2.7 million deaths each year from air pollution, 2.2 million are from indoor pollution and 80 per cent of the victims are rural poor in developing countries. The poor are most exposed to fumes and polluted rivers and least able to protect themselves.

An estimated 1.1 billion people were without access to clean drinking water in 1994 and 2.8 billion people lacked access to sanitation services. Waterborne diseases infect some 250 million people each year, about 10 million of whom die.

Currently, 166 million people in 18 countries are suffering from water scarcity, while almost 270 million more in 11 additional countries water stressed.

The future scale of environmental and health problems depends on action taken today. Most farming already is unsustainable, meaning that the land can't support it forever. Methods used around the world often cause erosion, pollute waterways, and waste fresh water. Also, most of the land on Earth that can be used for growing food is already being used. Pushed by the population growth, farmers will need to find ways to raise more food on the same amount of land.

For the past 50 years, food production has kept ahead of rising demand. The future is difficult to predict since natural conditions, technology and consumption and distribution patterns are constantly changing. If countries need to purchase food to feed their population, resources may be diverted from social and economic development.

80 countries cannot produce enough food to feed their own populations from existing land and water resources.

According to FAO, world food production will have to double in order to provide food security for 7.8 billion people expected by 2005.

Each year, an estimated 5 to 7 million hectares of agricultural lands are lost to accelerating land degradation and rapid urbanization.

At the local level, women are the group most affected by environmental problems – yet women also have the most potential to create change. Equal to access to education, credit and land, and the enforcement of legal rights would not only benefit women as individuals, but also contribute to the environmental and economic well-being of their families and communities.

In every part of the developing world, rural and urban, women are primarily responsible for finding water and fuelwood and for the preparation of food. Smoke from fuelwood and dung is more dangerous to health than tobacco smoke.

In rural areas, women are often responsible for the care of livestock and for tending the crops yet they are denied ownership of these resources by law or tradition. When women have control over economic resources - whether land, income or credit – they are more likely than men to spend their earnings on food, clothes and other basic needs, as documented in examples from countries such as Bangladesh, Cote d'Ivoire, Guatemala and Sri Lanka.

NEW DIRECTIONS

Promote reproductive rights

Respect for reproductive rights is contributing to slower growth rates, which means less pressure on natural resource. With slower growth rates, countries will have more time to prepare for the still inevitable, if smaller, population increases to come.

Improve the status of women

To protect the environment and slow population growth, look towards women the group most affected by environmental degradation and also the group able to effect the greatest change. Education for girls and women, reproductive and sexual health information and services and opportunities to earn income are some of the most important areas for action.

Share environmentally sound technologies

Industrialized countries need to use existing technologies and develop new ones that minimize damage to natural systems and to make these technologies more widely available to developing countries.

Change consumer behaviour

The high consumption, high–waste lifestyle of the top learning fifth of the world's population, most of whom live in the North, cannot continue without comprising the right of the lowest-earning fifth of the world's population to satisfy their basic needs. Conservation strategies can dramatically diminish energy consumption, for example.

Reduce poverty

Poverty alleviation is crucial to long term economic and environmental sustainability. North–south cooperation is vital to success in ending absolute poverty, as are fair markets, debt reduction, aid for development and foreign direct investment. The ultimate goal is sustainability in all areas of economic activity, including agriculture, industry, forestry, fisheries, transportation and tourism.

BUIDLING AWARENESS AMONG STUDENTS: SCHOOL-BASED PROGRAMS

With more children than ever in school, these institutions are an efficient way to reach young people and their families. In the last five years alone, the number of children enrolled in primary school in developing countries has jumped by some 50 million. There is substantial evidence to show that education has a profound effect on the reproductive health of young people. An extra year of schooling for girls reduces fertility rates by 5-10 percent. Young women who are in school generally delay marriage and childbearing, which enables them to develop their decision-making and negotiating skills, self-esteem and economic earning potential.

Introducing reproductive health programs at schools can have added benefits. At relatively low cost, these programs can help prevent early pregnancy, HIV/AIDS and STDs. School staff can also refer students to local health or counseling services when appropriate. By providing reproductive health programs early, it is possible to encourage the formation of healthy sexual attitudes and practices. This is easier than changing well-established unhealthy habit later. Finally, many of the elements needed to build school-based programs already exist. Some countries have ongoing school health programs that can be expanded to include reproductive health.

School health programs vary tremendously. Building support for ARH programs among government leaders, parents and the community at large can be a challenging task. Through research and program development work conducted by the Health and Human Development Program at Education

Develop-ment Center, Inc. (EDC) the following eight factors were identified to be key in bringing about organizational change.

Vision

It is a challenge to move school administrators and teachers away from daily practices to adopt new ones. More often than not, change occurs as a result of outside pressures. A vision about the ways in which schools can improve their quality and efficiency is an important factor in galvanizing human interest and motivation.

In numerous projects directed at changing policies and practices within schools, the existence of national guidelines and the involvement of respected leaders have been primary reasons cited by state and local agencies for their participation. The World Health Organization (WHO) suggests that school health programs be introduced by a country's ministry of education in collaboration with its ministry of health.

Leadership skills

To guide planning, implementation and evaluation of a school-based program, it is important to establish a leadership team of committed individuals who have a stake in seeing their vision become a reality. This team should consist of school administrators, students, parents, teachers and community leaders.

Data are invaluable in all phases of school-based reproductive health programs. At the outset, timely data can help ensure that programs focus on the real health needs, experience, motivation and strengths of young people, rather than on problems as perceived by others. Findings from the assessments can help to frame the main objectives of the program.

It is important to consider the social norms of school practitioners—their beliefs, daily practices, and view of young people—as well as their individual responsibilities and roles. Conflicts over values and norms are likely to arise and to be in a position to respond, schools need to involve parents and community leaders in the design and delivery of programs. Parent-teacher associations, adult education classes, formal presentations, open houses, religious center activities and community group meetings are appropriate settings for fostering collaboration.

Administrative and management support

Advancing the reproductive health of young adults through schools often requires the creation of multi-disciplinary and multi-agency management structures. Clearly defined roles, responsibilities and communication channels in structures that cut across territorial boundaries and the traditional roles of agencies are an important part of the implementation process.

For innovative programs to become rooted in individual institutions—whether it is within one ministry, one school or one clinic—requires local ownership. This is often achieved through involvement and adaptation of ideas and strategies to local concerns. Few programs, if any, are truly replicated. Almost all, like evolving organisms, are adapted and thrive in a specific culture or milieu.

Implementation of any new program in schools takes at least three to five years. Patience is required in the change process. When teachers or health workers try to master new skills, there is often an initial dip in proficiency, followed by improvement and mastery. Too often policymakers, planners and evaluators attempt to measure changes as a result of innovations too early in the experiment learning phase. Dedicating adequate time and resources to the process affects the success of implementation and ultimately the impact of the program.

Eements of ARH curricula offered in schools

Students should not only receive sexuality/ reproductive health information in the classroom, but also explore their own values and attitudes to acquire the personal skills they need to maintain healthy behavior. Effective programs provide teachers with training in the use of the health curriculum. In many countries it is possible to select from existing curricula and make minor adaptations to meet locai needs. Elements of some school-based curriculum include:

By exploring and clarifying their values through debates and discussions, students are able to reflect on the implications of their sexual decisions and the attitudes and values that influence them. This clarification can help equip them with the knowledge and skills necessary to negotiate safer sex.

Many existing programs are information-based and focus on anatomy, the biology of reproduction and symptoms of STDs. This information alone rarely equips young people with the resources they require to lead healthy sexual lives. Learning activities are needed to focus on skills for responsible behavior in the context of specific reproductive health issues and to build confidence in using the behaviors.

Age and development appropriateness

Curricula that are designed as a sequence from the primary through secondary levels respect the idea that sexuality is an evolving life experience. They should be age appropriate both in content and teaching methods and take into account changing physiology and sociology.

Placement in school curricula

Strategies include (1) implementation of a separate course or unit; (2) infusion of material into core subjects taught by different teachers; (3) utilization of outside educators willing to discuss sexual matters and help students gain access to community health services; and (4) introduction of reproductive health issues through new or existing HIV/AIDS-prevention programs.

Issues in training teachers to implement ARH programs

Active, informal, personalized and participatory teaching methods have been shown to be most effect in influencing the development of attitudes and changes in sexual behavior. Learner-centered and interactive teaching methods have a positive impact on the relationship between teachers and pupils and help to improve classroom behavior, young people's enjoyment of learning, attendance rates and teachers' job satisfaction. To ensure ARH programs are successful, the following issues for training teachers should be considered:

Selection of instructors: Teachers, parents, youth, and medical and health professionals can potentially fill the role of a reproductive health educator. Not all individuals within these groups, however, are ideal candidates for the responsibility. Knowledge, skill, enthusiasm, character and ability to create trust with students are key factors.

Pre- and in-service training for teachers: Teachers can function as healthy role models, advocates for healthy school environments, gatekeepers for students in need of services, resource people for accurate information, and effective instructors. They generally need training, however, to assume these roles. A valuable means of preparing teachers is through reproductive health programs in teacher training institutions and universities. If teachers have not received this training, they should participate in extensive in-service courses, continuing education classes or intensive seminars. Teacher interest can be stimulated by involving them in planning of training sessions, paying for release time, offering continuing education units or re-certification credit, providing free materials and offering reimbursement.

Content of teacher training programs: Included in training should be a review of national and local policies; concept of the health promoting school; mechanisms for program delivery; when, how and to what extent staff should be involved in the prevention and/or early intervention of pregnancy, STD infection, and HIV/AIDS; and an understanding of behavior change principles and techniques.

Innovative learning techniques such as role plays, cooperative group activities, community involvement activities and games and case studies should also be addressed. Content should include such issues as risk factors; policies and procedures for handling sensitive matters; mechanisms for referrals to community-based services; and reassurance that classes and presentations among educators will vary. A critical component of training is to help instructors feel comfortable discussing sexual topics. There should be a mechanism for them to raise questions after they have tried out new subject matter in the classroom. Newsletters, informal get-togethers and meetings enhance their skills and relevant knowledge.

Teacher training materials: Numerous guides and materials are available to assist individual teachers, institutions and governments develop training sessions. Multinational assistance organizations provide diverse materials for appropriate for different age groups and urban, rural and remote settings. In-country ministries of health and education are also good sources for materials. Teachers and students themselves can generate teaching and learning aids.

Linking health services to school-based ARH programs

Schools can link education to services so that students may bridge knowledge and attitudes with action. School nurses and counselors can help overcome barriers that discourage young people from utilizing health centers, including lack of confidentiality, transportation, inconvenient appointment times, prohibitive costs and general apprehension about discussing personal health matters. They can help young people clarify their feelings and make responsible decisions. WHO's materials in this area have been used in more than 60 countries since 1986. There are creative ways in which schools can provide contraception to students and promote availability among community sources. Condoms can be provided in bathrooms and promoted in posters. Male and female peer promoters can distribute them to their fellow students. Ideally condom distribution should be supplemented with education and counseling.

The promotion of young people's reproductive health through a coordinated school-based approach is desirable for financial, developmental and practical reasons. By building on what is known in this field, policy and program planners can tailor specific efforts to their own cultural, economic and political realities.

Comprehensive school wide reform (CSR)

A central component of current efforts to improve schools is comprehensive school wide reform (CSR), which focuses on changing teaching and learning through school wide restructuring intended to impact all aspects of schooling. CSR models now in use around the country are demonstrating the importance of teachers' contributions both in effectively implementing a reform model and in using the model's instructional strategies to improve student achievement.

Without the wide-scale commitment and involvement of the teachers in a school, implementation of CSR will likely be slow and incomplete, affecting only a few select teachers and their students instead of the whole school. As evidence of the importance of teachers' active participation in program implementation, many programs require that at least 80 percent of the school's faculty vote for their model before they allow the school to adopt it. Teachers who share a vision that large-scale fundamental changes in school structure and classroom practice are necessary to improve student outcomes are likely to support implementation of a model, as are those who see implementation of a model as a major and permanent initiative, instead of just another passing reform.

Active participation in the choice of the whole-school reform design model to be used by their school increases teachers' commitment to the model. Teacher involvement in the selection process also increases the rate and success of CSR implementation. In fact, making teachers partners in the decision-making process from the outset creates a natural accountability that positively influences the implementation of the design and is essential to achieving successful classroom-level changes; teachers who, conversely, perceive top-down decision making are more apt to resist the restructuring effort. CSR is most successful when schools have decision-making autonomy in administration and instruction.

Good coordination of program curriculum with Federal, state, and district requirements, such as student assessments, increases a program's attractiveness to teachers. Whereas they may be supportive of the program's learning goals, teachers also need reassurance that using the model will not impede students' mastery of the skills required by state-mandated tests or prevent more basic instruction in academic skills that at-risk students need.

Conventional standardized assessments do not cover many valued student outcomes, especially those emphasized by many reform models (e.g., higher-order thinking). To determine how well a program meets its own student achievement goals, teachers can develop alternative assessments and/or can benchmark progress based on student outcomes such as higher attendance rates, lower dropout and discipline referral rates, and better student post-high school planning. In addition, many schools have obtained district waivers from traditional school requirements, but this only calls attention to the tension between standardized assessments and the curriculum and instructional methods of some CSR programs.

Teachers also prefer models that fit with the school's overall environment, staffing, and student population, and those that mesh with reforms already in process, thus increasing the coherence of the school's efforts, and requiring less change for them.

Teachers role in implementation

Schoolwide reform requires a new vision of professionalism, where teachers assume a major role and responsibility for the schools. It necessitates making fundamental changes in the way instruction is provided, and, usually, redefining roles and relationships, reconsidering allocation of control and resources, and managing conflict effectively. Implementation of the most ambitious models may extend over several years, depending on both school factors and the complexity of the model; it requires teachers to focus on multiple goals, such as governance changes, collaborative planning, and fundamental changes in curriculum and instruction.

Providing teachers with adequate resources for implementation, such as materials, professional development, and time for planning, promotes their support. Districts that give more money to schools for professional development and teacher planning tend to have better implemented CSR designs. Not only are resources important in themselves, but their allocation is a key mechanism by which teachers judge the commitment of the school's leadership to the reform. Having adequate time for all the work involved has been a consistent and primary frustration for teachers trying to implement school reforms. They need time for training, curriculum development, preparation, and planning, and for interactions with other teachers. Some teachers have, in fact, noted that time for meeting as a team was critical to the model's effectiveness.

Allocation of adequate time for implementation has been problematic in restructuring schools, however, largely because it is difficult to predict the amount of time needed to adopt a school wide reform. Most schools underestimate the extent of change and staff involvement required to implement a design fully, and, thus, the amount of time for implementation and the cost of teachers' additional work.

Professional development

Professional development is at the heart of school change efforts. Its type, level, and quality are linked to successful implementation of CSR models. The CSR model's design team needs to be actively involved at the school to address the fact that teachers in the same school vary significantly in the way and the extent that they implement the school's CSR model. The team can also promote teachers' commitment and adjustment to the implementation of the selected reform model. Team members provide training in instructional techniques; suggest new forms of interactions between parents, teachers, and students that promote cooperation and understanding; and, perhaps most important, establish collaborative opportunities for teachers.

Some models provide development through regional facilities, others rely on design team personnel visits to the local site, and still others rely primarily on written material. The quality of support and communication between the design team and individual schools affects the level of implementation and teacher support. Teachers in restructuring schools report a preference for frequent training, proximity to the design developers, and the availability of already established sites where they can observe the program in operation and receive hands-on assistance.

Professional development tailored to their specific needs is the most helpful, as are models that provide substantial information about implementation. Teachers especially want clear information about the extent of the changes required, the time that implementation will take in general, and the time required of them personally. They also support models whose design teams help them develop the capacity to envision and plan organizational change.

Instructional strategies

Some CSR models are very prescriptive and provide curricula and assessments (e.g., Success for All), while other models rely more on the school to develop materials that support the philosophy of the reform (e.g., Coalition of Essential Schools). The models which provide more prescriptive materials, curriculum, and assignments have faster implementation rates. The most effective professional development involves school wide training, facilitators, and extensive training days. Several factors facilitate the implementation of reform efforts for most teachers, including provision by the designers of a structured curriculum, concrete examples of instructional practices reflecting the reform, and specific, practical mechanisms for achieving the higher standards established as a goal. These aids are even more helpful when they take into consideration the individual needs of the school, its particular population, and the experiences of its teachers.

HOLISTIC APPROACH TO POPULATION CONTROL

India is first among the countries which adopted an official family planning programme, as early as 1950. However, fifty years later this has not prevented the population touching the one billion mark. It is obvious that despite good intentions and concerted efforts we have failed in controlling our population. Considering the seriousness of the situation it is appropriate to introspect and ascertain as to what went wrong. The problem, though very complex, can be discussed under two headings:

i) the available methods for contraception and

ii) the users.

It will be evident soon that it is much easier to discuss the former rather than the latter. It is obvious now that there cannot be an ideal contraceptive, suitable for everybody. A careful choice has to be made among the current available methods, depending on the gender, country, socio-religious and cultural practices. According to available information the most accepted methods are the two terminal methods, vasectomy in the case of the male, and tubectomy in the case of the female. These are methods of choice for all those who have completed their family size and to use them is a conscious decision made by the couple. The next most commonly used methods are the barrier methods, still popular in spite of a high failure rate.

The other methods such as the use of contraceptive pills, intrauterine devices and injectables are used by a relatively small percentage of the population. It is also evident that except for the barrier method and vasectomy there are no methods available for male contraception, in contrast to the variety of methods available and in use for the female. Does this mean that the available methods are not adequate for the requirements and this inadequacy is the reason for uncontrolled population growth? The answer is firmly in the negative.

The available methods are more than adequate but what is lacking is the will to use them. This brings in the philosophical question as to what is meant by will and why the will is not there. It is for this reason that it was mentioned earlier that the issue of the user is a complex one. The users are both male and female, and with limited options available to the male, the entire burden of limiting the family is shouldered by the female. However, except for a miniscule percentage of the female population, the majority are passive participants in the process with no decision-making capacity.

It is in this context that population control was given a new dimension, namely reproductive health, which to a large extent centres around the female. The concept of reproductive health recognizes the diversity of the special health needs of women before, during, and beyond child bearing age, as well as the needs of men and the quality of life of the people involved. Considering this new emphasis, it is evident that population control programmes and reproductive health go hand in hand and are interdependent.

Why was there a shift to reproductive health from the much-advertised Family Planning Programme? As mentioned earlier the success of Family Planning is closely linked with the reproductive health of the woman. To quote the words of eminent clinical endocrinologist and reproductive biologist Dr S Roy: "Reproductive health includes human health, safe motherhood, women's development, child health and development, adolescent sexuality, adolescent education and health, effective choices of family planning prevention and management of reproductive disorders, infertility, STD's, genetic disorders and reproductive health care of the aged person". Dr Roy's statement needs to be considered carefully as it has been seen that unless each aspect is taken care of there cannot be a successful family planning programme. It has been well documented that several factors influence reproductive health of women starting from their health during infancy, childhood, adolescent nutritional status and status in the family.

It is common knowledge that despite claims of progress in the nation the girl child is still neglected in many communities; the opportunities for education and medical care are unsatisfactory and these have resulted in adverse effects on the general health and well-being of women. It needs to be emphasized that an important factor which has considerable influence on woman's reproductive health, is the age at which the first child is born.

In spite of all the laws that exist girls are still married much earlier than the stipulated age and this has an adverse effect on physical development; they are exposed to the risks of teen-age pregnancy, for which they are not prepared both psychologically and mentally. As a consequence of repeated childbirth, they are exposed to a very high risk of ill health and death.

The consequences of early pregnancy are the increases in female mortality and morbidity, which are very high in India. This is because of lack of adequate facilities for child birth as more than 20% of deliveries are carried out at home by untrained or inadequately trained personnel. Further, in cases of unwanted pregnancies, there are no facilities for safe abortion.

The most ideal situation would be that every pregnancy is a planned one with every child being cared for. It is essential to recognize that an unwanted pregnancy is a specific health risk for women and their families. It can not be over emphasized that problems of street children or children who are begotten out of unwanted or unplanned pregnancy may result in neglected or abandoned children who may also have to face family violence.

It should also be noted that in spite of all the regulations, there are several practices which hinder the overall development of women. Female infanticide is a still a common practice; there is a high dropout rate of girls from school. Women are discriminated against right from the cradle to the grave and even before they are born.

Due to the preference for a male child, technologies like amniocentosis are used for sex determination followed by female infanticide. To quote Dr Roy again: "Women's health cannot be improved and maternal morbidity and mortality cannot be significantly reduced without the overall development of the women. The status of woman in the society reflects the status of the nation. Women are important change agents for development".

A closely linked problem with women's health, development, and empowerment is the problem of child health, child survival and child development. The cumulative consequence of an early pregnancy, child bearing at an young age, the lack of decision-making capacity and unsafe abortions, is the high rate of child death, be it during pregnancy or later.

High rates of child death also result in high birth rates, leading to a vicious cycle associated with rapid population growth and increase in maternal mortality and morbidity. The child who survives in spite of the odds develops into a child with poor health, is malnourished, and often, is unwanted. When children reach adolescence - a very critical stage in human development - the lack of information an adolescence and sex education - results in children who display deviant behaviours. If not corrected at the right time, the problems of juvenile delinquency could result in these children.

It is evident from the discussion above, that the central point in this is the woman's health, be it general health or reproductive health. This is possible only when she has the opportunity for education, which will provide her with a decision-making capacity, which is the key to the rest of her development and future. Coming back to the question with which we started, what is wrong with our population control programme is that unless the status of women in society is improved there is no hope of curtailing our population growth.

The woman alone should decide what method to choose, when to choose and how many children she wishes to have. Her status in society is the key to the success of the population control programme in India. Having identified the problem, the obvious question to ask is what is the solution? Are we in such a situation that there is no hope? With the population crossing the one billion mark and birth the rate hovering around 3%, the situation is still grim. It should be noted that although 89% of the people favour the use of contraceptives, only 45% account for actual users. Thus more than 50% of the people have yet to be covered with the available methods. As mentioned earlier, the educational status of women and the age at which they are married has a direct relationship to compliance with contraceptive usage.

Considering the present rates of maternal morbidity and child survival, these fears are justified. However, it should be possible to educate people about other effective methods like copper IUD, oral pills, injectables and steroid hormonal contraceptives. Finally, there is still no effective method for male contraception other than vasectomy, which is a terminal method. Thus there is an urgent need to develop newer, more effective, suitable methods of contraception for the male.

The key to the successful implementation of the family planning programme is the effective communication skill of providers who motivate potential users. The job of the field worker will be much easier if he or she can convince people that contraception is a better option than the risks faced due to repeated pregnancy.

Considering the large percentage of illiteracy in rural areas, there is an urgent need to improve the literacy rates particularly that of the women. There is also an immediate need to improve the conditions of primary health care centres, which are the nodal points for any reproductive health activity.

Due to the lack of basic as well as transportation facilities in case of emergencies, thousands of patients particularly women and newborn children die following delivery or unsafe abortion and even dehydration in the case of children.

A national consensus has to be arrived at to uplift the facilities of the primary health care centres so that maternal and child mortality is reduced, if not totally prevented. It has been well documented that the uncertainty of child survival is the one reason which drives people to have more children as a means of security for old age in India. India's population growth is a cause of worry, but the problem is not one without solutions. But regulations will not help solve the problem.

The sense of responsibility should come from within every individual. While the educated male should change his attitude towards his female counterpart, granting her the dignity which is due to her, there is also an urgent need to change the status of the millions of underprivileged, illiterate women who are discriminated. Unless they are involved in the decisionmaking process, there is little hope for the future.

11

Pilot Activities in Population Education

This chapter reviews a series of pilot activities in population education in nine countries of Latin America, Africa and Asia under the inter-regional project: "Integration of Population Education into Programmes for Out-of-School Rural Youth". The objective is to identify project strengths and weaknesses and to draw lessons from the diverse country experiences, which can strengthen future FAO work in the area of population education.

BACKGROUND

"I wish I would have had the opportunity to participate in the training on reproductive health as a teenager, rather than learning about sex the hard way at the street comer", said a 21-year old woman at the launching of the FAO/UNFPA population education programme for 50 young men and women youth leaders in Ascencion de Guarayos, Bolivia. In Bolivia, like in many other developing countries, population education initiatives for young men and women in rural areas are few and far between, despite the fact that lowering fertility rates is a stated priority in terms of government policy for most countries that participated in this inter-regional project.

Despite substantial achievements in lowering fertility rates and limiting population growth during the past decades, significant differences in fertility rates between urban and rural areas persist, with substantially higher fertility rates in rural areas. In Peru, for example, rural fertility rates at 5.6 are still twice as high as urban fertility rates at 2.8.

Even more significantly, perhaps, the highest fertility rates are reported for disadvantaged groups working in agriculture (6.0), particularly those without access to formal education. In fact, in many cultures, young women are still encouraged to marry and have children early in life, despite the serious health, socio-economic and demographic consequences of adolescent childbearing.

In several countries in Asia and the Pacific, rapid socio-economic development is resulting in a delay in age at marriage and thus in a growing pool of unwed teenagers, according to a recent study on Adolescent Reproductive Behaviour in the Asian and Pacific Region. This trend may contribute to an increase in the risk of transmission of sexually transmitted diseases and in unwanted pregnancies and single motherhood. The study further points out that most countries lack the information needed for appropriate policy and programme responses to these issues and recommends the collection of data not only from married women, as is currently done, but also from unmarried teenagers and young women, regarding their sexual behaviour, contraceptive practices, pregnancy and childbearing. In addition, as Governments may be reluctant to provide contraceptive services to youths, innovative strategies to reach sexually active young men and women are becoming all the more urgent.

Rural-to-urban migration is yet another problem in many of the pilot countries, with far-reaching implications for population education programmes. In Thailand, many young men and women migrate from rural to urban areas before the age of 25 and become exposed to risks and conditions for which they are ill-prepared. Population education could contribute to easing this transition from rural to urban life. The examples above highlight the growing need for population policies and for information, education and communication (IEC) strategies targeted to youth in rural areas.

Population education is particularly critical for adolescents, who begin making decisions about their sexuality and about education, migration and other demographically relevant choices, and are increasingly exposed to risks, such as teenage pregnancy, STDs, HIV/AIDS, etc. Information and educational programmes on population issues are particularly relevant for young men and women in rural areas who do not attend school or drop out at an early age, and therefore do not have access to school-based population education nor to adult population education information.

Population education is defined in the FAO population education leader guides as a "learning process that enables people to understand how rapid population growth affects their quality of life or standard of living. The goal of population education is to give people enough information to be able to make responsible decisions about family size in a way that is personally meaningful and socially relevant."

In many developing countries, up to 70% of the young people between the ages of 15 and 25 live in rural areas with few primary schools and poorly qualified teachers. Of those that do attend school, 30% drop out during the first few years. In some regions of the world, as few as 10% of the children continue their education beyond primary school. Of that 10%, less than one-tenth finish secondary school. According to UNESCO statistics, there are between 130 and 150 million out-of-school youth worldwide. These numbers are increasing, not falling. Over two-thirds of these out-of-school youth are girls and young women.

For the purpose of planning population IEC programmes, youth is usually divided into an in-school and an out-of-school cohort. While in many countries population education has been introduced in formal school curricula, the means with which to reach out-of-school youth are still not as developed. The lessons learned from this inter-regional project may contribute to the development of appropriate strategies for methodological approaches and institutional channels.

PROJECT OBJECTIVES, TARGFT GROUP AND STRATEGY

The inter-regional project was designed with the long-term objective

> "...to have institutionalized the process of bringing population education to rural youth and young farmers so that these young men and women will have the opportunity to understand the effects of rapid population growth and be in a position to make informed decisions about family size and responsible parenthood."

Out-of-school rural youths (ranging from 15 to 24 years of age) were identified as the priority audience of the pilot population education activities for the reasons outlined above.

The-project strategy was premised on a set of population education prototype materials. designed for use by the leaders of rural youth groups in an earlier population education project (INT/88/P98: "Integration of Population Education into Programmes for Rural Youth in Low Income Countries"). It was foreseen that through this inter-regional project, these prototype materials would be introduced to new settings, with the necessary adaptation to different cultural backgrounds and translation into local languages. Population education for out-of-school rural youth would thus be introduced in participating organizations and countries and the strategies and materials would be disseminated widely.

The above-mentioned leader guides translate abstract concepts, such as national growth rate, population density and dependency ratio, into terms that are relevant to rural young men and women their families and their communities. Young people learn about family planning methods within the wider context of population change as it relates to agricultural, environmental, health, nutrition and community development issues.

The main channels used by INT/92/P94 to make non-formal education and training in population Responsible Parenthood education accessible to out-of-school rural youth were governmental organizations, such as agricultural extension services and young farmer programmes, and non-governmental youth organizations, such as Boy Scouts, Girl Guides and 4-H groups, the YMCA/YWCA, religious organizations, etc.

The project operated on an inter-regional basis from FAO Headquarters in Rome, initially in close collaboration with the FAO Advisors of the UNFPA Regional Teams in Harare and Addis Ababa. Most of the pilot activities in the nine countries were developed by FAO Rome in collaboration with national partner organizations. The operational instruments for setting up pilot activities were direct allotments to FAO Representatives in Ethiopia, Zimbabwe and China and "Letters of Agreement" between FAO and Ministries of Agriculture or national youth organizations in all other countries. The project did not include a Chief Technical Advisor or equivalent long-term expert, as the coordination of project activities was carried out by FAO Agricultural Extension and Education Service staff.

The project document had foreseen a number of regional and sub-regional meetings to introduce the leader guides and to develop pilot activities for field testing and for the adaptation of project strategies to local conditions. A regional meeting took place in 1994 in the Philippines, financed under the FAO Technical Cooperation Programme. This meeting gave Asian countries participating in the pilot activities the opportunity to exchange ideas, discuss bottlenecks and highlight successful project components. In particular, the workshop focused on preliminary pilot experiences and assisted the country teams in the development of pilot programmes or follow-up proposals. Even though originally foreseen, regional planning meetings and workshops for the exchange of experiences, other than the above-mentioned workshop in the Philippines, did not take place for operational reasons, as the project came to a close before participating countries had completed pilot activities.

According to the project document, inter-regional activities would be considered complete once the materials and programme strategies were adopted by institutions at the regional and national level. Follow-up activities at the national level would then be required to expand the programmes, utilizing country level resources. Assistance from the UNFPA country programmes was mentioned in the project document as a potential source for the further expansion of pilot activities.

TERMS OF REFERENCE

The Rural Youth Population Education Consultant will be responsible for the documentation of the impact of INT/92/P94 in participating countries, and the collection and synthesis of all related reports and financial records of the project. This will involve international travel to selected countries in direct support of project activities in Asia, Africa and Latin America.

Specific duties include:

1. Write a report documenting the impact of all INT/92/P94 project activities based on a synthesis of country progress/final reports, including lessons learned, successes and failures. An in-depth study will be carried out on rural youth population education activities under INT/92/P94 in one country of each of the three regions of Asia, South America and Africa.

2. Over the course of the consultancy, write several briefs (maximum one page) on significant accomplishments and/or points of interest related to the implementation of INT/92/P94 for circulation to UNFPA, New York, Country Support Teams and Country Programmes through the Office of the FAO Population Programme Coordinator.

3. To the extent possible, work towards the continued involvement of UNFPA Country Directors and Regional UNFPA Support Teams in project implementation and assessment of progress towards the goal of incorporating a rural youth population education component into UNFPA Country Programmes as a follow-up to this inter-regional project.
4. Design a monitoring and evaluation system for the implementation of future activities.
5. Carry out other duties related to INT/92/P94 as requested.

EVALUATION PROCEDURES AND METHODS

The assessment of the pilot activities presented below seeks to bring into sharp focus the relevance, long-term impact and sustainability of population education for out-of-school rural youth. To this effect, the consultant viewed his role as an intermediary between those participating in project implementation at the grassroots level and those involved in executing and funding the pilot activities. In other words, this evaluation has attempted to go beyond a mere analysis of inputs, outputs and immediate impact of the said activities. Such a limited focus would not reflect the diversity of the pilot activities in terms of the critical role of the institutional context and the socio-cultural environment.

ANALYSIS OF THE PROJECT APPROACH & OF PILOT ACTIVITIES

This section analyses methodological and operational issues related to the implementation of the inter-regional project. The purpose is to identify successful elements and bottlenecks of the population education approach and of the implementation modalities used by INT/92/P94 to stimulate discussion within youth programmes, FAO and UNFPA, as well as among these organizations to further develop population education concepts and programmes.

Population education in the leader guides and in the pilot training activities followed an integrated approach in that:

1. it was of an interdisciplinary nature, integrating concepts from demography, ecology, biology, economics, sociology, agriculture and nutrition;

2. issues dealt with in the leader guides, such as population growth and production, natural resources or migration, and sex education and parenthood were accompanied by the imparting of life skills (e. g. negotiation, decision-making, and leadership skills);

3. information and education on population issues was combined with practical activities (e g. tree planting, soil conservation, income generating projects) that were directly relevant to the lives of rural young men and women;

4. socio-economic phenomena, such as population growth-induced changes in agricultural production systems, environmental degradation and socio-demographic changes in rural communities were related to reproductive health and family planning issues.

This approach had the following advantages:

— By dealing with less sensitive issues first (such as agriculture and the environment), participants "warmed up" and got acquainted with each other. This created a favourable environment for discussing sex education and family planning at a later stage, described by trainers and trainees as "sensitive subjects".

— By discussing reproductive health and family planning in the context of socio-economic changes at the community level, the interrelationship between individual behaviour and quality of life was highlighted.

— The integrated approach to population education stimulated the interest of the youth who participated in the pilot activities. In Bolivia, for example, initially, registration for

> a population education training course in Guarayos was slow. Once the organizers, however, produced a poster highlighting the integrated training approach and advertising sessions on agriculture, the environment, income, nutrition, health family and family size, etc., within a few days, many more youths came to register than the course could train.

Youth leader training sessions in Bolivia will involve services of local resource institutions, such as the "Asociación Ecológica del Oriente", the "Colegio de Ingenieros Agrónomos", the "Escuela de Padres", the "Hospital de Guarayos" and the "Dirección Distrital de Educación." Thus the population education pilot activity intends to introduce the concept of population education not only among youth leaders, but also among several local institutions with an educational mandate. The Bolivia pilot activity is, therefore, pioneering a programme approach, enhancing mobilization of community and district level resources.

In Ethiopia, "the most exciting and appealing part of the population education programme, according to the young people who have participated in the project, has been taking part and planning and carrying out income generating activities decided upon by each group, " according to the training consultant of the project. The rationale for making income-generation part of the population education curriculum arose from the training modules on "Population and Agriculture" and "Population, Employment and Income."

Integrating population education with income-generating activities takes into account the particular circumstances faced by youths that are not able to attend school. "One of the most pressing issues for out-of-school youth is their lack of resources. Many do not attend school because they either lack the financial means to pay school fees or because they need to work to support themselves or their families" said the FAO Population Advisor in China, underscoring that "population education for youths outside the school system needs to serve the self-interest of young men and women".

The need for income-generating activities was also expressed in Zimbabwe. However, in this case, as training resources were spread over six different organizations, sufficient funds were not made available to set up practical projects for the youth at the village level. A leader of the Boy Scouts pointed out this constraint as follows: "In the modules, there are proposals for practical activities and for income-generating projects. However, without funding we cannot develop them with the youth."

The pilot activity in Ethiopia was implemented during a period of profound political and institutional change. The Ministry of Agriculture, which was the implementing agency, had to rely on its extension workers to create ad hoc youth groups. One of the major achievements of the population education pilot activity under these difficult circumstances was the official recognition of the need for a National Young Farmers Programme, which - once established - could serve as one of the channels for the implementation of the National Population Plan of Action.

In conclusion, the variety of themes and topics of the FAO population education curriculum stimulated discussion and a useful exchange of ideas among youths. In some countries, e. g. Bolivia, the integrated character of the population education curriculum led to a programme approach, involving various types of local resource institutions (schools, hospitals, agricultural research and education institutions) in population education training at the community level. The lessons of this innovative approach to population education should be closely monitored and documented vis-a-vis the traditional focus of working with youth organizations alone. In addition, the integration of population education and income-generating activities was found to be an effective mechanism for meeting the immediate needs of out-of school rural youth.

However, it should be noted that while project pilot activities were based on a conceptual framework with holistic population parameters, the FAO definition of population education in the leader guides lagged behind. Therefore, the FAO definition of population education as used in the leader guides needs to be revised to encompass - in addition to population growth - other population parameters (fertility, mortality, migration) that affect the quality of rural life (production and income levels, nutrition and food security, and health).

INSTITUTIONALISATION OF POPULATION EDUCATION

As stated above, the project's long-term objective was "to have institutionalized the process of bringing population education to rural youth and young farmers ". Special attention was thus paid on reaching "out-of-school" rural youth. The strategy for institutionalisation was based on three components:

— *Training*: national youth programme staff and volunteer leaders receiving training in population education concepts and in the use of the FAO population education leader guides;

— *Adaptation*: revising and translating the population education leader guides into local languages; and

— *Integration*: making the population education curriculum a part of the organization's own programme.

The project worked with non-formal youth programmes of government extension services (Ethiopia, Thailand, Indonesia), as well as non-governmental youth organizations (Bolivia, Colombia, Vietnam). In most countries, project activities were organized by only one organization, but in Zimbabwe, the arrangements were made with an NGO Umbrella Organization and training activities were carried out by six different youth organizations. In Peru, the pilot activity was jointly organized by the "Consejo Regional de Población" (CONAPO) at the local level, with technical support from the 'Universidad Peruana Cayetano Heredia (UPCH)".

Institutional networks to reach out-of-school rural youth differed significantly from country to country. The Vietnamese Youth Federation, for example, was described as having "an excellent network throughout the country with which to reach rural youth", while the pilot activity in Bolivia did not have an existing institutional network for out-of-school youth in rural areas. Some of the institutions had an explicit mandate to work in rural areas (such as Agricultural Extension Services) while others did not distinguish in their mandate between urban and rural youth (YMCA, YWCA, Scouts, etc.).

Given the differences in the number, role, and capacity of the participating institutions, the institutionalisation of population education received a different emphasis and was hampered by different constraints in the various pilot projects.

The three elements of the institutionalisation strategy - training, material adaptation and integration of the training curriculum - have been used to integrate population education in school curricula on many occasions. Under INT/92/P94, these strategic steps were applied to integrate population education into the programmes of non-formal youth organizations with the following results:

— The leader guides have been translated and adapted to local conditions in Peru (Spanish), Ethiopia (Amharic), China (Chinese), Vietnam (H'mong). Modified versions are still expected from Colombia and Bolivia (Spanish), Thailand (Thai) and Indonesia (Bahasa).

— "The Boys Brigade" in Zimbabwe prepared a draft booklet on "Population Education for the Boys Brigade of Zimbabwe" based on the FAO Leader Guides. Population Education has also been included into regular training activities, for which club members earn badges.

— The Vietnamese Youth Federation, with FAO and UNESCO assistance, developed an additional leader guide on HIV/AIDS and Drug Use - both of which were identified as important risks for youth. This shows how the pilot activities stimulated youth organizations to develop their own educational priorities within the population education framework. The new booklet could serve as prototype material and stimulate discussion among youth on HIV/AIDS and drugs issues in other countries as well.

A large number of cooperating organizations pointed out problems in continuing population education training activities beyond the pilot phase. The institutionalisation of the population education curriculum was hampered by financial, institutional, operational and conceptual obstacles. For example: The National Coordinator of YMCA in Zimbabwe pointed out: "Our programmes depend to a large degree on funds that we receive for carrying out specific projects for various donors, while our core funds are quite limited. With the small amount of unrestricted funds that we have, it was not possible to continue with training in population education after the funds from the pilot activities were exhausted." He further underscored: "The population education booklets alone are not sufficient to carry out population education. If you want a resource person (e. g. a nurse) to assist in the training and you take him/her away from other duties, you need to pay for his/her services."

Similarly, most youth organizations pointed out that after the leader guides were adapted to local conditions, for population education to continue funds would still be required for:

— the transport of trainers and monitoring staff to the training location;

— honoraria for resource persons;

— printing and distribution of additional materials on new topics such as HIV/AIDS (Peru), Population and Forests (Bolivia, Vietnam), Population and Culture (Zimbabwe);

— materials and resources required for practical activities as proposed in the leader guides (e.g. tree planting, income-generating activities, etc.).

In view of the lack of viable non-formal educational programmes for rural youth, the pilot activity in Bolivia is being organized in close collaboration with the school system. "We will explore ways in which the formal school system can take on responsibilities for work with out-of-school -youth", said the director of the Associacion Cristiana Feminina. The lessons to be learned from the Bolivia experience might point to new channels for the institutionalisation of population education into on-going youth programmes.

Lack of control and ownership of grass roots organizations over the pilot process may have also hampered the institutionalisation of population education into on-going youth programmes in some countries. This was expressed by the director of NANGO in Zimbabwe:

> "The funding of the pilot activity should have left us with more freedom in shaping the process. There was not enough time and resources to systematically look into the feasibility of the pilot activities and to familiarize the participating youth organizations with the concept. The task was to test the booklets in a certain time and it was sometimes difficult to move according to the pace of the various institutions."

In conclusion, the following issues need to receive attention in the planning of future activities:

a) *Institutional Capacity*: Institutionalization requires a minimum of resources on the part of partner organizations. Therefore, an assessment and an analysis of available resources and of resource constraints is necessary, if appropriate, institution-specific strategies for institutionalisation are to be developed. Such an assessment would need to consider:

   — the ability of partner institutions to reach out-of-school youth on a continuous basis;

   — the capacity to carry out activities with the organization's own human, financial and technical resources and/or the ability to mobilize the necessary resources from elsewhere; and

— the ability of an organization and its members to draw a long-term benefit from the activities.

b) *Methodology*: The methodology used for pilot activities needs to systematically build ownership on the part of the cooperation partner. This could, for example, be achieved by building each pilot activity on the findings of a training needs assessment and by developing educational materials in-country accordingly.

c) *Time*: The duration of the pilot activities, and, in particular, the timing of fund allocation needs to be adapted to the requirements of the partner organizations.

In addition, in transfering the concept of institutionalisation from school-based (formal) to non-school-based (non-formal) educational systems, the considerable differences between these systems need to be taken into account.

Table 1 highlights some of the characteristics of school-based and non-school-based educational systems. This is only a rudimentary framework, however, primarily aiming to stimulate discussion on institutionalisation in out-of-school contexts. Table 1 shows that the institutionalisation of an educational process in a non-formal setting is likely to be more difficult and complex than it would be in a school-based system.

For instance, volunteer leaders in non-formal systems, who are often former youth group members, provide less continuity to educational activities than school teachers who are permanent staff. In addition, resource constraints and the dependency on short-term donor allocations for specific projects are obstacles to long-term planning for out-of-school activities. Lastly, as youths participate in non-formal programmes on a voluntary basis, their mobilization is more difficult than it is in schools where attendance is obligatory.

Table 1: School-Based (Formal) and Non-School-Based (Non-Formal) Education Characteristics

	Formal Education Systems	Non-Formal Education Systems
Staff	civil servants NGOs) (could be civil	partly volunteers (e. g. in servants in government extension systems)
	long-term/permanent	short- to medium-term (particularly in NGOs and projects)
Participation	obligatory	voluntary
Coverage	national	national or local
Financial resources	government dependent	donor or project dependent
Learning Materials	standardized	purpose-oriented

These significant differences in the characteristics of formal versus non-formal education imply that the strategies used for the institutionalisation of population education in school systems may not be appropriate for non-formal educational systems. This was, for example, pointed out by the Population Advisor of the FAO/UNFPA Women, Population and Development Programme and Organizer of INT/92/P94 pilot activity in China, who said: "We cannot assume that we have a college structure out there in which we can integrate population messages as if we were in a classroom".

Pilot activities also showed that the term "out-of-school rural youth" is not specific enough to design effective IEC strategies. 'O'-level school leavers who participated in the pilot activity in Zimbabwe, for example, found the population education leader guides "too shallow". In Vietnam, the leader guides had "too much text and too few illustrations" for illiterate youths. Therefore, the target group "out-of-school rural youth" needs to be further specified and defined in terms of the social, economic, political and demographic realities of each country. A clarification of what is meant by "out-of-school rural youth" and a further conceptualization of strategies for reaching out-of-school youth would need to include the following variables:

— *Age and Education*: Out-of-school rural youth could include children not enrolled in school despite the fact that they may be of school age (e. g. 10-14-year-old school drop-outs), or adolescents that do not go to school because they have already finished a first school. These two categories constitute different target groups that may require different IEC strategies.

— *Employment Status*: The employment status of out-of-school rural youth needs to be specified. Are young men and women employed in the formal sector considered out-of-school youths, or does the definition only include those working in the informal sector or those not working at all?

— *Gender*: In some cultures, the term "youth" comprises only young males. To avoid discrimination, a clear target group definition would need to explicitly refer to young men and women. This is particularly important in view of the fact that in many developing countries girls/young women drop out of school at an earlier age or grade than boys/young men.

In terms of communication channels, out-of-school approaches usually imply that education takes place outside the school system. However, the dividing line between formal and informal education systems is often not clear cut. For example, some non-governmental youth organizations, such as boy scouts or girl guides in Zimbabwe, work with out-of-school youth in organized clubs. Some of these clubs may meet on school campuses, club members may be school pupils, volunteer leaders may be school teachers, and club activities may be extracurricular school activities.

Some youth organizations, such as boy scouts, girl guides, YMCA, YWCA, girls brigades and boys brigades traditionally catered for the children of the middle and upper classes. In Zimbabwe, for example, until 1980, only white young men could be members of YMCA. Consequently, some youth organizations may not necessarily target those without access to population education in school. Purely educational programmes may result in targetting those youth who already have access to school-based education.

As mentioned above, integrating population education into activities that serve the self-interest of youths - which for most out-of-school rural youth are likely to be activities from which they can derive immediate or short-term economic benefit - may be the most viable channel for reaching out-of-school youth. The potential of having community-based programmes or rural development projects serve out-of-school youth may not have been fully exploited by the interregional project. The FAO Representative in Bolivia, for example, stated that different types of FAO projects could integrate programmes and activities for rural youth, including population education, once the necessary support infrastructure for such components was in place.

To conclude, despite the keen interest for population education created through the pilot activities of the inter-regional project, preliminary findings from the field assessment show that short-term project funding has not been sufficient to sustain the integration of population education into non-formal educational programmes for rural youth. The concept of institutionalisation has not proved to be transferable from a formal to a non-formal educational setting, due to considerable differences in the resource base, staff and membership between school- and non-school based educational structures. Future population education activities would need to be based on an assessment of the institutional capacity of youth organizations in catering for out-of-school rural youth on a long-term basis.

Alternatives to short-term pilot activities in population education could include:

a) a concerted long-term effort on the part of donors to collaborate with youth organizations in order to strengthen national institutional capacity and integrate population education into these larger efforts; and

b) an identification of alternative channels and strategies for reaching out-of-school rural youth, such as rural and community development programmes.

FRAMEWORK FOR IMPLEMENTING THE INT/92/P94 PILOT PROJECT

1. Form National Implementation/Training Teams composed of a project coordinator, a training/volunteer leader development specialist and monitoring and an evaluation specialist.
2. Form a Rural Youth Advisory Committee to monitor activities, offer suggestions for strengthening the implementation of recommended strategies for follow-up and the institutionalisation of population education into rural youth programmes
3. Plan, carry out and evaluate national train-the-trainers workshop, which may have the following components:
   - review and revise text and illustration of the leader guides;
   - effective volunteer leadership development;
   - educational methodology for the incorporation of population education into ongoing rural youth programme activities;
   - concept of population education and its relevance for the needs of the country; and
   - use of the FAO leader guides as a pan of a comprehensive population education programme for rural youth.
4. Make revisions as needed, translate and print leader guides. Train volunteer leader, who should develop strategies of how to use the leader guides. Under guidance of volunteer leaders, youth groups should go through a series of at least

ten sessions over a period of six to nine month. Carry out mid-term evaluation.

5. For monitoring and evaluation the following should be present: evaluation of knowledge attitude and practices through pre- and post testing measures. Evaluation should include the following steps: review, discuss and document lessons learned, suggest revisions in leader guides, assess and document the value of the materials effectiveness in the educational process. Strategies for the institutionalisation of the use of the FAO population education materials and those monitoring progress of project activities should be developed.

THE TRAINING PROCESS

Training of professional trainers, youth leaders and youth in population education issues and in the use of the population education leader guides was a key component of all the pilot activities.

Within this broad framework, the implementation of the pilot activities differed significantly from country to country, particularly in terms of the role and function of the training participants, the training location, the subject matter content, and the intensity of the training at various stages of the training-of-trainers cycle.

The leader guide series contains a section on what to consider when using a resource person in training. However, the series does not provide any further guidance on how to set up a (pilot) training programme. In addition, as there was no common training for the national project implementation teams prior to the pilot activities, the capacity, skills and experience of the national project teams became the key determinants of the quality of the pilot process and account for the differences in the effectiveness of the various country pilot programmes.

Implementation team members pointed out that detailed guidelines on pilot project implementation would have been useful, particularly in reference to:

— how to organize a pilot project implementation team, including terms of reference, team member qualifications, and time requirements (full-time versus part-time staffing);

— how to carry out participatory training needs and resource assessments, including the use of tools such as Knowledge, Attitude and Practice surveys, Participatory Rural Appraisal, socio-economic investigations, etc.;

— how to select participants at the level of training of trainers and youth leaders and how to establish selection criteria (age, gender, education, etc.);

— how to mobilize local resource institutions and build linkages to related country level programmes;

— how to elaborate needs assessment-based training curricula;

— how to monitor and evaluate pilot activities and how to document the results of the pilot training and testing; and

— how to mobilize resources at the country level for mainstreaming population education within youth organizations.

Drawing on the experience of the project implementation teams of INT/92/P94, such guidelines for setting up pilot activities efficiently and effectively could be developed through an exchange of lessons learned in regional workshops for Asia, Africa and Latin America, as originally foreseen in the project document. In fact, most of the organizers were looking forward to and were expecting such an opportunity for exchange. However, due to the limited flexibility in funding and implementation procedures, it appears that these final workshops are not likely to take place.

The majority of partner organizations suggested a thorough review of the training-of-trainers model used in the project. A typical training sequence, for example, in Vietnam, included three steps:

a) a trainer workshop for youth organization field staff;

b) training of community volunteer leaders through trained field staff; and

c) local leaders using the population education leader guides with youth groups.

The role of training and the importance given to each of the three levels of training varied considerably from country to country. Some partner institutions placed a high emphasis on the training-of-trainers effect. In Zimbabwe, for example, only 18 master trainers were trained in the national workshops, but through the involvement of six different youth organizations, some 1000 youths in total were sensitized in population education issues during the exercise.

In other countries, emphasis was placed on reaching a relatively large number of trainees with high quality training in the first training session. In Peru, for instance, 71 young men and women from 43 communities and various districts were trained in the first workshops, while the total number of youth reached in the exercise is estimated at 500.

The experience of the pilot activities suggests that training-of-trainers involved trade-offs between the number of youth reached and the quality of the training. The first level of training in a training-of-trainers exercise was reported to be of higher quality than subsequent trainings carried out by trained trainers. This was expressed by a trainee in Zimbabwe as follows:

"While we as master trainers received quality training, we need to keep in mind that we could not give the same quality of training that we received to the youth leaders. Most of them received only one day of training". Another leader said: "Some of the trainers just took the booklets and read them to the youth. And then they called this a workshop."

Similar concern was expressed in Ethiopia about the viability of using a training-of-trainers approach. The final report states: "Any future project would have to ensure that the group leaders involved in population education would receive the full training. It does not seem that the development agents [extension workers who were trained as master trainers] will, with some exceptions, carry out this population education training properly."

In Vietnam, where the entire training process was organized tightly within a period of less than three months, national and provincial monitoring and evaluation officers participated in training at the community level and recorded results and experiences. In many other countries, however, monitoring and evaluation of the activities of trained trainers at the community level was hampered by logistical and financial constraints.

Due to the absence of an institutional network for reaching out-of-school rural youth, the pilot activity in Bolivia placed less emphasis on training-of-trainers. The national project implementation team organized the pilot activities as a community level seminar series in population education. Given the above limitations of the training-of-trainers approach, community level training of youth may be an alternative to training youth organization field staff alone, particularly in areas with weak institutional networks. However, the impact and cost implications of such an alternative approach would need to be examined in detail.

In conclusion, training was a crucial component in the implementation of pilot activities. While through a training-of-trainers approach a relatively large number of youth was reached at low cost, the quality of training was not in all cases satisfactory. Alternatively, direct community level training, particularly in areas with weak institutional infrastructure for youth work, is worth exploring as an alternative strategy. For future pilot exercises, detailed guidelines on how to organize pilot training would need to be developed, building upon the experience of INT/92/P94 country implementation teams.

THE ROLE OF THE LEADER GUIDES

The FAO population education leader guides, developed under the earlier inter-regional population education project INT/88/P98, were designed to enable youth leaders to carry out structured learning activities with existing youth groups, incorporating population messages into topics of interest to youth.

As pointed out earlier, the definition of population education in the leader guides needs to be revised, on the basis of the experience and lessons learned from the pilot activities, highlighting the rural-specific components of population education.

The leader guides constituted the backbone of pilot training activities. By translating the guides and adapting them to local conditions, youth organizations were brought into contact with population education issues. As mentioned above, the Boys Brigade in Zimbabwe adopted the booklets using its own institutional cover and format. The Vietnamese Youth Federation describes the booklets "as an effective technical instrument that can provide helpful service for the youth cadres to carry out the social tasks in compliance with their function of mass mobilization."

Introducing and reviewing the booklets stimulated discussion even among organizations that decided not to adopt population education as part of their mandate. The National Catholic Youth Council in Zimbabwe participated in the review of the population education leader guides, but subsequently decided not to take part in the pilot activities. The proceedings of the meeting highlight the sensitive nature of population education:

> "Since there is expected exhaustion of land resources what actually should be done? Isn't there an underlying premise that the future series of the leader guides will introduce "the pill" for example thereby exhorting people to use family planning? So, already we expect some debate between the priests, nuns and youth."

The process of revising the leader guides for the training activities varied substantially within countries. In Peru, for example, the adaptation of the population education leader guides to local agro-ecological conditions was carried out by a team of national experts before the pilot training, while in Bolivia, the adaptation of the leader guides is expected to build upon the experience of the pilot training, with the final version of the leader guides to be completed after the exercise.

The example from Peru where the leader guides were adapted to local agro-ecological conditions with some success raises the issue of the preparation of the leader guides on a regional or sub-regional basis for groups of countries with similar agro-ecological zoning, socio-cultural conditions and gender relations which would be ultimately better adapted to local realities.

The quality of the vernacular versions of the leader guides also differed from country to country. While some versions of the booklets (such as the Spanish version which was adapted to the Amazon region of Peru), were well received, others were not of satisfactory quality. The Ethiopia country report states, for example, that "the standard of production and quality of materials and drawings as promised by the Ministry of Agriculture Extension Department has been a big disappointment." As vernacular versions cannot be reviewed in FAO Rome, one way to ensure a high standard for the leader guides would be to have professionals review the revised versions, as was proposed in Thailand, where UNESCO supports a Population Education Clearing House.

The pilot activities in Zimbabwe had such a strong focus on introducing and using the leader guides that the project became known as the "booklets" project. However, the youth organizations used the booklets in the English version rather than translating them into the local languages of the pilot region, despite the fact that the actual training at the community level was carried out in the local languages. Revisions for the adaptation of the leader guides to local conditions have been proposed, but have so far not been included in the booklets as the national counterparts are awaiting to receive a copy of the prototypes in a word-processing format from FAO Rome.

Adjustments in the text and illustrations of the leader guides were made or else were suggested in nearly all the pilot activities. Some general recommendations for the development of leader guides at the inter-regional level are highlighted below:

— A key problem was that the population education leader guides were used without being tailoring to a specific target age range or education level. In the words of the Chief Commissioner of the Boy Scouts in Zimbabwe: "We were working with 0-Level School Leavers. Most of the participants felt the exercises in the leader guides stimulated discussion, but the information provided in the guides was rather shallow. The guides could be supplemented by a reference book that provides in-depth information to the leaders."

— In Vietnam, as the pilot activities involved a large number of illiterate youth, there was a proposal to modify the leader guides so that they could be used with non-literate audiences: According to the final project report, "a peculiar shortcoming noted among the H-mong youths is the high rate of illiteracy of both national Vietnamese and ethnic H-mong languages. The leader guides therefore would be more appropriate to them, if the messages were more abridged and more colourful illustrative drawings were added."

— In Peru, one volunteer leader highlighted the need for in-country adaptation of the population education leader guides, maximizing local resources and indigenous knowledge:

> "While the guides have been adapted to the local conditions, they still do not fully reflect our reality. For example, our parents and grandparents used effective traditional methods and herbal medicines to prevent and cure diseases. Some of this knowledge is being lost today. It would be good if leader guides could be developed here, so that they build on our traditional knowledge and on the resources that we have here in the jungle."

— Also in Peru, it is argued in the final report that the project did not explicitly address the gender dimension. Even though many of the pilot activities were targeted towards young men and women, the relationship between the sexes was not adequately dealt with in the leader guides, despite the fact that it is a key issue in family life education.

— In nearly all the pilot activities, it was pointed out that the leader guides were useful, but not sufficient to set up training programmes. In Ethiopia trainees "...want extra finance for each group to enable them to pay for a doctor/nurse to come and spend a day explaining in greater detail and give practical exhibitions of methods of contraception and contraceptives. " (this issue is discussed in detail in the section on institutionalization).

— The Boy Scouts in Zimbabwe had bound the 11 booklets together in one set and commented on the constraints of using the booklets in the field: "If those who developed the guides would know, what it means to travel by public transport with 20 sets of 11 booklets each for field testing, the type would probably be smaller and the booklets would be more compact". A loose leaf format would render the guides more practical for field use and allow project implementation teams to select certain exercises from the booklets that are relevant in a given country for adaptation to the vernacular.

During the review, several proposals were made to supplement the population education curriculum with additional booklets. The Vietnam final report proposes "to develop more leader guide volumes on other topics, for example, "Youth and Afforestation" "Population and Forest/Land Protection" or some special kind of newsletter/leaflets for rural/mountainous young readers." In Bolivia it was proposed to develop a guide on "Population and Forest Resources'', while in Zimbabwe, an additional guide on "Population and Culture " was suggested.

Summarizing the pilot experiences, it appears that the leader guides were instrumental in introducing population education topics to young men and women. For example, in Ethiopia "the content of the modules was praised as being very relevant to the lives of the participants and to date they have enjoyed the format of discussion and question and answer and group participation, " according to the national consultant of the project. However, the leader guides in participating countries remained rather similar in format and content to the prototypes, even after adaptation. Most organizations called them the "FAO Leader Guides," indicating that ownership was still with an international organization rather than with a local institution or with the youth itself.

As expressed in the above example from Peru, the need for local ownership of educational materials calls for a change in the role that prototype materials should play in future population education projects. Guides designed to be used worldwise need to focus more on how to introduce population education topics, rather than on providing already prepared sessions. This implies that methodological guides, e. g. on how to conduct training needs and resource assessments, how to introduce sensitive topics such as sex education in group discussion, how to organize and prepare training materials or how to evaluate a training session need to receive higher priority than they have so far.

In conclusion, while the leader guides were adapted to local conditions, training participants argued during the review that if the guides had been prepared in the region or in-country, they would reflect more accurately the local realities. This would be particularly important for the guides that build upon distinct agro-ecological conditions or cultural norms. FAO may be in a position to assist such a process by facilitating exercises on how to prepare educational materials and organize training programmes locally. Thereby standard information (such as technical aspects of family planning methods) could be provided on disk, CD or other electronic medium in a word-processing format as external inputs.

GENDER

The central role that gender plays in the success or failure of population education may appear obvious, but certainly needs to be underscored. It is only when young men and women understand about how rapid population growth affects their quality of life and standard of living, and decide jointly about family size issues that family planning can be effective. Thus, it is essential that population education programmes initiate a dialogue between young men and women on these issues, that they address the inferior socio-economic and socio-cultural status of women and their specific needs, and that they impart life skills that enable women to negotiate with men. Population education programmes targeting and/or addressing men alone have, in other words, little chance of success. In this context, the gender dimension of the inter-regional project constitutes a critical component of the entire pilot exercise.

The significance of gender did not receive the necessary attention in all of the pilot activities. This is reflected in the project documentation, which for the most part does not adequately address gender issues (including constraints, opportunities, the special needs of women, etc.), with some exceptions cited below. In particular, project country reports do not consistently document how many young men and women were trained as trainers or as youth leaders nor how many men and women were actually reached by the pilot activities.

In Ethiopia, the near absence of young women from the pilot activities was repeatedly identified as a major obstacle to the success of the project by one consultant, who argued that "all groups are male dominated because the development agents have traditionally involved male farmers and because education is generally considered the prerogative of the male. " She continues: "The fact that 80% of the participants in the pilot project are male is no accident. It seems that female home extension agents who deal with women in farming communities have been deliberately excluded from the training workshop. Despite repeated instructions during the workshop that participation in the youth groups should be 50/50 male/female, the development agents chose male leaders who formed almost exclusively male groups because they decided that this kind of education (and more specifically the family planning sexual reproduction part) is not suitable for females... "

In Peru and Bolivia, there appears to have been an equal number of young men and women participating in the pilot activities. This may have been a result of the fact that in Peru, the training was not based exclusively on training-of-trainers and project implementation teams applied their own criteria for selecting the youth leader participants. In Ethiopia, the majority of the training participants was selected by trained trainers and not by the project implementation teams. This meant that the selection criteria became diluted. In effect, national project implementation teams needed training on how to set up proper training programmes, including how to select training participants, and how to ensure that women are among these participants, that they are not marginalized in the training process itself, and that they are empowered to participate in equal terms in the training as men.

In addition, it was found that population education concepts need to be gender sensitive both in terms of the messages imparted and in terms of the educational approach being used. In particular, the leader guide methodology on sex education is in need of further refinement. In Peru, for instance, it was underscored that the methodology on sex education requires additional adaptation and tailoring for specific audiences. Thus, to reach Peruvian indigenous communities in the Amazon, a different approach is needed from that used for non-indigenous communities. Furthermore, as the culture, norms and socio-economic status of Peruvian Indian women are different from those of non-Indian women, a different gender approach would also be needed.

Findings from the field assessment of the pilot activities also point to the fact that each region has specific gender problems that need to be addressed in population education for youth. In Asia, for instance, the traditional preference for male children, which is reflected in the saying: "You may have all the wealth in the world, but if you do not have a male child, it is for nothing, " is a population education issue: in several countries, the preference for male children is leading to a proportionally higher abortion of female fetuses. The FAO population education leader guides, however, do not address this issue of fetal/child discrimination nor of female infanticide, which is a pressing problem for many women in the region.

In China, male out-migration from rural areas is a major concern for young men and women alike. As men are the first to migrate and male children have a priority in attending schools, it is the women and girls that are left behind with the responsibility of farming. This has both negative and positive implications: on the one hand, women assume an even greater burden, but, on the other hand, this may eventually lead to the erosion of the traditional supremacy of the male and give women some financial independence. Population education could assist in promoting the positive ramifications of this "feminization of agriculture." The FAO leader guides could make a substantial contribution in this direction by addressing this issue and making population education relevant to the immediate concerns of young men and women in China.

In Latin America, family relationships and problems in the family (including male/female roles, alcoholism, drug abuse, incest, etc.) are important issues for young men and women. These concerns, again, would need to be reflected in the leader guides, if they are to capture the attention of the youth in Latin America.

MONITORING AND EVALUATION

Monitoring is defined as a continuous assessment both of the functioning of project activities in the context of implementation schedules and of the use of project inputs by targeted populations in the context of design expectations. Monitoring is an internal project activity and an essential part of good management practice. Evaluation is the periodic assessment of the relevance, performance, efficiency and impact of the project in the context of its stated activities.

"No evaluation can be better than the quality of the facts and figures on which it was based. Facts and figures are never given, they are always produced by somebody." This statement highlights the importance of setting up a framework for monitoring and evaluation which ensures the collection and analysis of data at various levels of project implementation. Particularly relevant is monitoring and evaluation information in pilot projects, as this allows for testing innovative methodologies, approaches or materials. Thus, "producing" and documenting lessons learned, is, in effect, an implicit project output.

The original project document included a monitoring and evaluation table, which provided a general indication of the types and frequency of monitoring as well as progress indicators and means of verification. The suggestions made therein are relevant mainly for the inter-regional level of project implementation, such as annual progress reports (from FAO to UNFPA), mission and workshop reports.

The country implementation teams were provided with a framework, in which Knowledge, Attitude and Practice surveys with pre- and post-testing for measuring project impact were proposed. It was also recommended to review, discuss and document lessons learned, as well as to make revisions in the leader guides, and to assess and document the value of the effectiveness of the materials.

However, the implementation framework did not include specific agreed-upon guidelines on what type of information to collect and analyze in the pilot process, or how to do this. It was left up to the country implementation teams to develop strategies for monitoring the progress of project activities. As a result, the quality of the information base for monitoring and evaluation was not uniform, but depended on the emphasis that national project teams placed on this aspect of project implementation.

Several teams reported that the budget of the pilot projects did not adequately cover the cost of collecting, monitoring and evaluating information. For example:

— The national project coordinator in Ethiopia highlighted budget limitations in her reports: "With regard to on-going field evaluation, the structure which has developed to date is that the consultant/coordinator visits approximately four development agents per week with the two chief supervisors. Observations and notes are compared and discussed at the end of each set of visits....Overall, the biggest disappointment has been the inability of the consultant to carry out a proper evaluation of all the youth group projects due to the non-availability of transport and the lack of follow-up resources to develop this work."

— The project implementation team in Vietnam had set up a sophisticated procedure for monitoring and evaluating the pilot training through national and provincial officers. However, the final report of the Vietnam pilot activity was accompanied by a letter which also highlighted budget limitations, as was the case with Ethiopia: "As you are aware, this project, as planned with great distances to travel to and from project sites, large range of educational themes requiring long duration of two level training workshops and three field testing drives, a big number of participating youths and field testing sessions, is probably too small for such time-, effort-, and finance-consuming components."

— A report on the pilot activity in Peru further pointed out the financial constraints involved in monitoring and evaluation: "The budget constraints of the project limit adequate follow-up of the trained leaders and the groups they established in their respective communities. In some cases there might not have been a multiplicator effect in the dissemination of the leader guides and training of groups through the trained leaders."

— The difficulty in setting up a uniform monitoring and evaluation procedure for each of the participating youth organizations was explained by the National Project Coordinator in Zimbabwe: "Each organisation had been given an opportunity to plan its own agenda. Some organisations do have full time staff others do not. ... Some are more active during school holidays, while others have their target groups at hand during the school term ... There is a strong need to allow the project fit into the normal on-going practices of youth group activities."

The felt shortage of funds for monitoring and evaluation may be related to the fact that the concept of "piloting" was not sufficiently elaborated in the project document. Also, it appeared during the field assessment that the concept of "piloting" was not adequately communicated to the participating institutions. As adaptation, testing and training in the use of the leader guides were introduced in the countries as "pilot projects", the expectation was created that after the pilot phase, a main phase would follow. In some cases, this lack of follow-up led to disappointment on the part of the counterpart institutions. The Chairman of SCANVYO in Zimbabwe, for example, said: "Why does one embark on a pilot project to test a methodology, when there are no funds for a main phase?

Regional workshops could play an important role in monitoring and evaluation. Networking and exchange of programme priorities among implementation teams of the various countries could be used to set up a system of self-evaluation. In the beginning of the pilot process, participating institutions could meet to agree on monitoring and evaluation criteria, which are especially important to observe during the pilot process, and to jointly develop pilot plans. At the end of a pilot sequence, lessons learned in each country and possibilities for follow-up could be discussed. As some of the INT/92/P94 pilot activities are still on-going, FAO and UNFPA could still hold the originally planned meetings to discuss the pilot experiences of implementation teams from South America (Peru, Bolivia, Colombia) and Asia (Indonesia, Thailand).

A uniform summary sheet on the experience of participants and participating institutions at the country level prepared before the implementation of the pilot activities would facilitate the review of the pilot experiences at the inter-regional level. Such a brief structured summary could include standardized as well as open-ended questions reviewing the relevance and impact of the project on the beneficiaries, the successes and constraints experienced by the country level implementing agency and the need for support services needed from international organizations.

The pilot activities produced a wealth of information and valuable lessons on integrating population education into different non-formal settings. As a pilot exercise, however, more emphasis would have been needed to develop in the early stage of the project a common structure for analysis, to assist the implementation partners to collect information and to analyze and document lessons learned. The difference in quality of country pilot activity reports suggests that training of implementation teams in monitoring and evaluating pilot projects should be considered an essential component of future population education pilot projects.

IMPACT OF POPULATION EDUCATION TRAINING

The impact of the project in most participating countries was assessed through formal questionnaires, including Knowledge, Attitude and Practice surveys, before and at the end of the training exercise. Using this procedure, most countries reported that the training had a positive impact.

An extensive baseline and impact survey of approximately 300 youths was conducted in Zimbabwe. The following table shows some of the results:

Table 2: Impact of Population Education Pilot Activity in Zimbabwe

	Baseline Survey January 1994	Impact Survey April 1994
Percentage aware of dangers of early motherhood	69%	76.4%
Percentage agreeing to youth having access to contraceptives	55%	65%
Percentage discussing population issues	79.4%	85%
Average number of children wanted per couple	3.4%	2.5%

According to the survey, population education in Zimbabwe had an impact on the awareness of young men and women of the dangers of early motherhood, the acceptability of using contraceptives, and the number of youth discussing population issues. Most importantly, perhaps, the training seems to have had an impact on the desired number of children young people wanted to have.

The Vietnam final report also highlights the positive impact of the population education training among the youth:

> "Analysis of the workshop report, evaluation sheet and questionnaires completed by every trainee showed that all the trainees knowledge and awareness of the training subject was enhanced, their grasp of working methods, their application of working skills was improved and they were

> obviously well prepared for the role as group leaders for field testing sessions at their bases".

The pilot activity in China was similarly evaluated positively: "Through evaluation we can see that this project was a success, and has achieved good results. Through the population education programmes the young participants have benefited in the following ways:

a) They have improved their knowledge of the relationships between population growth and distribution of the resources needed for agricultural production.

b) They have improved their understanding of the relationships between population, employment and quality of life; and ability to identify employment opportunities for youth through proper utilization of local resources.

c) They have learned practical skills and increased competitiveness in the market economy

d) They have learned the knowledge of proper nutrition, health care and the importance of breast feeding for the child and the mother. They have now paid more attention to sanitation facilities.

e) They have now understood the advantage of a small family (fewer children) and the country's family planning policy of one couple one child."

In the interpretation of these results, however, it is important to recognize that Knowledge, Attitude and Practice surveys were administered shortly after the training, when the subject matter was still fresh. Also, as exposure to training and materials was limited in terms of duration, monitoring changes in knowledge, attitude, and practice over a longer-term period would yield a more accurate assessment.

On the basis of such concerns, the training organizers in Peru were reluctant to report a change in knowledge, attitude and practice among youths. According to the final report, "programmes in population education using the leader guides need to be integrated into a long-term educational process, where the educational contents are internalized and translated into a change of attitude and practice. No leader guide and no discussion by itself will produce changes when they are not accompanied by a systematic and long-term process." The implementation team consequently proposed that "to know results in knowledge, attitude and practice changes, a longer-term follow-up of the experience with the participating groups is necessary."

FOLLOW-UP TO PILOT ACTIVITIES AT NATIONAL LEVEL

The project document pointed out that country level pilot activities would be considered complete once the leader guides were adapted to the local conditions, and that thereafter, resources from other national programmes would be needed to expand upon activities with out-of-school rural youth.

UNFPA country programmes were mentioned in the project document as a potential source of funding for follow-up activities at the country level. At the 1994 International Conference on Population and Development in Cairo, adolescents received high priority. In fact, the conference programme of action states that:

> "Countries should aim to meet the needs and aspirations of youth, particularly in the areas of formal and non-formal education, training, employment opportunities, housing and health, thereby ensuring their integration and participation in all spheres of society, including participation in the political process and preparation for leadership roles."

The leader of the UNFPA Country Support Team for East and South East Asia described adolescents as a priority audience for UNFPA-supported programmes and attributed special significance to working with youth in rural areas, given their limited access to educational opportunities. In addition, he specifically underscored the potential for FAO/UNFPA collaboration in working with out-of-school youth.

Despite the increasing importance that UNFPA has been placing on working with rural youth, the transition from inter-regional project activities to follow-up through national programmes proved to be difficult for the following reasons:

— UNFPA Country Directors maintained that they had not been involved in the planning of the pilot activities and were, therefore, not able to make timely adjustments in their country programmes. Some had only been informed of the pilot activities after these had already started. The UNFPA Country Director in Zimbabwe, for example, expressed her concern regarding FAO Headquarters-initiated projects imposing programmes on a country without first consulting with the Country Office. This may well be an obstacle in planning project follow-up activities that are in line with the country programme.

— The population education pilot activities were not coordinated with other programmes at the country level. In Zimbabwe, for example, the UNFPA programme had recently funded a population education project with the Boy Scouts, using a different set of population education materials. The FAO pilot activity was thus partly duplicating these earlier efforts.

— Some counterpart institutions of the regional project were not considered to have sufficiently-developed institutional capacity to implement larger follow-up activities.

On the part of the counterpart institutions, the pilot activities in effect created considerable interest in follow-up:

— The 'Consejo Regional de Población (COREPO)' in Peru prepared a proposal for follow-up, which was submitted to UNFPA and FAO. UNFPA indicated interest in continued support for population education for out-of-school youth in Loreto Region, but mentioned that FAO should provide a framework (e. g. a technical cooperation project) in which population education could be integrated. As the COREPO proposal still needs further refinement, both FAO and UNFPA could provide technical support.

— In China, the UNFPA country programme has so far not indicated interest in supporting follow-up to the pilot activities. However, some continuity to the pilot training was provided through the FAO/UNFPA Population, Women and Development Programme, but this is also coming to a closure.

— Interest in follow-up was also expressed by the Vietnamese Youth Federation. Their terminal report states: "... we very much hope that with the serious and fruitful efforts already shown by our project staff in the capacity as practical tester of the series .... FAO could favour us with affirmative response so that this guidebook series could be made available to the Vietnamese rural youth leaders and youth cadres." A proposal for a follow-up project "Popular Use of FAO Leader's Guides in Vietnam" was drafted during the FAO training workshop in Manila, 17-20 October 1994. This was revised, reformulated and formally submitted to FAO Headquarters in March 1995.

— The director of the National Association of Non-Governmental Organizations (NANGO) in Zimbabwe, the counterpart institution for the organization of pilot activities pointed out: "The Letter of Agreement should have foreseen some resources for a local consultant to organize follow-up to the pilot activities in Zimbabwe." Proposals for follow-up to the programme are available. However, donors still need to be identified. This requires fundraising on the part of the umbrella NGO, which was not foreseen in the project document as part of the counterpart institution's responsibilities.

Many participating youth organizations in Zimbabwe maintained that they had not received adequate support for follow-up and were "left in the middle of the pilot exercise":

— The national secretary of the Girls Brigade in Zimbabwe said: "We would have expected a donor to look into the evaluation study of the pilot activities and to tell us if we could continue with population education."

— The chief commissioner of the Boy Scouts pointed out: "As proposed in the leader guides, population education would need to be integrated into practical activities, such as planting trees, rabbit keeping, marketing horticulture products, but so far we did not receive funds to continue work along these lines. "

— The national youth coordinator of YMCA pointed out: "The major weakness in the implementation of the pilot activities was that nobody really had thought about "What next". We have stimulated and excited the youth, but nobody has gone back to fulfill the expectations that were created."

— The chairman of the Standing Conference of Voluntary National Youth Organizations expressed his concern for follow-up as follows: "Why does one embark on a pilot project to test a methodology, when there are no funds for a main phase?"

In conclusion, the population education pilot activities created considerable interest as well as high expectations in terms of a full-fledged project on the part of the organizations that work with young men and women at the grass roots level. However, so far, follow-up action at the country level has been difficult due to a lack in resources on the part of youth organizations and the absence of involvement and coordination of the pilot activities with UNFPA country programmes.

CONCLUSIONS AND RECOMMENDATIONS

1. The need for population education for out-of-school rural youth was further confirmed through the INT/92/P94 pilot activities. The FAO population education concept of integrating education in issues related to agriculture,

employment, income and community development with family life education, including sex education, family planning, health, nutrition, and child care proved to be useful and relevant for the youth leaders and the youth that participated in the pilot training activities. In some countries, the integration of population education with income-generating activities was successful in establishing an avenue for reaching out-of-school rural youth. Further efforts, however, are needed to identify opportunities and constraints of income-generating activities and their suitability as strategic carriers of population messages for out-of-school rural youth.

2. Field assessment findings show that short-term pilot activities have not been sufficient for the sustained integration of population education into non-formal educational programmes for rural youth. Given the considerable differences in the resource base, staff and audiences of formal and non-formal educational structures, the institutionalisation of population education in non-formal educational settings appears to have been hampered by serious financial and capacity constraints. The fact that donor funding of youth organizations is largely geared towards short-term projects does not leave them sufficient financial leeway to sustain long-term population training programmes with their own resources.

   Future population education activities targeted at non-formal rural youth organizations would need to be based on an assessment of the institutional capacity of these organizations in terms of staff, volunteer support, financial resources, technical capabilities and their ability to cater for out-of-school rural youth on a long-term basis. Based on the results of such an assessment, population education would eventually need to be integrated in a long-term concerted effort on the part of donor organizations to strengthen rural youth organizations.

3. In some population education pilot locations, institutional networks for targeting out-of-school rural youth were non-existent. Population education training in some of these sites, (as was the case in Bolivia), was carried out as a coordinated effort between local resource institutions (schools, hospitals, and agricultural education and research institutions), which organized a community level training seminar series in population education for youth leaders. The results of this collaborative effort may be useful in the identification of alternative channels and strategies for reaching out-of-school rural youth. In addition to working with rural youth organizations, potential channels for future population education activities could include, for instance, rural and community development programmes of both FAO and other executing/implementing agencies.

4. Through training-of-trainers - a key component in the implementation of pilot activities - a relatively large number of youths was reached at low cost. However, the quality of population education in the second training cycle by trained trainers was in some cases reported to be inadequate. Also, some country reports stated a male bias in the selection of training participants. Future pilot activities would therefore need to place more emphasis on familiarizing national project implementation teams with how to plan, implement, monitor and evaluate a pilot training programme. Thereby, it would be particularly important to base future training programmes on a training needs assessment in-country, in order to make the training curriculum relevant to local problems.

5. The FAO population education leader guides constituted the backbone of the inter-regional project pilot training activities. During the pilot process, the leader guides were translated into several local languages and adapted to local conditions. However, training participants mentioned during the project evaluation that if the guides had been prepared in the region or in-country, they would have reflected the

local realities more accurately. This would be particularly important for those leader guides that build upon distinct agro-ecological conditions or cultural norms. Also, in-country preparation of educational materials would make it easier to tailor them to specific audiences, such as illiterate youth or indigenous communities.

Given the fact that population education prototype materials need country-specific and target group adjustments, and that population education materials are a necessary, but not sufficient, component of population education training for out-of-school rural youth, future FAO assistance in population education would need to focus on building national capacity for the preparation of educational materials and for the organization of professional training programmes in population education, rather than on providing ready-made booklets. In addition, the preparation of population education prototype materials on the basis of agro-ecological zoning, socio-cultural characteristics and gender variables rather than on a continent-wide basis could be explored. This core information could be provided by FAO on disk, CD or other electronic media in a word-processing format.

6. As a pilot exercise, more emphasis may have been necessary in the early stages of the project to develop common criteria for monitoring and evaluation, to assist the implementation partners in collecting information, and to analyze and document lessons learned. National coordinators of pilot activities maintained that a briefing on and discussion of pilot project objectives, implementation and monitoring and evaluation procedures among various teams of each region at the outset of the exercise would have been useful and would have enhanced project implementation. In addition, it was repeatedly stated by national project implementation teams that regional meetings to set up a system for self-evaluation, in which the implementation teams themselves would hold the

responsibility for project evaluation would have further enhanced the pilot process.

In particular, the implementation teams in Bolivia, Peru and Thailand expressed a keen interest in sharing the lessons learned in their country exercises with other teams in the region. In view of the fact that both the Peru and Bolivia country exercises operated in a rural area that did not have institutional infrastructure for youth programmes, a regional workshop comparing the Latin American experiences would be especially relevant and useful to the entire pilot exercise.

7. The results of Knowledge, Attitude and Practice Surveys (KAP) conducted in some of the pilot countries suggest that population education based on the FAO youth leader guides has had a positive impact on training participants in terms of the frequency that population issues were discussed, awareness of the risks of early pregnancy, and changing preferences towards a reduced number of children. However, assessing the long-term impact of the exercise on the basis of these KAPs may not be adequate, as most of these changes in behaviour were measured immediately after the training. As was pointed out in the Peru pilot activity, long-term impact requires a long-term educational process rather than a limited number of population education sessions delivered over a brief period of time.

8. The pilot activities created considerable interest as well as high expectations in terms of a full-fledged project among youth organizations. However, so far, follow-up action at the country level has been difficult due to a lack in resources on the part of youth organizations and the absence of involvement and coordination of pilot activities with UNFPA country programmes.

INDEX